THE IMPACT OF SOCIAL FACTORS ON HEALTH

A CRITICAL READER FOR THE PHYSICIAN ASSISTANT

Revised First Edition

By Darron T. Smith
University of Tennessee Health Science Center

and Tasha E. Sabino
Christian Brothers University

Bassim Hamadeh, CEO and Publisher
Michael Simpson, Vice President of Acquisitions
Jamie Giganti, Managing Editor
Jess Busch, Graphic Design Supervisor
Monika Dziamka, Project Editor
Natalie Lakosil, Licensing Manager
Mandy Licata, Interior Designer

First published in the United States of America in 2015 by Cognella, Inc.
Cover image: Copyright © 2012 by Depositphotos Inc./ ginosphotos1

Trademark Notice: Product or corporate names may be trademarks or registered trademarks, and are used only for identification and explanation without intent to infringe.

Printed in the United States of America

ISBN: 978-1-63189-170-0 (pbk)/ 978-1-63189-171-7 (br)

www.cognella.com   800-200-3908

CONTENTS

PART III: THE ROLE OF PROVIDER INTERACTION AS A SOCIAL DETERMINANT OF HEALTH

91

ACKNOWLEDGMENTS

We are eternally grateful to the members of Cognella publishing who patiently assisted in the concept and design of this project and waded through numerous draft delays and relocations in the completion of this manuscript. They provided us with encouragement and criticism, both of which were needed to bring about a well-developed and impactful volume. We would like to thank our reviewers who took much of their time to read the chapters contained within this book and offer up cogent responses, providing rich insight and much needed direction for many of the chapters. We are also excited to introduce this volume to our PA colleagues across the nation and hope they find value within the covers of this book.

ABOUT THE EDITORS

Darron T. Smith is an Assistant Professor at the University of Tennessee Health Science Center in the Department of Physician Assistant Studies. His background includes 17 years of medical experience as a primary care health provider with an attention to the medically underserved, including work at community health centers, the National Guard, and Native American reservations in southeast Utah. Since entering the field of PA education, Dr. Smith has focused his research on improving the social factors that cause disease, particularly in communities of color. His current research, for which he received a Physician Assistant Education Association (PAEA) grant, focuses on healthcare workforce discrimination involving African American physician assistants. He is an active leader at the national level, serving as a member of the PAEA Diversity and Inclusion Committee and a state delegate for the Tennessee Association of Physician Assistants.

Dr. Smith is a Renaissance man, examining race in many different theoretical terrains from family and religion to sports and healthcare. He is the co-author of *White Parents, Black Children: Experiencing Transracial Adoption* as well as the co-editor of *Black and Mormon*. His current book, *The Truth About the Honor Code: When Race, Religion & Sports Collide*, is scheduled for release in 2014. He is a frequent political and cultural commentator for *Huffington Post* on various issues of US-based oppression. He has also contributed to various forums, from *Religion Dispatches* and *ESPN*'s Outside the Lines to the *New York Times* and *Chicago Tribune* op-ed sections.

Tasha Sabino is a clinically practicing physician assistant with experience in urgent care, family medicine, and orthopedics. She is a physician assistant educator where she teaches as adjunct faculty in the Physician Assistant Department at Christian Brothers University in Memphis, Tennessee. Ms. Sabino, likewise, is a researcher in which her focus is on the social determinants of health and health inequities as they impact vulnerable populations in the US. She received her Master's degree in Physician Assistant Studies from the University of Utah. Prior to a career as a PA, Ms. Sabino taught high school science, health, and sports medicine and practiced as an athletic trainer. Her undergraduate degree is in Exercise and Sports Science with a specialization in Athletic Training from the University of North Carolina at Chapel Hill.

INTRODUCTION

C urrently some 48 million people in the United States are without health insurance. This number has risen sharply since 2009 due to the unpredictable economy, which resulted in high unemployment and a decline in employer-offered benefits (Galewitz and Villegas, 2010). The cost of health expenditure per person is at an all-time high (and disproportionately so when comparing the Gross Domestic Product to other countries), and yet, there is little to show for it in terms of patient outcomes. The United States continues to lag behind other developed nations in the health status of our people. The US morbidity and mortality is among the highest in the developed world. And within our own country, the disparity in health and health care between the haves and have-nots is astounding and steadily increasing.

This critical physician assistant reader focuses on various topics related to the social factors that influence health and disease, otherwise known as social determinants of health (SDOH), which remain a significant and growing problem in US society. The contributions in this manuscript cover a range of key social, economic, political and historical issues as they relate to medicine and healthcare, and specifically as they apply to physician assistant studies. This project evolved from the need to examine in more detail how social processes and the environment interface to cause degenerative disease (i.e., cardiovascular disease, certain cancers and obesity).

An individual's health status is one social indicator where the evidence of inequities is especially glaring and speaks volumes to our national priorities. Because US healthcare has been a for-profit enterprise, there is a clear link between income and health status. Centuries-old oppressive structures like racism, classism, sexism and other forms of stratification in this society gave rise to the fact that certain groups have paid a much heavier price on their health and well-being than other more advantaged groups. Whether from lack of health care insurance or under-insurance, inadequate access to primary care health providers, or the unequal care from those providers, the research literature suggests that high quality medicine is not for the disadvantaged or poor, but instead for the most privileged and wealthy Americans.

We feel it is important that physician assistants understand the evidence-based interaction between the social environment and health status of their patients and expand their investigative tools of inquiry during their professional health care education and eventual practice. To gain this knowledge, we feel it is imperative that this reality of health care is incorporated into the curriculum. PA faculty members are key to expanding the thinking of students beyond the perfunctory nature of medicine, thus teaching them to think more critically about the social world and their responsibility as care givers in it.

Given the expansion of health care coverage via the Affordable Care Act, more American citizens will be eligible for coverage, which will likely include a more diverse patient populace than ever before. From the very young to the aging baby boomers, each group is poised to overwhelm healthcare delivery services. As it currently stands, primary health care professionals are out of step with the patients they will likely serve in the coming years. This book is designed to increase the knowledge base and understanding of how the mind and body are intimately connected. Further, it will serve to emphasize the greater roll that the physician assistant can play in better understanding this delicate interaction and, in turn, treating and educating patients in a fair and equitable manner in efforts to strengthen overall physical and emotional health. We hope this book will begin the conversation in PA schools that will lead to a different type of patient care and, ultimately, a different type of human care professional—one more keenly aware of and empathic of how social factors contribute to disease progression in a multitude of ways. In this book, we will cover a few important topics related to Social Determinants of Health.

—Darron T. Smith, Ph.D., PA-C
The University of Tennessee Health Science Center

—Tasha E. Sabino, MPAS, PA-C
Christian Brothers University

POLICY RELATED SOCIAL FACTORS

HEALTHCARE STATISTICS

United States Healthcare Disparities in Access and Treatment, 2012

By Cardell K. Jacobson, Ph.D.

D espite having a high standard of living compared with most countries in the world, health care in the United States lags behind several similar modern nations in the world. In this chapter we examine reasons for this disparity.

The evidence for the disparities comes primarily from two standard measurements of the health of a nation: life expectancy and infant mortality rates. They can be used to compare health cross nationally. Many nations are clustered near the top of life expectancy and have low rates of infant mortality. The United States is not far behind the leading nations. Nevertheless, the United States falls below at least forty-nine other countries according to these standards. The remainder of the chapter will contextualize the national number by examining the disparities of income in the United States and the attendant disparities in health care. Once these contextualizing factors are considered, I argue that the United States has very good health care, for those who can afford it. Unfortunately, not all Americans have adequate access to health care; these are primarily the poor[1] and working classes and members of minority populations. Thus, the result is that the overall health care figures for America are lower than they could and should be considering the overall wealth of the nation.

---

1 "Poor" is generally considered to be below the federal poverty level; high income is generally considered to be four times the federal poverty level.

COMPARING LIFE EXPECTANCY AND INFANT MORTALITY ON THE WORLD STAGE

Life expectancy and infant mortality are indices used around the world to assess each nation's level of health. They have been proven to be indicative of the nation's other health statistics. The Central Intelligence Agency's *World Factbook* estimates that life expectancy in the United States (in 2011) was 78.37. While that life expectancy is very good, it is only fiftieth among the 221 countries listed by the CIA (CIA Life Expectancy, 2011). The United States lags four years behind Japan, a country with one of the highest estimated life expectancies (82.25). Life expectancy in the United States is also well below Singapore, Hong Kong, Australia, Italy Canada, France, Spain, Switzerland, Sweden, Israel, and other countries that all have estimated rates above eighty years. Even Jordan, Greece, and South Korea have higher estimated life expectancies than the United States. Within the United States, life expectancy for Whites is four years higher than it is for Blacks (78.4 and 74.3, respectively, in 2008—the last year for which the *Statistical Handbook of the United States* has actual data and not projections). This disparity is expected to grow. The *Statistical Handbook* estimates that in 2015, life expectancy of Whites will be 79.5 compared with 75.0 for Blacks. While it does not provide estimates for other ethnic groups, the numbers for other disadvantaged minorities are likely similar.

Results for infant mortality portray much the same picture. Infant mortality is the number of children per thousand born who die before achieving the age of one. While the infant mortality rate for the United States is a relatively low 6.06 (estimated for 2011), that figure is higher than infant mortality rates in more than fifty other countries. The CIA examined 222 countries (CIA Infant Mortality, 2011), and as is the case with life expectancy estimates, many of the countries are small and have relatively homogenous populations. Further, the wealth disparity is lower in many countries than in the United States. Hence, many of the same countries have both lower infant mortality rates and higher life expectancy than the United States.

What is particularly disconcerting about these health outcome numbers is that they are worse than essentially all other countries in the United States, despite the fact that the United States spends a higher proportion of its gross domestic product (GDP) than any other country in the world on health care (15.2 percent compared with the world average of 6.1 percent). The country with the next highest expenditure (as a percentage of GDP), Switzerland, spends 10.2 percent of its GDP on health care (World Health Organization annual report, 2011).

These rates for the United States reflect a number of factors. The reader might suspect that the United States, with its high expenditures for health care, has more doctors and other medical practitioners than other countries. In fact, this is not the case. The number of physicians, dentists, and hospital beds (per 10,000 people) is not particularly high. The United States has 26.7 physicians per 10,000 people compared with Switzerland (40.7) and Germany (35.3). Similarly, the number of dentists in the United States per 10,000 people is 16.3 compared with Japan at 41.4. Finally, the number of hospital beds per 10,000 people in the United States is 31, compared with 53 in Switzerland, 82 in Germany, and 138 in Japan (all numbers from the World Health Organization 2011 annual report). Thus, the number of physicians, dentists, and hospital beds does not appear to be the primary reason for the high cost of medicine in the United States.

In truth, many factors are responsible for the cost of health care in the United States. For example, elective surgeries such as cosmetic surgery, obesity-related surgery, and joint replacements drive up health care costs. Further, the number of specialists is high, and most hospitals and health care providers in the United States are for-profit organizations. But two significant explanations lie in the lack of equal access to health care and the inequity in the actual care provided to some groups in American society. Thus, the ensuing discussion focuses on the inequality of income and inequality of access to health care.

DISPARITIES WITHIN THE UNITED STATES: NATIONAL HEALTHCARE DISPARITIES REPORT

In the United States, there is a significant divergence in health outcomes between the rich and the poor, between Blacks, Whites, and other groups, and these outcomes reflect health care inequities. Documentation of the disparities in access to health care comes from the government itself. Each year since 2003, the Agency for Healthcare Research and Quality (AHRQ), which is part of the US Department of Health and Human Services, has tracked disparities in health care in the United States (http://fodh.phhp.ufl.edu/files/2011/05/AHRQ-disparities-2010.pdf). The Agency does so under mandate from the United States Congress. Much of its report, the National Healthcare Disparities Report or NHDR, is concerned with progress toward health care goals (NHDR, 2010). The report uses three dozen databases and focuses on nine general topics: effectiveness of care, patient safety, timeliness of health care delivery, patient centeredness, care coordination, efficiency of the healthcare system, health systems infrastructure, access to health care, and priority populations (minorities and the poor). It also incorporates recommendations from a number of agencies and organizations as well as its own priorities. The most recent National Healthcare Disparities Report, a truly vast and detailed report of 248 pages, argues that while health care *quality* overall is improving in the United States, *access* to health care and the *disparities* in health care are not improving.

The overall summary of results is as follows:

- Palliative and end-of-life care, and patient and family engagement are said to be improving.
- Population health, safety, and access to health care are said to be lagging.

Despite long-term concerns for health care equality, the annual report shows striking disparities in the care of America's underserved communities, specifically the poor and individuals in minority communities. The report attributes the disparities primarily to differential access, provider biases, poor communication between providers and recipients, and poor health literacy. Here is a summative statement from the Agency report:

> Unfortunately, Americans too often do not receive care that they need, or they receive care that causes harm. Care can be delivered too late or without full consideration of a patient's preferences and values. Many times, our system of health care distributes services inefficiently and unevenly across populations. Some Americans receive worse care than other Americans. These disparities may be due to differences in access to care, provider biases, poor provider-patient communication, and poor health literacy. http://fodh.phhp.ufl.edu/files/2011/05/AHRQ-disparities-2010.pdf (Highlights, p. H−1).

The NHDR focuses on the disparities, not on the causes. Because the report has to be politically neutral, it does not often place American health care disparities in the context of the larger issues and disparities within American society. (Hence, the section on poverty is the last section in the report.) As the report notes, all Americans should have equal access to high-quality care. Instead, the authors find that racial and ethnic minorities and poor people often receive poorer quality of care and face more barriers when trying to access care.

A brief summary of the report focuses on the racial and ethnic[2] disparities:

Most minority group individuals received both worse care and had worse access to care than did Whites. First, here are the results on <u>access</u> to care:

- Blacks had worse access to care than Whites on one-third of core measures.
- Asians and American Indians/Alaska Natives had worse access to care than Whites on one of five core measures.
- Hispanics had worse access to care than non-Hispanic Whites on five of six core measures.
- Poor people had worse access to care than high-income people on all six core measures.

The results for <u>actual care</u> were reported as follows:

---

2   The report uses the conventional naming of racial and ethnic groups, and I do as well. At the same time, I would emphasize that these classifications are not biological classifications, but rather social classifications or designations, and most are based on self-identification.

- Blacks and American Indians/Alaska Natives received worse care than Whites on about 40 percent of core measures.
- Asians received worse care than Whites on about 20 percent of core measures.
- Hispanics received worse care than non-Hispanic Whites on about 60 percent of core measures.
- Poor people received worse care than high-income people on about 80 percent of core measures.

The NHDR finds improvement in only two of the areas it examined, palliative and end-of-life care, and patient and family engagement. Further, while the report states that overall health care quality is improving in the United States, quality and access are "suboptimal" for minority and low-income groups (NHDR, p. H–2). The report concludes that patients receive appropriate acute care services on average (only) three-quarters of the time. Nevertheless, those figures vary greatly depending on one's location, race and ethnicity, and particularly income status. If the other quarter of the population received appropriate care services, the life expectancy and infant mortality rates of the overall population would be much closer to the best in the world. Sadly, all of the areas examined in the report showed disparities related to racial, ethnic, and socioeconomic status. These disparities are substantial across the nation, and the report finds no signs of improving.

The largest differences in the NHDR are between the lowest and highest income people; the report notes that the poor receive worse health care on 80 percent of the core measures. Unfortunately, the income differences are conflated with minority/white differences since most members of racial and ethnic minority communities have lower incomes. Large racial and ethnic differences exist between Whites and Blacks and between Whites and aboriginal groups (American Indians and Alaskan Natives or AIAN). Blacks, American Indians and Alaska Natives, and Hispanics (who can be part of any racial classification) all received worse care than Whites on about 40 percent of the core measures in the survey. Asian Americans, despite having higher income than Whites in the 2010 census, still reported about 20 percent worse care than Whites. In sum, the report notes that disparities in quality of care are common, and as noted earlier, the report indicates that the disparities are not diminishing. Health care is improving for all groups, but gaps remain between minority groups and Whites.

The one complaint of the NHDR is that the numbers do not portray the full picture because the represented groups are often conflated; the poor and minority groups are often one and the same. Most racial and ethnic groups are worse off than Whites economically. As reported in Section 10 of the NHDR, 24 percent of Blacks and 21 percent of Hispanics, but only 10 percent of Asians and 8 percent of Whites, are poor (section 10, p. 12). The differences between these various groups in the AHRQ report are often merged with the differences between the wealthy and the poor. For example, 19 percent of the poor experienced decreased quality of care compared with high-income people. But 21 percent of African Americans experienced worse quality of care compared with white Americans (AHRQ, Figure H.1 p. H–4). Whether or not these are the same people is not addressed. The report does not break out how many poor black, white, Hispanic, or other groups did *not* have good access to good health care or did *not* receive good health care. While the report details statistical regression (using several variables to predict outcomes) analyses for changes in health care, it does not report similar analyses detailing what factors are related to access or care for the subpopulations.

The AIAN group in the NHDR report, unfortunately, is combined with several other groups, namely the Asian groups. The Asian groups generally have higher income and educational levels than Whites, but the AIAN group has significantly lower educational and income levels than Whites. Thus, the conclusions presented in the report for the combined group do not accurately reflect either group (Asians or AIAN), and the combination of the two groups does not allow accurate conclusions to be drawn about either group. The results from the generally high income of the Asian groups masks the effects of groups with lower incomes: American Indians and Alaska Natives who are likely to have poor access to health care.

Just as the "Asian" group consists of a heterogeneous blend, the Hispanic classification in the report masks great variability among the various Latin groups—Mexican Americans, Puerto Ricans, Cuban Americans, and others. Still others identify as being of "more than one race" or as "none of the above," a classification in the census data and many governmental surveys. The NHDR does not report how individuals who are biracial or who check "none of the above" are classified in the results. Thus, members of these "groups" likely differ in terms of access to health care as well. In any case, the racial, ethnic, and differences by poverty status are profound and disturbing.

WEALTH GAP AND RACIAL DIFFERENCES LINKED TO QUALITY AND ACCESS OF CARE

A large imbalance exists in the healthcare system within the United States. Much of this lies in *quality* and *access* of care for its recipients. The lack of access to health care is tied directly to the fact that the United States does not have universal health insurance. In addition, the United States has underserved groups of people referred to above: lower incomes and minorities. These are individuals and families that struggle to find affordable health insurance for themselves or their families, and those without health insurance often ignore health problems until their illnesses become critical. Critical care, which is associated with much greater expenses and worse outcomes (e.g., early death), consequently becomes the care of choice.

Another related reason for the substandard health care statistics in the United States, as noted earlier, is the disparity of incomes and wealth in the United States. A recent report by the Organization for Economic Co-operation and Development (OECD) shows that the United States has the fourth-highest income disparity in the world after Chile, Mexico, and Turkey (accessed May 1, 2012). The disparity between the rich and the poor is greater in the United States than in all other developed economies. This wealth gap is correlated with higher rates of mental and physical health problems for the total society, worse education, higher crime rates, and a variety of other social problems (see Wilkinson and Pickett, 2009).

The OECD study is based on a measurement known as the Gini coefficient. The Gini coefficient ranges from 0 to 1, where zero indicates perfect equality and one indicates all wealth goes to a single individual. The report finds growing rates of income inequality everywhere in the world. Between the mid-1980s and late 2000s, the average Gini coefficient for OECD countries rose annually by an average of 0.3 percent, and now sits at 0.31. The *Washington Post* (among others) also notes that the income disparity has been increasing over the past several decades (*Washington Post*, June 19, 2011). For comparative purposes, the Gini coefficient for Chili is 0.50 whereas the United States is 0.38, both above the world average. Other advanced nations fare better than the United States; New Zealand's is 0.34 and Australia's is 0.33. The nations with the most equality are Iceland and Switzerland (OECD). Thus, the United States has relatively high income inequality compared with other developed countries.

Consequently, part of the reason for the relatively high infant mortality and lower-than-need-be life expectancy is that the high income disparity corresponds with the lack of good access to medical care for some, typically those near the bottom of the socioeconomic ladder. In the United States, the very poor have access to health care through Medicaid, a federal program for the poor. Those just above the poverty rate (considered to be just over $11,000 for one person and roughly $23,000 for a family of four), however, often have less than good access to quality medical care since they do not qualify for government aid and cannot afford private health insurance.

The report also found that residents of the inner city and rural areas tend to receive worse quality of care than other areas. This is particularly true in large central cities, but also in areas the report defines as micropolitan (counties with an urban cluster of twenty thousand to fifty thousand people adjacent to metropolitan areas) (NHDR, p. H–11). This pattern reflects what William Julius Wilson (1996) reports as concentration effects. His argument is that as middle-class African Americans and others fled the nation's inner cities and these urban areas became a concentration of poverty, crime and drug use. The single-parent households left behind could not provide as much oversight or resources to their youth. We should, therefore, not be surprised that a deficit of health care and access is prevalent in these areas.

In seeking care, the poor are far more likely to visit emergency rooms than are others in society (Garcia et al. 2010). Garcia's report, based on 2007 National Health Interview Survey statistics, reported that one in five people in the United States had at least one visit to the ER in one year's time. For those below the poverty level, the rate was nearly 30 percent. Whereas for the wealthy (those making more than four times the poverty rate), just over 15 percent visited the ER; the highest proportion of those were by people over the age of seventy-five.

This also involved a higher percentage of non-Hispanic Blacks. Hispanics were less likely than Whites or Blacks to visit the ER, but this reflects their younger age and, possibly, their immigration status.

Interestingly, the uninsured under the age of sixty-five were no more likely than the insured to visit ERs (Garcia et al. 2010), possibly because they deferred treatment or could not afford treatment. People with Medicaid were more likely than others to have used emergency departments more than once in the past year; approximately 15 percent had two or more visits, compared with 7 percent of the uninsured and 5 percent of the insured (data from the Centers for Disease Control, http://www.cdc.gov/nchs/). Medicaid patients could receive treatment, even though they were poor and thus more likely to go for treatment. In other words, the poor are likely to use emergency health care as a first option, but the uninsured (who typically include those that lie just above the poverty line as well as middle-class households) do not. Both groups often wait, likely as a result of cost and not seeking medical care until it becomes more dire or critical. The result is more serious health problems that require more expensive procedures. The National Healthcare Disparities Report draws attention to the polarity in the access and quality of care between differing populations. With the adjustment of the Medicaid qualifying rates and the introduction of the Affordable Care Act passed by Congress and signed by President Barack Obama in 2010, the number of new people with access to quality medical care is set to increase by thirty million and, hopefully, begin to reduce some of the disparities between the various groups. At present, however, considerable disparities exist. For example, the following are a few disparities as reported by the Centers for Disease Control (CDC) (http://www.cdc.gov/nchs/data/databriefs/db74.htm, accessed October 27, 2011).

Infant Mortality

In 2007, the infant mortality rate for non-Hispanic black women was 2.4 times the rate for non-Hispanic white women. American Indian/Alaska Native (AIAN) and Puerto Rican women also had relatively high infant mortality rates. The higher infant mortality rate for non-Hispanic black and Puerto Rican women, compared with non-Hispanic white women, was primarily due to their higher levels of preterm births and preterm-related causes of death.

In contrast, the higher infant mortality rate for AIAN women was mostly due to causes of mortality rates at term and near-term, and not to a higher percentage of preterm births.

Higher infant mortality rates from sudden infant death syndrome contributed the most to the infant mortality gap between AIAN and non-Hispanic white women. The infant mortality rate for non-Hispanic Blacks was 13.31 percent compared with 5.63 percent for non-Hispanic Whites. The next highest rate was for American Indians and Alaskan Natives (grouped together).

While such disparities reflect multiple factors, many of the factors stem back to income differentials. Residing within urban areas exposes individuals to higher carcinogenic environments, stress, and concentrations of crime, drug use, as noted earlier. Wilson (1996) has discussed the concentration effects of urban poverty. But as the NHDR notes, much of the differentials also reflect lack of access to good, quality health care. Essentially, those individuals who make up the racial and ethnic minorities in the United States suffer from concentrations of poor health care and poor access to health care compared with those in the middle and upper socioeconomic classes in America. As the NHDR report notes, the most defining characteristic of poor health care in the United States is poverty.

HIV Infection

A second example of unequal health care is the rate of HIV infection. The CDC reports rates of HIV perinatal infection by racial and ethnic group. During 2004–2007, the average annual overall rate of diagnoses among non-Hispanic black children was 12.3 per 100,000, compared with Hispanic children (2.0) and non-Hispanic white children (0.5) (MacDorman and Mathews 2011).

Cancer Rates

Still another example of disparities by racial and ethnic groups is the rate of cancers in the United States. As the CDC reports, for all *new* cancers combined among men, "The rate of new cancer cases is highest among Black men, followed by White, Hispanic, Asian/Pacific Islander, and American Indian/Alaska Native men." And the death rates from cancer are also reported to be highest among black men compared with all other groups (CDC 2010, accessed October 27, 2011).

The NHDR report notes similar disparities for cancers among women in the United States. There is, however, an unfortunate irony for women. The rate for *new* cases of cancer is highest for white women, followed by black, Hispanic, Asian/Pacific Islander, and American Indian/ Alaska Native women. At the same time, the death rates from cancer are highest among black women, followed by white, American Indian/Alaska Native, Hispanic, and Asian/Pacific Islander women (CDC cancer rates 2010, accessed October 27, 2011). The clear reversal of these rates between new cancers and death from breast cancer (for white and black women) is a strong indictment of access to health care and health care treatment. In other words, the discovery of new cancers likely reflects the better access to health care that white women have, leading to a higher detection rate, while access for women of color lags. Black women are also more likely to postpone seeking treatment, and thus more likely to die from cancer than white women.

One final example regarding cancer rates is the recent documentary about Dee Dee Ricks. *The Education of Dee Dee Ricks* is an HBO documentary about the availability of treatment for breast cancer for black and white women. The documentary discusses the efforts of one white woman, Ricks, a breast cancer survivor herself, to help black women who lack adequate health care because of a lack of insurance (ABC *Nightline*, October 26, 2011). The documentary portrays Rick's own struggle with cancer and a double mastectomy, and then reports her efforts to obtain treatment for black women by raising money. The film depicts, on a personal level, the dramatic difference in accessibility by black and white women for breast cancer treatment.

SUMMARY

The disparities reported by the CDC and other agencies mirror the numerous other health care disparities in the NHDR. And as the NHDR report notes, much of the lack of access and care is related to lower income and worse access to health care by the poor or the near-poor. A 2011 report in *USA Today* (October 5, 2011) also notes that the worst-rated hospitals treat a larger share of the poor. Among other findings, the article reports that those same hospitals treat twice the proportion of elderly black patients and poor patients than the best hospitals, and their patients are more likely to die of heart attacks and pneumonia. Many of these "worst" hospitals are in the South where African Americans represent a larger proportion of the population than in the nation as a whole.

The *USA Today* report on the worst hospitals is strikingly similar to the conclusion of Wilson's (1996) work on "concentration effects" for cities. While Wilson emphasizes concentration effects in the cities, the South also has concentrations of the poor and minorities. Just as the well-to-do people fled the inner cities in other parts of the nation, wealthy (disproportionately white) flight and more motivated people (black flight) fled the rural South to urban centers in the South and North. This internal migration left pockets of people in the South who tend to be disproportionately poor and African American. This is also where the *USA Today* article found the worst hospitals to be located.

In sum, the healthcare system in the United States lags behind other industrialized countries on major measures of quality, efficiency, and access to care. The disparities suggest that the wealthy in America may be keeping up with the rest of the world, but good health care treatment for the poor and minority groups is disproportionally lagging. Americans die far more frequently than people in other countries as a result of preventable or treatable conditions (Levey, 2011). According to Levey, the United States has made progress, but other countries have made greater progress in treating such conditions. His report points directly to the lack of insurance, which in turn prevents people from obtaining good access to health care or having prescriptions filled. For example, one-third of American adults have such problems compared with just 5 percent in England.

Although reports such as the NHDR reflect the health of the nation, they do not yet fully reflect the post–great recession conditions. Numerous reports in recent years have pointed to the decline of middle-class incomes, even before the "great recession." We can only surmise how profoundly the recent recession has affected the disparity in health care access and treatment.

REFERENCES

ABC's *Nightline. The Education of Dee Dee Ricks.* http://abcnews.go.com/blogs/health/2011/10/26/resources-for-the-education-of-dee-dee-ricks-treating-breast-cancer/. Accessed October 27, 2011.

Agency for Healthcare Research and Quality (2011). *National Healthcare Disparities Report.* http://fodh.phhp.ufl.edu/files/2011/05/AHRQ-disparities-2010.pdf.

CDC: *Cancer rates (2010).* http://www.cdc.gov/Features/CancerHealthDisparities/. Accessed October 27, 2011.

CDC: *Racial/Ethnic Disparities Among Children with Diagnoses of Perinatal HIV Infection–34 States, 2004–2007.* http://www.cdc.gov/mmwr/preview/mmwrhtml/mm5904a2.htm?s_cid=mm5904a2_e. Accessed October 27, 2001.

CIA: *Infant mortality rate.* https://cia.gov/library/publications/the-world-factbook/rankorder/2091rank.html.

CIA: *Life expectancy.* https://www.cia.gov/library/publications/the-world-factbook/rankorder/2102rank.html.

Garcia, Tamyra Carroll, Amy B. Bernstein, & Mary Ann Bush. (2010).

"Emergency Department Visitors and Visits: Who Used the Emergency Room in 2007?" *NCHS Data Brief, No. 38.* May 2010. http://www.cdc.gov/nchs/data/databriefs/db38.pdf. Accessed April 12, 2012.

Levey, N. N. "American health care trails other countries." Tribune Washington Bureau, as reported in *Anchorage Daily News,* October 18, 2011. http://www.adn.com/2011/10/18/2126700/health-care-in-us-trails-other.html#ixzz1bFafl5kj. Accessed October 27, 2011.

MacDorman, M. F., & T. J. Mathews. "Understanding racial and ethnic disparities in U.S. infant mortality rates." *NCHS Data Brief, No. 74.* Hyattsville, MD: National Center for Health Statistics. 2011.

New York Times. "Welfare Limits Left Poor Adrift as Recession Hit." http://www.nytimes.com/2012/04/08/us/welfare-limits-left-poor-adrift-as-recession-hit.html?pagewanted=1&_r=2&nl=todaysheadlines&emc=edit_th_20120408. Accessed April 12, 2012.

Pear, R. (October 25, 2011). "Top Earners Doubled Share of Nation's Income, Study Finds." *New York Times.* Accessed October 26, 2011. http://www.nytimes.com/2011/10/26/us/politics/top-earners-doubled-share-of-nations-income-cbo-says.html?_r=1&nl=todaysheadlines&emc=tha23.

Statistical Handbook of the United States: http://www.census.gov/compendia/statab/2012/tables/12s0105.pdf, table 104. Accessed May 1, 2012.

USA Today (October 6, 2011). "Study: Worst hospitals treat larger share of poor." http://yourlife.usatoday.com/health/healthcare/story/2011-10-05/Study-Worst-hospitals-treat-larger-share-of-poor/50670780/1. Accessed October 15, 2011.

Washington Post. "Polls Find Americans Uneasy as Income Inequality Increases." June 19, 2011, p. A1, A16.

Wilson, W. J. (1996). *When Work Disappears: The World of the New Urban Poor.* New York: Knopf.

World Health Organization Annual Report. 2011. http://www.who.int/gho/publications/world_health_statistics/EN_WHS2011_Full.pdf. Accessed April 29, 2012.

Wilkinson, Richard G., & Kate Pickett. *The Spirit Level: Why Greater Equality Makes Societies Stronger.* London: Bloomsbury Press, 2009.

A BRIEF LOOK AT THE PATIENT PROTECTION AND AFFORDABLE CARE ACT OF 2010

By Vasco Deon Kidd, DHSc, MPH, PA-C, MS

INTRODUCTION

The United States healthcare system is in a state of transition after passing the Patient Protection and Affordable Care Act (PPACA, or commonly referred to as the ACA), which is designed to improve health disparities, reduce health care costs, provide coverage to the uninsured, and improve the quality and delivery of health care. Over the past several decades, the US healthcare system has been spiraling out of control. Racial and ethnic disparities are increasing at a time when the country is becoming more diverse. The number of uninsured Americans remains high while health care costs continue to outpace inflation and wages. According to a report in 2009 by the Centers for Medicare & Medicaid Services, health care spending accounted for 17.3 percent of the US economy, more than any other industrialized nation (Pickert, 2010).

Yet, even with out-of-control spending on health care, our system of health delivery is neither better nor more equitable than the rest of the industrialized world. Further, high unemployment coupled with a fragmented US healthcare system has led to substantial social inequalities in health in recent years. Racial and ethnic minorities not only lack adequate insurance and access to health care, but also are more likely than Whites to die prematurely of chronic diseases (Bahls, 2011). The looming question is how does society correct these imbalances in order to facilitate improvements in health outcomes, life expectancy, and quality of life?

It is estimated that 48.6 million people were uninsured in 2011 (Fox, 2012). Recent research indicates that as many as 44,500 deaths per year in the United States are linked to the lack of health insurance (Fox, 2012; Wilper, Woolhandler, Lasser, McCormick, Bor, and Himmelstein, 2009). One of the most effective ways to shrink the health disparities gap and improve quality of life is to expand access to health care and control the costs of medical coverage. Expanding medical coverage among low-income adults increases healthcare utilization, improving health and wellness while reducing the financial burden carried by the most vulnerable. Without these improvements, those most vulnerable will continue to delay or deny medical care due to cost (Healthday, 2011).

THE AFFORDABLE CARE ACT

The Patient Protection and Affordable Care Act, signed into law on March 23, 2010, was created to address coverage gaps and pressing health inequities while improving health outcomes and reducing health care costs. The ACA includes a multitude of provisions that will be implemented in stages over several years, but the major provisions involved are health insurance reform, expanded coverage, extended requirements of public programs, health insurance exchanges, and the creation of patient-centered medical homes.

Health insurance reforms will prevent insurance companies from denying protection to consumers with pre-existing conditions and instituting a lifetime maximum of coverage that they will pay out on an individual/family consumer. Additionally, reforms will ensure that preventative care will be provided with no deductibles, co-insurance, or co-payments. Preventative care ranges from the annual visit, including a physical examination with lab work, to procedures and tests such a colonoscopy or mammogram (http://www.commonwealthfund.org/Health-Reform/Health-Reform-Resource.aspx).

Another major specification of the ACA is the expanded coverage for children and young adults. Since young adults, aged nineteen to twenty-nine, rank among the highest uninsured population (http://kff.org/health-reform/issue-brief/uninsured-young-adults-a-profile-and-overview/), the ACA increases the age of health insurance coverage to twenty-six years of age for those children still living at home. Thus, this nation can significantly improve coverage rates among the uninsured.

The Affordable Care Act also provides for an expansion of Medicaid to 133 percent of the federal poverty level (FPL), casting a wider safety net to include childless adults whose income meet Medicaid requirements in efforts to shrink the coverage gap (http://kff.org/health-reform/issue-brief/expanding-medicaid-to-low-income-childless-adults/). The FPL was $11,000 for an individual and $20,000 for a family of three in 2012. The Centers for Medicare & Medicaid Services' (CMS) Office of the Actuary has estimated that, as a result of the expansion, the number of Medicaid enrollees will increase by 14.9 million in 2014 and by 25.9 million in 2020 (GAO, 2012). Federal funding has been allocated to cover the states' costs of new enrollees into the Medicaid program, as seen in Table 1.

Table 1: Federal funding designated to states for Medicaid expansion

100% for three years from 2014–2016
95% federal funds in 2017
94% federal funds in 2018
93% federal funds in 2019
90% federal funds in 2020 and beyond

http://www.idph.state.ia.us/hcr_committees/common/pdf/hbe/medicaid_expansion_under_the_aca.pdf.

Many citizens lacking health insurance coverage fall into a middle-class window that is above 133 percent of the federal poverty level. The Health Insurance Exchange or HIX is one significant way the remaining coverage gap can be reduced. Simply put, a health insurance exchange is a marketplace where insurers compete for customers. Health insurances exchanges are a relatively new concept to most states. Consumers can use these exchanges to purchase insurance policies. Those consumers whose incomes fall between 133 percent and 400 percent of the federal poverty level can apply for subsidies through the exchange. By 2014, all states will be required to have implemented health insurance exchanges (the federal government does provide technical and financial assistance to help states become compliant). The exact configuration and governance of a health insurance exchange will vary from state to state, but the idea is to create an easy-to-use price and benefits comparison for the consumer (http://kaiserfamilyfoundation.files.wordpress.com/2011/04/8061-021.pdf).

Notably, the ACA has added provisions to strengthen the primary care system through increasing reimbursement rates for providers, incentivizing primary care, and the adoption and promotion of a concept called Patient-Centered Medical Homes (PCMH) in which greater connection between provider and patient is designed to aid in improving health care delivery and, hence, health outcomes. PCMH is a model health care setting that creates partnerships between patients (and family members, when appropriate) and their individual health care provider and other members of the health care team, with the purpose of facilitating "continuous and coordinated care" (http://www.acponline.org/advocacy/state_health_policy/hottopics/pcmh.pdf). The PCMH increases provider accessibility to its patients in a number of ways, including fielding questions and offering consultations electronically and rendering care in suitable, multicultural, and linguistic ways. The PCHM is a model that considers building relationships in ways that are supportive of differences with team members. Additionally, this model evaluates the whole patient with an eye toward improved patient experiences and health outcomes in the intimidating world of health care (http://www.pcmh.ahrq.gov/portal/server.pt/community/pcmh_home/1483/pcmh_defining_the_pcmh_v2).

Healthcare reform is designed to improve patient coverage and outcomes while reducing costs. The Patient Protection and Affordable Care Act addresses significant shortcomings in the current US healthcare system; however, various arms of the act are dependent on one another for success. For example, one controversial piece of the legislation has been the individual mandate, which requires everyone to show proof of insurance by 2014 or risk paying a penalty. Though some citizens and lawmakers have objected to this concept, the justification for this design is to control costs by spreading the risk to all individuals, thus affording insurance companies the ability to keep premiums down and improve payouts. The ACA includes a multitude of provisions focusing efforts on the end goal of improving the quality of life for all US citizens.

IMPLEMENTATION OF THE PPACA: OBSTACLES AND ADVANTAGES

Even though the federal government has committed financial resources to improve access to care, obstacles remain. In June 2012, the Supreme Court upheld the constitutionality of most of the Affordable Care Act, but struck down a key provision that forced states to expand Medicaid eligibility to 133 percent of the FPL. Under the ACA, states were required to participate in Medicaid expansion set by the federal government, and failure to cooperate and comply with the expansion would result in withdrawal of matching federal funds from the current Medicaid program. The Supreme Court ruled that Congress had exceeded its constitutional authority with this provision (Liptak 2012), thus allowing states to opt out of the Medicaid expansion efforts if they so choose. For those states that choose to opt out, it is unclear how their residents who are above the state Medicaid threshold yet below the government eligibility for subsidies (133 percent to 400 percent of FLP) will be covered. In addition, many states do not make Medicaid available to childless adults at any income level. This could possibly leave many Americans without suitable and affordable health care coverage unless a solution is formulated.

Another obstacle that may result during the healthcare reform is access to health care providers. With an already growing disparity in access to care, only about half of American physicians accept new Medicaid patients (Cunningham and May, 2006); hence, increasing health insurance coverage does not necessarily translate into improved access to care. In addition, there continues to be a decrease in the number of clinicians interested in pursuing primary care fields. During the past decade, many physicians have shied away from primary care due to rising patient load, lower reimbursement, job dissatisfaction, and administrative paperwork in exchange for a more lucrative and prestigious career in specialty care (Brewster, 2008). Also, the number of medical students who plan to practice primary care medicine has dropped 51.8 percent since 1997, according to the American Academy of Family Medicine. This comes at a time when the United States is facing a looming physician shortage. It is estimated that 45,400 to 65,800 primary care providers will be needed between 2020 and 2025 (AAMC 2008). The perpetual shortage of primary care practitioners could have a negative effect on implementation of healthcare reform, which is designed to focus principally on the primary care sector (Gopal, 2012).

Fortunately, there are retention provisions imbedded within the ACA to incentivize clinicians to remain in the practice of primary care. The federal government now offers a 10 percent bonus to primary care providers such as internists, pediatricians, family practitioners, physician assistants, nurse practitioners, and other clinical nurse specialists or APRNs who render professional services in a health professional shortage area (Anderson, 2010). To be eligible for such bonus payments, 60 percent of a provider's Medicare-allowed charges in a prior period must be for primary care services (Anderson, 2010). Also, the PPACA will offer loan repayment strategies for eligible providers practicing in "public service" and "high-needs" areas (low income, low access to care) (AAMC, 2012).

One of the major benefits of the Affordable Care Act is its focus on addressing health and health care disparities (http://kff.org/disparities-policy/). Most notably is the ACA goal aimed at providing insurance to those who cannot afford coverage. As noted previously, this tends to be those in the lower SEC who make just above the poverty line ($11,000 per individual) and, as such, do not qualify for public assistance. These individuals are typically people of color. It is estimated that from 2003 to 2006, the cost of racial/ethnic disparities in the form of direct medical expenses and lost productivity in the United States exceeded $1 trillion (Laveist, 2009).

The PPACA attempts to further address disparities in health with key provisions in such areas as childhood obesity and public health innovations. Health economists estimate the indirect costs of adult obesity at $506 per obese worker per year due to lower worker productivity, resulting in $4.3 billion a year for absenteeism (Gates et.al, 2008). Spending in the United States on obesity-related illnesses may rise by as much as $66 billion a year by 2030 (Gerlin, 2011). Unfortunately, the impact of obesity on worker productivity is felt disproportionately among people of color, who have higher rates of the disease and subsequent comorbidities compared with Whites (Blackwell, 2010). Childhood and adult obesity rates are higher in the United States than most developed countries, and if current obesity trends are not reversed, they will continue to progress toward diseases of slow accumulation in the form of heart disease, stroke, hypertension, and diabetes.

Under the PPACA, $25 million will be allocated over four years to address child obesity. Further, the US Department of Health and Human Services will provide guidance to health care providers and obesity-related services available for Medicaid enrollees. At the same time, public health innovations will include funding research in public health services and systems to examine best-prevention practice. Public and private partnerships will be created to conduct an education campaign on national prevention and health promotion outreach. Additionally, the Department of Health and Human Services will allocate funding for federally qualified health centers (FQHC) to continue to service the poor and underserved.

Obesity is just one condition that is a result of health inequities in American life. Another area where the ACA will address health care disparities is in the form of training more health care practitioners to meet the growing demands of a rapidly changing and increasingly diverse and aging populace. Under the PPACA 93.150, primary care residency programs will see an increase in funding for the expansion of physicians trained in general internal medicine, general pediatrics, and family medicine residencies (ACA, 2010). Awards of $80,000 are given per expanded position per year (ACA, 2010). Likewise, millions of dollars in funding are now available through the Department of Health and Human Services for the expansion of physician assistant training programs by funding new student stipends, reasonable living expenses, educational expenses, and indirect costs to support higher enrollment. The objective is to increase the number of physician assistants in primary care (ACA, 2010).

Medical education is beginning to recognize the importance of developing curricula that exposes students to different cultural norms, beliefs, and traditions, which will likely be encountered during clinical practice. The health care professionals of the twenty-first century must understand how social and cultural factors associated with access to care, medication non-adherence, alternative therapies, and end-of-life decisions all influence treatment modalities and care. Under the PPACA, the Department of Health and Human Services supports the development of model curricula in health profession education to train medical professionals in cultural competency, health disparities, social determinants of health, and prevention. Any curriculum model should teach health care providers how internal biases can influence clinical decision making and demonstrate appropriate strategies for managing such biases.

Other benefits of the PPACA in addressing health care disparities include $95 million for investing in and improving school-based health centers to strengthen safety nets that provide poor children and adolescents with needed health services. Also, the PPACA appropriates grants to study both current gaps and also research-based improvements needed in existing measures of health care quality for use in government health programs (Hillsman, 2010). These grants help establish an effective framework to collect and analyze aggregate data on health care quality as well as report on efficacy data and level of resources used by various therapies in health care delivery (Hillsman, 2010). These and other provisions will lead to meaningful reform of both public and private health programs.

Despite the additional funding to medical education and incentive payments to clinicians practicing in primary care specialties, it is yet to be determined whether the PPACA will stabilize and expand the primary care workforce. What is known is that given the current shortage of primary care physicians and increased patient demand, the US healthcare system will invariably develop a greater reliance on mid-level providers (physician assistants, nurse practitioners, and advanced nurses) who seek an expanded scope of practice in their training (Feltes and Vrabel, 2010).

CONCLUSION

In 2010, the 111th Congress took a bold step to revamp the US health industry by taking up health reform, and it did what its predecessors were unable to do. The PPACA has revolutionized the US healthcare system and may have set the nation on a path to universal health care for all its citizens. The primary goals of the PPACA are to provide health care coverage to thirty-two million uninsured Americans, improve access to care, and reduce health care costs. Further, the Supreme Court ruling and Congress's pronouncement of the PPACA as the law of the land now moves us into the discussion on how best to implement the legislation's provisions. This may pose a difficult task given the economic realities faced by some states, ongoing political brinkmanship, and a declining primary care workforce. In addition, the Supreme Court decision, which upheld the PPACA, may have complicated its implementation by allowing states to opt out of Medicaid expansion efforts, potentially leaving many Americans without coverage options. It is far too early to know the true impact of the PPACA until all the provisions have been fully implemented and evaluated, but this is the first effort made to reduce the enormous inequities in health and health care between the "haves" and the "have-nots." With renewed hope, there is new opportunity to strive toward equality, as every American deserves the right to have affordable health care to improve their quality of life.

REFERENCES

AAMC (2008). *The Complexities of Physician Supply and Demand: Projections Through 2025, Center for Workforce Studies*. Retrieved from https://www.aamc.org/download/158076/data/updated_projections_through_2025.pdf.

Anderson, G. (2012). "Expanding access to primary care services and general surgery services." Horne-llo.com. Retrieved from http://www.horne-llp.com/industries/health-care/resources/healthbeat-special-alerts-health-care-reform-series/expanding-access-to-primary-care-services-and-general-surgery-services.

Bahls, C. (2011). "Health Policy Brief: Achieving Equity in Health." *Health Affairs*. Retrieved from http://healthaffairs.org/healthpolicybriefs/brief_pdfs/healthpolicybrief_53.pdf.

Brewster, A. (2008). "The crisis of primary care physicians." *Boston Globe*. Retrieved from http://www.boston.com/bostonglobe/editorial_opinion/oped/articles/2008/05/29/the_crisis_of_primary_care_physicians/.

Condon, S. (2012). Television network report finds states opting out of Medicaid expansion could leave many uninsured. CBS News.

Deloitte Center for Health Solutions (2011). "Physician perspectives about health care reform and the future of the medical profession." http://www.deloitte.com/assets/Dcom- UnitedStates/Local%20Assets/Documents/us_lshc_PhysicianPerspectives_121211.pdf.

Cunningham, P. & May, J. (2006). *Medicaid patients increasingly concentrated among physicians*. Center for Studying Health System Change Tracking Report No. 16. Retrieved from http://www.hschange.com/CONTENT/866/?PRINT=1.

Feltes, J. & Vrabel, D. (2010). "One Bite at a Time: PPACA's Immediate Impact on Physicians." MDNews.com.

Fox, E. (2012). "Fewer Americans uninsured." US Bureau of the Census. CNNMoney. Retrived from http://money.cnn.com/2012/09/12/news/economy/census-bureau-health-insurance/index.html.

Gates, D. M. et al. (2008). "Obesity and presenteeism: The impact of body mass index on workplace productivity." *Journal of Occupational Environmental Medicine* 50 (1): 39–45.

Gerlin, A. (2011). "Expanding waistlines may boost U.S. health cost $66 billion a year by 2030." Bloomberg.com. Retrieved from http://www.bloomberg.com/news/2011-08- 25/expanding-waistlines- may-boost-u-s-health-cost-66-billion-a-year-by-2030.html.

Gopal, L. (2012). "Shortage of primary care doctors in US may render PPACA pipe dream." Medindia.net. Retrieved from http://www.medindia.net/news/shortage-of-primary-care-doctors-in-us-may-render-ppaca-a-pipe-dream-97598-1.htm.

Hartley, E. (2010). "Doctors in demand: Primary problem." Inforum.com. Retrieved from http://www.inforum.com/event/article/id/287260/.

Healthday (2011). "Medicaid coverage 'substantially' improves access to care: Study." http://health.usnews.com/health-news/managing-your-healthcare/insurance/articles/2011/07/07/medicaid-coverage-substantially-improves- access-to-care-study.

Hillsman, S. (2010). "Historic health reform legislation enhances the role of social science research in improving Americans' health." ASAnet.org. Retrieved from http://www.asanet.org/footnotes/apr10/vp_0410.html.

Hislop, R. (2010). "Health reform and Medicaid expansion." *National Health Reform Magazine*. Retrieved from http://www.healthcarereformmagazine.com/article/health-reform-and-medicaid-expansion.html.

H.R. 3590, *The Patient Protection Affordability Care Act (PPACA)*. Retrieved from http://healthyamericans.org/assets/files/TFAH_Timeline_March2010.pdf.

Koba, M. (2011). "Medicare and Medicaid: CNBC Explains." Retrieved from http://www.cnbc.com/id/43992654/Medicare_and_Medicaid_CNBC_Explains.

LaVeist, T. A., Gaskin, D. J. & Richard, P. (2009). "The economic burden of health inequalities in the United States." Washington, DC: *The Joint Center for Political and Economic*. Retrieved from http://www.jointcenter.org/hpi/sites/all/files/Burden_Of_Health_FINAL_0.pdf.

Liptak, A. (2012). "Supreme Court Upholds Health Care Law, 5-4, in Victory for Obama." *New York Times*. Online.

Palestrant, D. (2010). "Why physicians oppose the health care reform bill." Retrieved from, http://www.forbes.com/2010/04/28/health-care-reform-physicians-opinions-contributors-daniel-palestrant_2.html.

Pickert, K. (2010). "The unsustainable U.S. health care system." Time.com. Retrieved from http://swampland.time.com/2010/02/04/the-unsustainable-u-s-health-care-system/.

Shick, M. (2012). Student loan repayment information. *The Association of American Medical Colleges*. Retrived from https://www.aamc.org/advocacy/meded/79048/student_loan_repayment.htm.

The Government Accountability Office (GAO). *States' Implementation of the Patient Protection and Affordable Care Act. GAO-12-821*.

The Physicians Foundation (2010). *2010 doctor survey: Key findings*. Retrieved from http://www.physiciansfoundation.org/uploadedFiles/Survey%20Key%20Findings%20Nov%202010.pdf.

Wilper, A. P., S. Woolhandler, K. E. Lasser, D. McCormick, D. H. Bor, & D. U. Himmelstein. "Health Insurance and Mortality in U.S. Adults" *American Journal of Public Health*, vol. 99, no. 12, 2009, pp. 1–8.

UNDERREPRESENTED MINORITY RECRUITMENT IN THE PHYSICIAN ASSISTANT PROFESSION

By Michelle DiBaise

The Department of Health and Human Services defines underrepresented minorities (URM) as African Americans, Mexican Americans, Latinos, Native Americans, and Alaska Natives (Department of Health and Human Services [DHHS], 2006). Underrepresented minority enrollment in Physician Assistant (PA) programs has historically been higher than in other health professions (PAEA, 2012). The difference may be rooted in the history of the profession. The PA profession began with the graduation of three former military corpsmen from Duke University in 1967. In the early evolution of the PA concept, program training length ranged from 12–18 months and conferred an associate's degree, a bachelor's degree, or a certificate upon completion (Dobmeyer, Sonderegger, & Lowin, 1975). Alexander (1970) provided the first report on URM enrollment in the PA profession shortly after its commencement. The author discussed the shortage of minority physicians and posited that minority PAs could serve as the answer to this shortage, particularly in rural areas (Alexander, 1970). In Alexander's report, the National Medical Association (NMA), an organization comprised of minority physicians, not only endorsed the PA concept, but called for expansion of enrollment in PA programs to include "poor blacks" (Alexander, 1970, p. 429). Since PA training was relatively short and did not require a college degree at the time, the PA profession was seen as a viable option to increase the diversity of health care.

Despite the higher URM enrollment in the PA profession, there were indications that the distribution among programs was skewed. In the late 1970s, Schneller and Weiner (1978) surveyed 1,126 students who had matriculated in one of the 49 PA programs in existence. Findings revealed that 78 (6.9 percent) of the students were African American and nearly

40 percent of those students were enrolled in just two PA programs (Schneller & Weiner, 1978). The authors also demonstrated that the African American students were more likely to decrease their course load or withdraw from college altogether due to financial constraints compared to the white students (Schneller & Weiner, 1978). Weiner and Schneller (1981) followed the same students and tracked their graduation rate; two years later, the authors found that 65 percent of African American males, 75 percent of African American females, 90 percent of white males, and 92 percent of white females graduated.

Over the next two decades, the number of PA programs remained fairly stable, but URM enrollment began to decrease (Accreditation Review Committee for Physician Assistants [ARC-PA], 2011). He, Cyran, and Salling (2009) demonstrated this decline in URM enrollment in PA programs in the United States from 1980 to 2007. The percentage of African Americans declined from 9.5 percent in 1980 to 7.8 percent in 2007, and American Indian student numbers remained stable at 0.5 percent. While Hispanic or Latino populations increased from 5.4 percent in 1980 to 10.1 percent in 2005, the numbers subsequently decreased in 2007 to 8.2 percent (He et al., 2009). The most recent Physician Assistant Education Association (PAEA) Annual Report shows that of the 5,563 students who matriculated in 2012, 3.9 percent were African American, 1 percent were American Indian/Alaska Native, and 7.6 percent were Hispanic (PAEA, 2014a).

Barriers to URM Enrollment: Potential Factors Affecting the Decline of URM Applicants

There was a sharp increase in the number of PA programs beginning in the mid to late 1990s, a trend that shows no sign of slowing (ARC-PA, 2011). As of Spring 2014, there were a reported 181 accredited PA programs in the United States, with 65 additional programs set to begin by 2016 (ARC-PA, 2014; Glicken & Miller, 2013). And despite increasing numbers of programs, the ratio of applicants to available seats is anticipated to increase (PAEA, 2012). Yet, there remains a glaring disparity in URM student matriculation into physician assistant school.

In 2001, PAEA began using a Centralized Application Service for PAs (CASPA), which allows for tracking of applicant data (PAEA, 2012). In 2011, 88 percent of all PA programs participated in CASPA (Glicken & Miller, 2013). According to the CASPA data report that same year, 16,569 unique applicants applied to PA programs (PAEA, 2012). Each CASPA-member PA program received an estimated 759 applications, with each applicant applying to an average of six programs (PAEA, 2012). Of the 16,569 applicants, 4,731students matriculated into a PA program in 2011 (PAEA, 2012). The data on URM applicants demonstrate not only a continual decrease of applicants over the past six years, but a significant difference between the percentage of URM applicants and the percentage of URM matriculants (PAEA, 2012). While Hispanic students account for 8.43 percent of the applicants, only 6.8 percent of the matriculants are Hispanic (PAEA, 2012). The divide is greater for African American students, representing 6.55 percent of applicants, but only 3.5 percent of matriculants (PAEA, 2012). On the other hand, white students represent 65.5 percent of the applicants and show an increase in the percent of matriculants at 79.5 percent (PAEA, 2012).

Barr, Gonzalez, and Wanat (2008) studied students enrolled at Stanford University on a premedical track to determine the decline in interest in medicine. The authors found that the largest declines in interest in medicine occurred among female and URM students. The most common reason provided was a bad experience with a single course, most commonly organic chemistry, followed closely by poor academic advising (Barr et al., 2008). Here, additional factors are explored.

Academic Preparation

In 1998, the Association of Physician Assistant Programs (the forerunner of the current PAEA), in partnership with the American Academy of Physician Assistants (AAPA), convened a task force to determine the entry and terminal degrees of the profession (APAP, 2000). The published decision declared the bachelor's as the standard entry level and the master's as the terminal degree for PA programs (APAP, 2000). A master's as the terminal degree led to an increase of program length, with a range of 18–36 months and a mean program length of 26.9 months (PAEA, 2012). By the 2011–2012 admissions cycle, 87 percent of matriculants had a baccalaureate degree or higher upon entry into the PA program, and 91.2 percent of the accredited PA programs granted a master's as the terminal degree (ARC-PA, 2014; PAEA 2014).

Though there is currently no published literature available on the URM student enroll-ment compared to degree awarded in PA programs, there is growing concern, as URM students are typically left behind in health care occupations and the STEM (science, technology, engineering, and math) fields. Roderick, Nagaoka, and Coca (2009) found a widening gap between the college-bound aspirations of URM students and their ability to earn a four-year degree. The authors demonstrated that lower family income and African American or Latino students were less likely than white or affluent students to graduate (Roderick et al., 2009). The URM and disadvantaged students on average were less prepared in the core academic skills and generally required remediation in college. Roderick et al. (2009) also demonstrated that nearly 50 percent of white students, but only 25 percent of Latino and 12 percent of African American students, meet the minimum benchmark in mathematics on standardized tests (i.e., ACT). This is an area of fruitful inquiry for PA educators concerned with research directed at increasing the number of URM applicants, matriculants, and ultimately graduates.

Financial Issues

As stated previously, students from low-income families are least likely to complete a four-year college degree, and the reasons are multifactorial. Boyd, Hernandez, and Braun (2011) surveyed disadvantaged students and discovered that many had difficulties with finances. The problems they encountered included difficulty navigating the Free Application for Financial Student Aid (FAFSA), unreliable transportation, and the inability to afford living independently. For example, students that cannot afford rent and live with their parents must be claimed as a dependent. This negates their ability to file an independent FAFSA and decreases the aid award. Some students were concerned about identity theft if they filled out the FAFSA forms, and others feared they would pay higher taxes (Boyd et al., 2011). Students may also be required to work to afford school, which can adversely affect their grades while enrolled, while other students may drop out of school because they need to support their families financially (Boyd et al., 2011). A review of the literature in 2009 showed that only 26 percent of white students were considered poor (<100 percent of the Federal Poverty Level [FPL]) or near poor (100–199 percent FPL) compared to Hispanic students at 58 percent poor and near poor, African American students at 54 percent poor and near poor, and American Indian students at 57 percent poor and near poor (Smith, Nsiah-Kumi, Jones, & Pamies, 2009a). Financial factors might influence less affluent students to obtain courses through community colleges, potentially making them less competitive for a PA program.

Minority Faculty Mentors

A recent survey of the literature found that another barrier to URM enrollment in an institution is a lack of URM faculty to serve as mentors (Smith et al., 2009a). In a review of the demographics of PA faculty over the past three years, there has been a decrease in minority faculty. In 2008, 82.7 percent of PA faculty members were white; in 2012, 84.9 percent were white (PAEA, 2010; PAEA, 2014a) (See Figure 1). A lack of diversity among PA faculty may lead to a less-than-satisfactory mentoring experience for URM students. Students of color who have experienced such a dearth of mentors who look like them throughout their undergraduate studies may be hesitant to apply to professional graduate education at institutions that similarly lack diversity among its faculty and staff.

Anti–Affirmative Action Legislation

Taking into consideration the factors such as lower academic preparedness, greater financial strife, and a lack of minority faculty mentors, students of color have a long history of underperforming on admissions criteria. Hence, affirmative action laws were designed to provide equal opportunity to URM students who were at a disadvantage compared to the majority of white students, who on average have better educational opportunities, higher math and science grades, and higher scores on standardized testing (Smith, Nsiah-Kumi, Jones, & Pamies, 2009a). Critics of affirmative action claim that race-based criteria discriminate against white students and decrease the quality of the programs in which affirmative action is employed (Smith et al., 2009a). Though race-based quotas were eliminated in the 1978 Supreme Court case, *Regents of the University of California v. Bakke* (U.S. Supreme Court, 1978), the Court did allow for the establishment of admission procedures that could consider race, economic background, and other criteria as deemed important to the mission of the public institution under the strict scrutiny test. Strict scrutiny requires the institution to demonstrate a "compelling interest" in the race- or ethnicity-based decision that must be necessary to meet the mission of the program after race-neutral options are utilized (Smith et al., 2009b, p. 854). Recently, several states, including Arizona, California, Colorado, Florida, Michigan, Missouri, Nebraska, Oklahoma, Texas, and Washington have proposed legislative action challenging affirmative action policies (Smith, Nsiah-Kumi, Jones, & Pamies, 2009b). Of these states, Arizona, California, and Nebraska have successfully passed anti–affirmative action legislation, which blocks public institutions from considering race, gender, ethnicity, or national origin in the admissions process of public institutions.

In the 2003 case *Grutter v. Bollinger*, however, the Supreme Court upheld the decision made in *Bakke*, siding with the University of Michigan's ability to use race in the holistic and individualized application review (U.S. Supreme Court, 2003). In the 2013 U.S. Supreme Court decision in *Fisher v. University of Texas*, the Court again upheld its earlier decision in *Bakke*, but also stated that race-neutral approaches must have been tried and shown to fail to increase diversity within an institution, in addition to meeting the strict scrutiny test (Rosenbaum, Teitelbaum, & Scott, 2013). The latest decision also states that the lower courts have the ability to determine whether an institution meets both strict scrutiny and an adequate trial of race-neutral recruitment. The decision appears to open the door to additional legal challenges when race is used in an admissions process. Fear of legal action could lead some public institutions to decrease or stop targeted-recruitment of URM students. And without an improvement in financial and academic preparedness for students of color—starting with a refinement in early childhood education and equal funding between all public schools—URM students will continue to lag behind in applying to programs of higher education, including medical, dental, and other allied health professions.

Under-Recruitment of URM students

A study by DiBaise, Salisbury, Hertelendy, and Muma (2014) examines the perceived barriers to recruitment of URM students among physician assistant programs (see Figure 2). Thirty-four possible barriers were presented to PA program respondents. The most frequently cited perceived barrier was low undergraduate grade point average (GPA), noted by 82.5 percent of program respondents (DiBaise et al., 2014). Other barriers listed by a majority of respondents include poor science preparation (61.4 percent), absence of role models (61.4 percent), low educational achievement (59.6 percent), difficulty finding financial resources (56 percent), not enough minority faculty (52 percent), and lack of peer or community support (50.9 percent) (DiBaise et al., 2014). The perceived barriers in the study by DiBaise et al. are similar to an earlier study by Agrawal, Vlaicu, and Carrasquillo (2005), which examined medical school recruitment of URM students. The only difference among the barriers between the Agrawal et al. (2005) and DiBaise et al. (2014) studies is that PA programs cited financial barriers to be more of an issue than did medical schools. The cost of PA education has nearly doubled over the last decade, with private institutions being almost two times more costly than public institutions (PAEA, 2014a). Of course, the increasing cost of education may be a barrier to all students, not just URM students.

The Importance of Diversity in the Health Professions

The Institute of Medicine (IOM) asserts that increasing diversity of health professional students and faculty will improve cultural competence of all students in each respective program and will prepare graduates to effectively provide health care to a diverse population (Institute of Medicine [IOM], 2004). The federal government spends millions of dollars annually to increase the supply, diversity, and quality of health profession applicants. A core belief exists within the Department of Health and Human Services that a more diverse health profession will provide better patient satisfaction, decrease language barriers, and improve health care access and quality (DHHS, 2006).

Saha, Guiton, Wimmers, and Wilkerson (2008) sought to answer whether diversity in medical schools is associated with the students' plan to work in and preparedness to care for diverse populations in underserved areas. The authors performed a cross-sectional study of allopathic medical students over two years and found that white students at schools with higher diversity felt better prepared to treat diverse populations and that access to care should be equitable (Saha et al., 2008). This association was most significant when a threshold of 10 percent URM or 36 percent nonwhite, non-URM students was noted at the medical school under study. Higher URM populations, however, had no association with the desire of white students to work in underserved areas (Saha et al., 2008).

The Association of American Medical Colleges (AAMC) additionally examined the implications of a diverse student body in medical schools (Coleman, Palmer, Winnick, Holland, & Knight, 2008). The authors noted that increased diversity provides an enhanced quality education for all students and prepares a more culturally competent workforce, improves the knowledge base of health care disparities, and focuses the research agenda on cross-cultural issues (Coleman et al., 2008). Hence, AAMC provides a framework for the recruitment of URM students.

Furthermore, Price et al. (2009) noted that URM providers are more likely than their white counterparts to practice in underserved sites, but also noted they are more likely to care for patients of the same race or ethnicity, regardless of insurance status. Minority patients expressed greater satisfaction with their health care when performed by a provider of the same race or ethnicity (Price et al., 2009). Muma, Kelley, and Lies (2010), in a cross-sectional study of PAs in the United States, found that URM PAs are more likely than their white counterparts to provide health care for the underserved and more likely to work in primary care. In a follow-up survey by Smith, Muma, Burks, and Lavoie (2012), the factor that was found to most influence URM PA practice location was designation of the site as underserved.

Increasing URM Recruitment in the Health Professions

Decreasing URM numbers among health professions has led to the development of several recruitment and retention programs to address the diversity shortage. Individual recruitment strategies include increasing health profession visibility through presentations, workshops, and outreach programs. Emory University developed a mentoring program focused on URM high school students with an aptitude for the health sciences (Rohrbaugh & Corces, 2011). The program involved pairing a URM student with a URM faculty member to develop a health care research project over the summer months. Since the inception of the program, 39 students have completed the program. Forty-six percent of graduates are working toward a science-based degree, with 15.4 percent of graduates pursuing a health science goal (Rohrbaugh & Corces, 2011).

Project Access, an outreach program that started in 1987, targets URM middle and high school students with the goal of raising awareness of the PA profession and encouraging the students to consider a career in the health professions. Interest in the program declined after a few years, until it was reinvigorated at the 2009 annual AAPA conference in Atlanta. In 2011, the AAPA and PAEA provided 14 presentations to over 300 disadvantaged students in the Las Vegas area (Pomeranz, 2010). A *Project Access* toolkit is available online for PA members to download and use for local outreach activities. Many of these URM outreach activities are single events generally centered around increasing awareness, including presentations, hands-on workshops, production of literature, and research projects.

Taking these outreach programs one step further would be the development of a pipeline for URM students, preferably starting in secondary education and guiding them through college and to postgraduate medical studies such as physician assistant training. A pipeline would have numerous contact points throughout the educational careers of URM students.

There are several models of successful pipeline programs among the health professions discussed in the literature.

The Diversity Pipeline in the PA Profession

Historically, the earliest PA pipeline started in Seattle in 1968 at the MEDEX Northwest program and later expanded to rural areas of Washington, Idaho, Utah, Wyoming, and Alaska (Ballweg, Wick, & Johnston, 2003). The mission of the MEDEX program is to attract Alaska Natives, Native Americans, Hispanic farmworkers, urban African Americans, rural residents, military corpsmen, and disadvantaged students. The MEDEX mission is also designed to provide financial support through stipends and scholarships for PA training and to return the graduates to their communities (Ballweg et al., 2003). Over its history, MEDEX Northwest has trained PAs at up to five sites, with an average of 40 percent of the students from URM or disadvantaged populations (Ballweg et al., 2003). The MEDEX Northwest program has placed 43.2 percent of graduates in primary care, 20.5 percent in nonurban areas, and 34.5 percent practice in designated underserved settings (Wick et al., 2012). In addition, the MEDEX program has been unwilling to adopt the master's level degree, as concern exists that a degree change would adversely affect the diversity of the student population.

Stanford University Medical Center uses a decentralized network of community colleges and preceptors to recruit minorities from disadvantaged communities. Garcia and Fowkes (1987) examined the outcome of an integrated program, including: (a) admissions workshops; (b) media; (c) faculty mentors; and (d) small group teaching sessions. This integrated process led to a doubling in the proportion of minority students in each class, accounting for 54 percent of the class in 1983 and 44 percent in 1984 (Garcia & Fowkes, 1987). Though only one minority student quit for academic reasons, the overall attrition rate of the minority students was double that of their white peers in the 1983 and 1984 classes (Garcia & Fowkes, 1987). The Stanford University Medical Center continues to offer associate's, bachelor's, or master's degrees upon graduation from the PA program (Stanford School of Medicine, 2012).

The Diversity Pipeline in Other Health Care Professions

Other health professions have developed pipeline programs, some of which also have affiliated PA programs (i.e., Howard University, University of Oklahoma, University of North Dakota, University of Nebraska Medical Center, and Baylor). The literature primarily focuses on medical or dental school matriculation and does not discuss the number of URM or disadvantaged students who participated, and yet chose another health career path such as the PA profession.

The Texas A&M Health Sciences Center Baylor College of Dentistry developed a longitudinal series of programs designed to recruit and retain URM students into the dental school (Lacy, McCann, Miller, Solomon, & Reuben, 2012). In addition to educating students about the dental profession, they also receive courses to improve their academic performance, attend field trips, participate in Future Dentist Clubs, perform community service projects, participate in hands-on activities, and prepare for standardized testing, including the Scholastic Aptitude Test (SAT) and the Dental Admission Test (DAT). From 1997 to 2008, multiple programs were started, targeting various groups: elementary school, junior high, high school, and post-baccalaureate school. From 2000 to 2009, 91 percent of the students in the program applied to college, and 93 percent of those students were admitted (Lacy et al., 2012). Data from 1997 to 2009 demonstrate that 87 percent of the participants applied to dental school or another health profession with a 77 percent admittance rate (Lacy et al., 2012). Underrepresented minority enrollment in the dental school has nearly tripled since the inception of the program. Since 2006, Baylor College of Dentistry has maintained the highest percentage of URM students compared to any other nonminority dental school in the United States. What's more, the retention rate of these URM students is at 92.5 percent, compared to 95.7 percent for all dental students (Lacy et al., 2012).

In 1989, the Robert Wood Johnson Foundation began the Minority Medical Education Program (MMEP), later called the Summer Medical Education Program (SMEP), a six-week experience designed to improve academic and Medical College Aptitude Test (MCAT) performance, as well as provide clinical opportunities for college freshmen or sophomores (IOM, 2004). In 2003, the program was expanded to include dentistry and is now referred to as the Summer Medical and Dental Education Program (SMDEP). Since 1989, nearly 15,000 students have participated in MMEP, SMEP, or SMDEP, of which 61 percent applied to medical school and 64 percent of those matriculated (Smith et al., 2009a). (This does not account for the number of students who applied to other health-related professions, including dentistry.)

In the Phoenix area alone, there are SMEP offerings at the University of Arizona Tucson and Phoenix campuses and Northern Arizona University's Dreamcatcher Program, as well as the Mesa Community College Achieving a College Education (or ACE) Program. While these programs are focused on medicine as a future career path, not all of the participating students will eventually apply to medical school. The first goal of these programs is to help the students apply to college and focus on a science major. To meet this goal, students receive additional math, science, and English skills courses. The second goal is to provide them with a mentor, guiding them to a future health career. In addition to the PA profession, other medical fields are highlighted, including nutrition, public health, athletic training, nursing, and physical therapy. Students who continue in a pipeline, also called Health Careers Opportunity Programs (HCOPs), are more likely to successfully matriculate into the health professions. In fact, Smith et al. (2009a) noted that the most successful diversity pipelines for increasing URM student enrollment in the health professions are those that emphasize math and science enrichment, preparation for admissions, financial support, and exposure to professional options. Unfortunately, very few HCOPs are in existence due to the time-intensive and costly nature of conducting the program. In the 2012–2013 enrollment cycle, the CASPA application captured the number of students who stated they participated in a pipeline program. According to the CASPA data, of the 19,558 students who applied to PA schools, 196 (1 percent) of the students stated they had participated in an HCOP. Applicants who successfully matriculated include 34 HCOP participants (17 percent of all HCOP applicants and 0.55 percent of all matriculants) (PAEA, 2014b). Among the HCOP participants, 185 provided information regarding their race and ethnicity (see Table 1). The majority of the HCOP applicants were nonwhite and non-Hispanic; however, the majority of HCOP matriculants were white, non-Hispanic.

The Role of PA Admissions Faculty in Recruiting URM Students

The AAMC has established guidelines to assist medical schools with incorporating a race-neutral application process that places less emphasis on GPA and standardized test scores and incorporates a student's life experiences, community outreach, leadership, and interview as a holistic approach to admissions (Addams, Bletzinger, Sondheimer, White, & Johnson, 2010). The admissions faculty is vital to the success of a holistic process. But to ensure continued equality in admissions, faculty must engage in annual training and gain or maintain a clear understanding of the roles, responsibilities, and mission of the program (Addams et al., 2010). The AAMC recommends group interviews with at least two faculty and three or more applicants (Addams et al., 2010). Inter-rater reliability measures are important to assess that faculty interviewers understand the process and also that applicants are allowed to fully demonstrate their strengths and weaknesses to the admissions committee (Addams et al., 2010). Badura, Ramos, and Muma (2007) utilized race-neutral admissions criteria at the Wichita State University PA program over the course of four admissions cycles. The authors de-emphasized GPA standards over the study period and subsequently found a leveling of URM matriculation, where other schools were seeing a decrease (Badura et al., 2007).

Barriers to a holistic admissions process still exist. Some programs use the most competitive GPAs to select their incoming class, which puts the URM student at a disadvantage (Addams et al., 2010). In addition, a lack of URM faculty places an increased burden on the URM faculty who are able to participate in the admissions process, potentially leading to faculty burnout (Addams et al., 2010). A holistic admissions process can add time in prescreening applicants and interviews, which may be difficult in understaffed programs (Addams et al., 2010).

Recruitment Strategies to Increase URM Applicants in PA Programs

DiBaise et al. (2014) queried PA programs regarding the frequency of use and effectiveness of 20 recruitment strategies to attract URM students. The study found that the number of programs that use recruitment strategies was low and the frequency, on average, was about once per quarter. Approximately 50 percent or more of the PA programs used only four strategies. Three of these included site visits to an undergraduate institution (61.2 percent), preadmission counseling (58.2 percent), and minority student targeted presentations (47.8 percent) (DiBaise et al, 2014). Further, many programs consider the availability of student loans as a recruitment tool (at a rate of 57.6 percent), yet this does not truly define recruitment, or the *act* of seeking and enlisting new applicants (DiBaise et al., 2014). A low percentage of PA schools (9 percent) used enrichment programs, and yet they were rated as having the highest effectiveness in recruiting URM students. Programs that conducted more frequent recruitment or pipeline programs were correlated with higher URM enrollment. Compared to a study by Agrawal et al. (2005) on recruitment strategies in medical schools, utilization of these strategies ranged between 30 percent and 57 percent lower among PA programs than medical schools. Examining data on medical school matriculation shows that 59.2 percent of medical students in 2012 were white, 22.5 percent were Asian, and 18.3 percent were URM students (AAMC, 2012). Compared to medical students, there were fewer URM students matriculating into PA programs in the same year (12.5 percent) (PAEA, 2014a).

Conclusions

Since the inception of the physician assistant profession, training programs have increased in length and are now mostly at the graduate level. They have also increased the number of applicants-to-capacity ratio, but they now face a legal issue on the role of race in the admissions process. These changes have led to a steady decrease in the URM applicants for PA programs. In an attempt to thwart the continued decline of minority applicants, programs in various health professions have developed pipelines and other recruitment activities to improve the number of qualified minority applicants. A review of the literature shows that the majority of these recruitment programs are housed in public institutions. And yet, these same institutions are most at risk to legal challenges of using race as an admissions factor.

As a profession, physician assistants must increase outreach to all disadvantaged students. The largest areas of benefit, based on the research, appear to be in initial outreach to middle and high school students who have an interest in science. As the student progresses through their schooling, assistance in applying for financial aid and preadmissions counseling to both college and graduate programs becomes imperative. Additional assistance in strengthening math, science, and English skills is also beneficial in developing a successful candidate from a disadvantaged background.

The call to arms to increase diversity is nothing new. This call has been sounding for nearly four decades in PA education. As health care in the United States sits on the precipice of change, there has never been a better time to answer that call. If we fail to effect change, minority enrollment will continue to plummet. Recruitment efforts are necessary to increase the pool of qualified URM applicants. With provider manpower shortages in primary care (Smith & Sabino, 2012), particularly in urban and rural areas, and a decrease in minority enrollment in PA education, the need for patient care in the medically underserved communities is dire. Studies show that providers of color who look like those they serve tend to have higher levels of trust among their patients (Cooper et al., 2012). To overcome the inequities that exist in health care delivery services, PA schools must take responsibility in training more providers of color, which is an important factor in patient health outcomes.

REFERENCES

Accreditation Review Commission on the Education of Physician Assistants. (2011). *Accredited programs over time*. Retrieved from http://arc-pa.org/documents/Programs20over%20time9.2011.pdf

Accreditation Review Commission on the Education of Physician Assistants. (2014). *Accreditation actions*. Retrieved from http://arc-pa.org/acc_programs/

Addams, A. N., Bletzinger, R. B., Sondheimer, H. M., White, S. E., & Johnson, L. M. (2010).

Roadmap to diversity: Integrating holistic review practices into medical school admission processes. *Association of American Medical Colleges*. Retrieved from http://www.cossa.org/diversity/reports/Integrating_Holistic_Review_Practices.pdf

Agrawal, J. R., Vlaicu, S., & Carrasquillo, O. (2005). Progress and pitfalls in underrepresented minority recruitment: Perspectives from the medical schools. *Journal of the National Medical Association, 97*(9), 1226–1231.

Alexander, L. L. (1970). The physician assistant: A challenge toward bridging the gap. *Journal of the National Medical Association, 62*(6), 426–430.

Association of American Medical Colleges. (2012). Total Enrollment by U.S. Medical School and Race and Ethnicity, 2012, Retrieved from https://www.aamc.org/download/321540/data/2012factstable31.pdf

Association of Physician Assistant Programs. (2000). Association of physician assistant programs' degree task force final paper, September 28, 2000. *Perspective on Physician Assistant Education, 11*(3), 169–177.

Badura, D., Ramos, V., & Muma, R. D. (2007). Evaluation of a physician assistant student admission plan that considers race neutral factors. *Physician Assistant Education Forum, Poster* Retrieved from http://soar.wichita.edu/dspace/bitstream/handle/10057/1081/pa0705003_A1b.pdf?sequence=1.

Ballweg, R., Wick, K. H., & Johnston, J. (2003). A 15-year history of federal grants to MEDEX Northwest. *Perspective on Physician Assistant Education, 14*(2), 88–95.

Barr, D. A., Gonzalez, M. E., & Wanat, S. F. (2008). The leaky pipeline: Factors associated with early decline in interest in premedical studies among underrepresented minority undergraduate students. *Academic Medicine, 83*(5), 503–511.

Boyd, J. K., Hernandez, J. Y., & Braun, K. L. (2011). Engaging nurse aide students to develop a survey to improve enrollment and retention in college. *Progress in Community Health Partnerships: Research, Education and Action, 5*(2), 169–176 doi: 10.1353/cpr.2011.0015

Coleman, A. L., Palmer, S. R., Winnick, S. Y., Holland & Knight, L. L. P. (2008). Roadmap to diversity: Key legal and educational policy foundations for medical schools. *Association of American Medical Colleges.* Retrieved from http://uscm.med.sc.edu/strategicplan/AAMCRoadmaptoDiversity2008.pdf

Cooper, L. A., Roter, D. L., Carson, K. A., Beach, M. C., Sabin, J. A., Greenwald, A. G., & Inui, T. S. (2012). The Associations of clinicians' implicit attitudes about race with medical visit communication and patient ratings of interpersonal care. *American Journal of Public Health, 102,* 979–987.

Department of Health and Human Services. (2006). The rationale for diversity in the health professions: A review of the evidence. Retrieved from http://bhpr.hrsa.gov/healthworkforce/reports/diversityreviewevidence.pdf

DiBaise, M., Salisbury, H., Hertelendy, A., & Muma, R. D. (2014). Strategies and Perceived Barriers to Recruitment of Underrepresented Minority Students in Physician Assistant Programs. *Journal of Physician Assistant Education (submitted).*

Dobmeyer, T. W., Sonderegger, L. L., & Lowin, A. (1975). A report of a 1972 survey of physician's assistant training programs. *Medical Care, 13*(4), 294–307.

Garcia, R. D., & Fowkes, V. K. (1987). Recruitment and retention of minority students in a physician assistant program. *Journal of Medical Education, 62,* 477–484.

Glicken, A. D., & Miller, A. A. (2013). Physician assistants: From pipeline to practice. *Academic Medicine, 88*(12), 1883–1889. http://dx.doi.org/10.1097/ACM.0000000000000009

He, X. Z., Cyran, E., & Salling, M. (2009). National trends in the United States of America physician assistant workforce from 1980 to 2007. *Human Resources for Health, 7*(86), 1–10.

Institute of Medicine (IOM). (2004). *In the nation's compelling interest: Ensuring diversity in the health care workforce committee on institutional and policy-level strategies for increasing the diversity of the U.S. healthcare workforce.* Washington DC: The National Academies Press. Retrieved from http://www.nap.edu/catalog/10885.html

Lacy, E. S., McCann, A. L., Miller, B. H., Solomon, E., & Reuben, J. S. (2012). Achieving student diversity in dental schools: A model that works. *Journal of Dental Education, 76*(5), 523–533.

Muma, R. D., Kelley, J., & Lies, S. (2010). Relationships of demographic background and practice setting among practicing physician assistants in the United States. *Journal of Physician Assistant Education, 21*(2), 15–21.

Physician Assistant Education Association. (2009). *Twenty-fourth annual report on physician assistant educational programs in the United States.* Retrieved from http://www.paeaonline.org/index.php?ht=a/GetDocumentAction/i/87485

Physician Assistant Education Association. (2011). *Twenty-sixth annual report on physician assistant educational programs in the United States.* Retrieved from http://www.paeaonline.org/index.php?ht=a/GetDocumentAction/i/135135

Physician Assistant Education Association. (2012). CASPA cycle 10 report. *PAEAOnline.* Retrieved from http://www.paeaonline.org/index.php?ht=d/sp/i/138061/TPL/topblockacross/pid/138061

Physician Assistant Education Association. (2014a). *Twenty-eighth annual report on physician assistant educational programs in the United States.* Retrieved from http://www.paeaonline.org/index.php?ht=d/sp/i/243/pid/243

Physician Assistant Education Association. (2014b). 2012–2013 HCOP for applicants and matriculants. *PAEA Data Request.*

Pomeranz, H. (2010). Project access events at AAPA conference a success. *PAEA Networker.* Retrieved from http://www.paeaonline.org/index.php?ht=d/ContentDetails/i/108860

Price, E. G., Powe, N. R., Kern, D. E., Golden, S. H., Wand, G. S., & Cooper, L. A. (2009). Improving the diversity climate in academic medicine: Faculty perceptions as a catalyst for institutional change. *Academic Medicine, 84*(1), 95–105.

Roderick, M., Nagaoka, J., & Coca, V. (2009). College readiness for all: The challenge for urban high schools. *Future of Children, 19*(1), 185–210.

Rohrbaugh, M. C., & Corces, V. G. (2011). Opening pathways for underrepresented high school students to biomedical research careers: The Emory University RISE program. *Genetics, 189,* 1135–1143.

Rosenbaum, S., Teitelbaum, J., & Scott, J. (2013). Raising the bar on achieving racial diversity in higher education: The United States Supreme Court's decision in *Fisher v University of Texas. Academic Medicine, 88*(12), 1792–1794. http://dx.doi.org/ 10.1097/ACM.0000000000000022

Saha, S., Guiton, G., Wimmers, P. F., & Wilkerson, L. (2008). Student body racial and ethnic composition and diversity-related outcomes in US medical schools. *Journal of the American Medical Association, 300*(10), 1135–1145.

Schneller, E. S., & Weiner, T. S. (1978). The black physician's assistant: Problems and prospects. *Journal of Medical Education, 53*, 661–666.

Smith, B., Muma, R. D., Burks, L., & Lavoie, M. M. (2012). Factors that influence physician assistant choice of practice location. *Journal of the American Academy of Physician Assistants, 25*(3), 46–51.

Smith, D. T., & Sabino, T. E. (2012). Where's the doctor: PA and NPs on the front lines of U.S. healthcare. In C. Cook (Ed.), Voices in medical sociology. San Diego: University Readers, Inc.

Smith, S. G., Nsiah-Kumi, P. A., Jones, P. R., & Pamies, R. J. (2009a). Pipeline programs in the health professions, part 1: Preserving diversity and reducing health disparities. *Journal of the National Medical Association, 101*(9), 836–847.

Smith, S. G., Nsiah-Kumi, P. A., Jones, P. R., & Pamies, R. J. (2009b). Pipeline programs in the health professions, part 2: The impact of recent legal challenges to affirmative action. *Journal of the National Medical Association, 101*(9), 852–863.

Stanford School of Medicine. (2012). Stanford School of Medicine primary care associate program with Foothill College. *Stanford Medicine* Retrieved from http://www.pcap.stanford.edu

U.S. Supreme Court. (1978). *Regents of Univ. of California v. Bakke - 438 U.S. 265* Retrieved from http://supreme.justia.com/cases/federal/us/438/265/case.html

U.S. Supreme Court. (2003). *Grutter v. Bollinger - 539 U.S. 306.* Retrieved from http://supreme.justia.com/cases/federal/us/539/306/

Weiner, T., & Schneller, E. S. (1981). Black attrition in physician assistant training programs. *American Journal of Public Health, 71*, 425–427.

Wick, K. H., Evans, T. C., Larson, E. H., Brock, D. M., Gianola, F. J., & Ballweg, R. (2012). The MEDEX 40-year graduate survey: Workforce deployment and practice satisfaction. *Physician Assistant Education Forum, Poster 1122* Retrieved from http://static.coreapps.net/2012paea/handouts/524af9ad18ea f9cb58dd5ef0abba9a7d_1.pdf

Figure 1

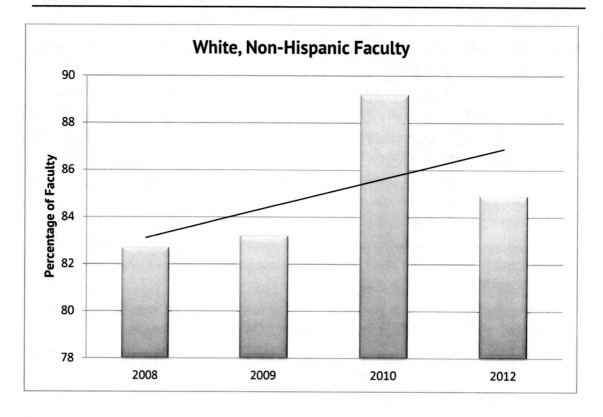

Figure 2

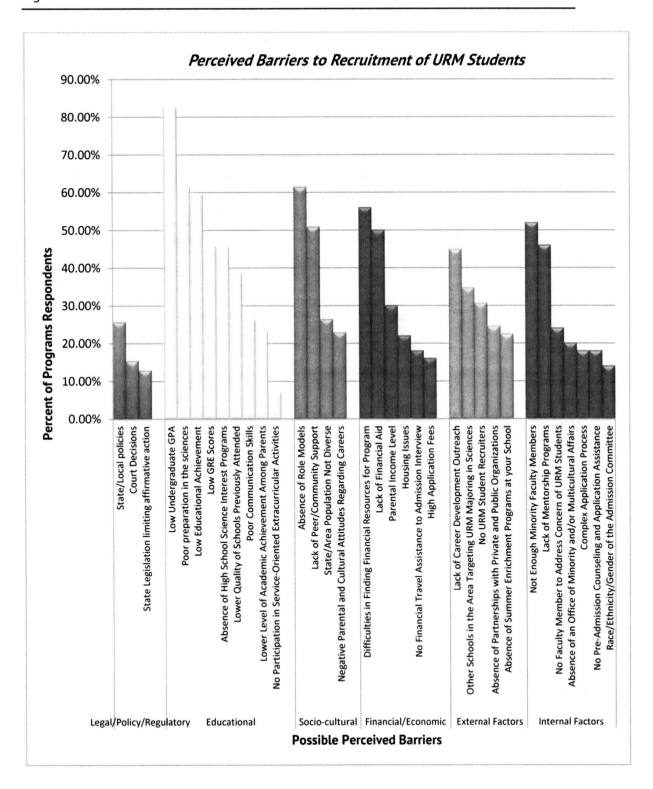

Table 1. PA Program Applicants and Matriculants in 2012–2013 Who Participated in a Health Careers Opportunity Program (HCOP)

	Applicants			Matriculants	
	n	% of all applicants	n	% of applicants	% of all matriculants
Non-HCOP	19,362	99.00%	6,159	31.2%	99.45%
HCOP	196	1.00%	34	17.3%	0.55%
Total	**19,558**	**100.00%**	**6,193**		**100.00%**
	n	% of HCOP applicants	n	% of HCOP applicants	% of all matriculants
HCOP Hispanic	44	22.45%	8	18.18%	0.13%
HCOP Non-Hispanic	141	71.94%	25	17.73%	0.40%
HCOP Not reported	11	5.61%			
HCOP White	70	35.71%	18	25.71%	0.29%
HCOP Non-White	115	58.67%	11	9.57%	0.18%
HCOP Not reported	11	5.61%			

II

UNDERSTANDING HOW PROVIDER PROFICIENCY IN SOCIAL DETERMINANTS OF HEALTH IMPACT PATIENT CARE AND HEALTH OUTCOMES

ADDRESSING SOCIAL DETERMINANTS OF HEALTH WITH CULTURAL COMPETENCE

By Lisa D. Hines, Ph.D., MSW

Many communities are plagued by structural and social conditions that support inequality, making it a challenge to eliminate global health disparities. The World Health Organization defines social determinants of health (SDOH) as those integrated, complex, and overlapping social systems and structures that include the health services, physical environment, and social environment. In other words, social determinants of health are structural and societal factors[1] that are responsible for most of the world's health inequities. Health care is, in fact, "shaped by the distribution of money, power and resources at global, national, and local levels" and, thus, influenced by policy choices (World Health Organization, 2013). The SDOH are those factors and resources that are essential to and influence the distribution of health and illness in the population, which is positively correlated with the persistence of health disparities[2] in the United States (CSDH, 2008).

It is important to understand why health disparities should be viewed as a social justice issue. Social justice is the view that everyone deserves equal economic, political, and social rights and opportunities (NASW, 2012). Throughout the world, health equity gaps are growing; it is unfair that people who are socially and economically disadvantaged are sicker and have a lower life expectancy than people in more privileged societies with higher social positions (CSDH, 2008; Irwin et al., 2006). Written by those in power, many policies and laws carry hidden discriminatory provisions—whether intentional or not—that benefit those at the top of the social hierarchy over those at the bottom and contribute to health inequities. Social science scholars identify those laws as examples of SDOH (Metzler, 2007; Braveman et al., 2011; Jones et al., 2009; Baker et al., 2005).

Racism, they argue, structures opportunity and assigns value based on the social interpretation of how one looks by giving some (those who possess the "right" look) greater value while others are given less value. And this indirectly determines health status. Thus, racism, ethnocentrism, segregation, stereotyping, and classism are tightly connected to health equity. They lead to lack of power, money, resources, and education, which may result in poor health care access, treatment, and outcomes. The elimination of avoidable health inequities is not only a matter of social justice but also a fundamental human right, many argue (Healthy People 2020, 2012; Hunt and Backman, 2008; Marmot, 2005; Marmot, 2007).

This chapter will briefly address how social determinants of health have influenced minority health, with particular insights into African American history, including medical care of African American soldiers during the Civil War and African Americans in research and clinical trials. Many African American and other minority patients feel uncomfortable going to the doctor. They cite mistrust and/or distrust based on prior experiences with traditional Western forms of health care. Patients of color are often viewed as not caring about their health—yet, in reality, they may display help-seeking behavior in nontraditional and unique ways. Second, this chapter will address the lack of cultural competence[3] or awareness in health care organizations and with health care providers (i.e., medical doctor, nurse practitioner, and physician assistant), which contributes to public health's failure to see and understand African Americans and other minorities, including immigrants, as whole people rather than a pathology that presents at the clinical encounter. Finally, this chapter seeks to offer several recommendations on how health care providers and public health professionals may continue to address this gap in its theoretical, research, and practice orientations through training and education.

AFRICAN AMERICAN HEALTH HISTORY, RACISM, AND HEALTH STATUS

In her book, *Intensely Human*, Margaret Humphreys (2008) revealed Civil War-era health disparities of African American soldiers, finding high rates of disease and death as far back as 1862. There were few African American physicians during the Civil War, and due to illiteracy, African American soldiers had to rely on white soldiers to advocate on their behalf. Medical care for African American soldiers during the war was mediocre at best. While the policy was to employ medical staff members for black soldiers with the same credentials as white regiments, there is evidence that this policy was abandoned in practice. Institutional racism[4] infiltrated every aspect of American life from church and schooling to the government and military. Slavery conditions and the inequities that followed have taken a toll on African

American human capital, indirectly causing a "reduction in the health and wealth" of the community (Gaskin, Headen, and White-Means, 2005 p. 1). Legal and government-sanctioned segregation, racism, and race-based discrimination continue to have intergenerational effects on the African American community.

Attempts to explain and eliminate African American health disparities in the United States have been difficult. Factors that include socioeconomic status, lack of health insurance, health behaviors, lack of effective communication, general mistrust of health care professionals, and genetic and biologic issues account for a portion of the disparities in health status between Blacks and Whites. African Americans, who represent 13.4 percent of the US population, are twice as likely to be uninsured, less likely to have any source of health care, and tend to receive lower quality health care than their white counterparts (US Bureau of the Census, 2008; IOM, 2003). Even when these variables are controlled for, however, the inequities experienced by African Americans persist (Krieger et al. 1993; Lille-Blanton and LaVeist, 1996; Navarro 1990, Gee 2002). How, then, do we account for the fact that African Americans have alarmingly higher rates of diabetes, stroke, cancer, and other chronic diseases than Whites (Office of Minority Health, 2013)?

A growing body of evidence suggests that the experience of discrimination and racism is associated with multiple indicators of poorer physical health (Stuber et al., 2003, Collins et al. 2000; Gee, 2002; Saha et al., 1999; Krieger, 1990). Findings by Hines (2010) support the theory that racism or even perceived racism plays a large role in explaining African American health disparities, particularly when levels of stress are examined (Pietrese and Carter, 2007). Experiences of discrimination have been shown to be associated with rates of hypertension (Krieger 1990), poorer self-rated health (Williams et al. 1997), and increased cigarette smoking (Ladrine and Klonoff 1996) among other health sequelae. For example, one study found that those African American college students on white campuses who reported experiencing racial/ethnic verbal harassment were twice as likely to use tobacco products due to increases in stress (Bennett et al., 2005). Additionally, an association has been found between low birth-weight children and mothers who experienced discrimination (Giscombé and Lobel, 2005; Collins et al., 2000).

Furthermore, perceived racism has been associated with health-related behaviors such as higher levels of psychological distress (Krieger, 1990) and depression (Wise et al., 2007), particularly among black women (Lepore et al, 2006). Perceived discrimination is defined as the perception that one has experienced differential and negative treatment because one belongs to a particular group (Barker, 2003). Whether racism is actual or perceived, it has been found to be an important predictor of health status and outcomes. In a qualitative study examining attitudes about HIV and cancer among African Americans, interviewees cited perceptions of racism, mistrust of doctors, and a desire for more African American health care professionals as reasons for low rates of screening by African Americans. Couple the stress of racism with the stress of limited income, poorer living conditions, lack of health care and insurance, decreased quality of education and poorer wages, and stress hormone levels remain elevated in a chronic daily state. Smith (2011) writes, "It is within the spaces of large, Black, segregated communities where stress wreaks havoc on Black bodies," leading to early deaths among African Americans.

CULTURAL COMPETENCE IN HEALTH CARE

Supporters of patient-centered care and advocates of cultural competence "emphasize the importance of expressing concern for the patient's well-being, showing respect, and incorporating the patient's views in decision making as valuable tenets of interpersonal relationships in health care" (Street et al., 2008 p 203). With ever-increasing demands on individual health care providers by the healthcare system and HMOs to see more patients in shorter periods of time, interpersonal interactions—such as rapport building, active listening, and patient-centered activities—may take a back seat to more stereotypical and bias interactions by providers (Burgess et al., 2007; Sinclair and Kunda, 1999). Yet, as health care professionals sought to offer appropriate care, Kai et al. (2007) found they often felt a sense of uncertainty and disempowerment. Medical providers feel helpless because they are unable to "treat" many of the social problems that accompany patients to their visits, such as housing, unemployment, and lack of education (RWJF, 2011).

At Creighton University Medical Center (CUMC), thirty-seven faculty and staff members participated in a study to assess of the cultural competency involved in clinical care and research (O'Brien et al., 2006). The authors found needs for continued cultural sensitivity/competency training to enhance group and interpersonal relationships, an understanding of certain aspects of minority cultures, perceptions of disease and wellness, and access to minority communities. In a separate study, Thom and Tirado (2006) recruited fifty-three primary care physicians at four diverse practice sites and enrolled 429 of their patients with diabetes and/or hypertension into their study. Patients completed a baseline survey, which included a measure of culturally competent behaviors displayed by their physician. Cultural competency training was then provided to physicians at two of the sites. At all four sites, physicians received feedback in the form of their aggregated cultural competency scores compared with the aggregated scores from other physicians in the practice. The primary outcome at six months was an increase in the patient-reported physician cultural competence score, increases in patient trust and satisfaction, and even more intriguing, improvements in patients' weight, systolic blood pressure, and glycosylated hemoglobin at the locations and among those physicians receiving cultural competency training.

In the recently instituted cultural competency training curriculum at the University of Hawaii medical school, the authors found that increased interest in global health training was shown to have positive effects on clinical skills and cultural competency of the participating residents (Carpenter, Kamaka, and Kaulukukui, 2011). Although most of the issues raised are not unique to Hawaii, participants' recommendations to teach students about the host culture and traditional healing practices identify as important themes not usually found in medical school curricula (Kamaka, Paloma, and Maskarinec, 2011). Additional research demonstrated how participation in a formal global health-training program for pediatric residents influenced perspectives when caring for diverse patient populations (Castillo et al., 2010). Findings suggest that participating in a global health-training program helped residents begin to acquire skills in cultural awareness. Kelly (2011) recommends cultural competency training that emphasizes moving from mere diversity exposure and the fostering of cultural awareness to obtaining cultural knowledge and cultural skills, and then applying the knowledge and skills to actual diverse patient populations.

In addition to improving patient care and access to health services, cultural awareness and sensitivity skills are needed to attract participants of color for research and clinical trials to aid in the advancement of medicine. In clinical trials, random sampling is desired to increase the validity of the results; however, the medical profession has historically been marred with controversy regarding its dealings with African Americans, making it hard to recruit Blacks for sampling purposes (Hagen, 2005; Gamble, 1997). The recruitment of African Americans as human subjects in clinical trails has a long and cruel history in the emergence of American medicine, and the Tuskegee Experiment[5] remains one of the most significant human rights violations in the Western world (Shavers et al., 2000; Gamble, 1997; Thomas and Quinn, 1991). Still others included the case of John "Fed" Brown, a runaway slave who once remarked in 1855 that the doctor who owned him produced painful blisters on his body to see how deep his black skin went (Savitt, 2002). The belief then was that black slaves had thicker skin to better withstand heat. And Marion Sims, known as the father of gynecology, would use reluctant slave women to perfect his new surgical experiments before operating on white women. Using women suffering from the deadly condition vesicovaginal fistula, which developed as a result of childbirth and caused complications from incontinence to infection, Sims operated up to thirty times without the use of anesthesia on one slave woman alone (Sims, 1884). Subsequently, medicine has experienced an inability to recruit and retain African Americans and other marginalized communities for sampling purposes in research and clinical trials following such gross abuse and mistrust. And, consequently, health disparities will not be eliminated until health professionals are able to reach out to the members of this population with a level of trust that encourages participation in medical research and health services.

A culturally competent health care provider, who demonstrates sensitive language and effective communication, conveys to his or her patients that they are valued. This strengthens levels of trust between the provider and patient, which results in improved patient compliance. Less effective patient communication by health care personnel can create a greater atmosphere of ambivalence by some. Such causes of mistrust along with additional factors such as a lack of African American physicians and other health care providers of color, a lack of outreach by researchers and scientists, and a lack of universal health care (free services on demand) make it hard to recruit African Americans and other patients of color for participation in research trials and health services (Hines, 2010; O'Brien et al., 2006; Vanderwaal et al., 2001). While more research is needed to combat the issue of health disparities among whites and people of color, the demand for cultural competence from medical providers is an additional evidenced-based intervention that would result in improved health behaviors and outcomes.

RECOMMENDATIONS AND ACTION STEPS

The World Health Organization (WHO) recommends interventions that are technically feasible, politically supportable, financially affordable, and socially desirable and acceptable through the lens of the social determinants—in other words, culturally competent (Allenye, 2005). The demographics of the United States are becoming increasingly diverse, and while race, gender, class, sexual orientation, age, ability, experiences, access, income, and individual spirituality/religious preference are not the most important aspects of a medical encounter, they have been determined to have an a significant impact on treatment and, thus, on health. Culturally competent care would reduce barriers in the clinician-patient interaction and decrease structural barriers that prevent patients from maintaining their health, but providers must first recognize that clinician bias has an impact on patient outcome.

To start, cultural competency involves providing services that are respectful of and responsive to the culture and linguistic needs of consumers, as language and culture relate in complex ways. Effective communication with patients is critical to the safety and quality of care. Barriers to this communication include differences in language, culture, and health literacy (Gregg and Saha, 2007). Evidence-based practices that reduce these barriers—such as adding on-site (or access to) interpreters, employing health care workers and providers that look like their patients, patient education centers, and employee education workshops—must be integrated into health care work processes (Schyve, 2007; Dohan and Levintova, 2007; Wu et al., 2007) to ensure equal treatment of those with language and health literacy barriers (Chen et al., 2007).

Physician assistants are in a unique position to connect with patients while providing effective and quality treatment. PAs can break down cultural, linguistic, or literacy barriers and improve the care of their patients in specific ways, including taking courses on inequalities that exist between racial and ethnic groups in US society (i.e., racism 101), living in communities in which they serve, and adding medical Spanish courses to their continuing education. PA schools can also aid in the training of culturally aware PAs by adding sociological-based courses for the inevitability of students working with patients of color, as well as robustly recruiting faculty members and students of color in the PA profession, and encouraging more professional association with providers of color. Overall, improving the quality of US health care is truly dependent on improving language and literacy services (Lavizzo-Mourey, 2007; Saha and Fernandez, 2007).

Secondly, there is a need to increase community-based initiatives to improve health in economically disadvantaged populations through actions on social determinants (Assai and Watts, 2006; Laborde et al., 2007; Uttal, 2006; Devieux et al., 2004). Some examples include collaborations with working-class, inner-city Latino and African American families (Muir et al., 2004), collaborations between local universities and the US Department of Health Services for training in public health preparedness (Peate and Mullins, 2008), and cultural competency training by facilitating physician-patient relationships (Kaholokula et al., 2008). Additionally, schools training medical providers (MD, DO, PA, and NP schools) can create a center for health disparities research (Deatrick et al., 2009), and hospitals can establish an office of diversity and human rights staffed by a social worker (Sulman et al., 2007). In the region where they are based, PA schools can establish a community-based health center with an interdisciplinary health care team to give students exposure and training with at-risk populations, thereby offering opportunities to give back to those communities in which the schools thrive (Bruner et al., 2011).

Thirdly, we must reconsider how health care is delivered in the United States and redefine what "healthy" means for Americans. This means developing a holistic approach to health care by integrating behavioral health and other social services into health care services—the model adopted by community health centers for decades. This approach, offering a variety of services from primary medical care to behavioral health care, is showing effectiveness across the country. One key service provided in community health centers that utilize a variety of programs such as patient-centered educational classes and a referral program to specialists is outreach services.

Outreach workers are defined as individuals who assist with reducing barriers to services and resources. They are generally indigenous, neighborhood people familiar with the culture of the targeted population. They have the knowledge and skills necessary to increase participation and motivate individuals to come into or stay in services. Outreach workers are trusted members of the community who can deliver realistic and honest messages to the targeted population. Their tasks may consist of increasing trust, communication and education on the needs of participation in the research, promoting health and improving compliance, educating on disease prevention, and providing support to change health behaviors such as diet, smoking, drinking, and exercise. They recruit and assist with retaining participants in health services, research, and clinical trials. Outreach workers are members of the case management team and are involved in case planning and follow up with clients and research participants (Zuvekas et al, 1999, Fowler et al., 2006). They are successful because they have the ability to gain the trust of their patients, discuss clearly the benefits to their community, and give full disclosure in plain language to obtain consents from their patients. They are culturally competent (Corbie-Smith et al., 1999).

Outreach through such methods as direct communication, use of volunteers, incentives and benefits, meetings with staff members where success stories are shared, verbal acknowledgements, gifts and volunteer luncheons, advertising, friends, and health fairs and clinics have been shown to be effective in health promotion and increasing compliance and retention (Kiger, 2003; Zuvekas et al., 1999; Fiske et al., 1999; IOM, 2003). Not only does this eliminate the load from the primary care provider, but outreach strategies can help increase trust, facilitate communication, and reduce ambivalence in members of the targeted communities. By incorporating community outreach workers or patient navigators into their services, health providers can increase patients' participation in their own health care, allowing for patients to take ownership of their healthy lifestyle and treatment plans.

Advocates of these models have administrators who have the desire, skills, and knowledge necessary to develop programs and assist organizations, systems, and/or individual providers to work effectively and provide services consistent with the cultural context of the client and knowledge of the diversity in human conditions and experiences. Further, services that utilize culturally appropriate outreach and recruitment methods increase the retention of patients in appropriate medical services, the recruitment of patients of color in research studies, and appropriate cultural outcome measures. Moreover, culturally healthy programs are implemented in diverse communities and use diverse objectives where a commitment to diversity is explicit in policies and practices (Godfrey, 2006; McNeil, 2003). Using cultural competence, an evidenced-based approach of addressing social determinants of health, shows a commitment to reducing health disparity gaps in the United States and around the world. Once this is attained, we can literally save and affect lives.

REFERENCES

Allenye, G. (2005). *Social determinants of health*. Caribbean commission on health and development.

Assai, M., Siddiqi, S., & Watts S. (2006). "Tackling social determinants of health through community-based initiatives." *BMJ*, vol. 333, October 21, 2006. bmj.com.

Baker, E. A., Metzler, M. M. & Galea, S. (2005). "Addressing Social Determinants of Health Inequities: Learning from Doing." *Am J Public Health*. 95(4): 553–555. doi: 10.2105/AJPH.2005.061812.

Balsa, A. I. & McGuire, T. G. (2003). "Prejudice, clinical uncertainty and stereotyping as sources of health disparities." *Journal of Health Econ*, 22, 89–116.

Barker, R. (2003). *The Social Work Dictionary*. Washington, DC: National Association of Social Workers.

Bennett, G., Wolin, K., Robinson, E., Fowler, S., & Edwards, C. (2005). "Perceived racial/ethnic harassment and tobacco use among African American young adults." *American Journal of Public Health* 95(2), 238–240.

Braveman, P., Egerter, S., & Williams, D. R. (2011). "The social determinants of health: Coming of age." *Annual Review of Public Health*, 32, 381–398. http://search.proquest.com/docview/858281469?acc ountid=15042.

Bruner, P., Davey, M. P., & Waite, R. (2011). "Culturally sensitive collaborative care models: Exploration of a community-based health center." *Families, Systems, & Health*, 29(3), 155–170. doi:10.1037/ a0025025.

Burgess, D., Van Ryn, M., Dovidio, J., & Saha, S. (2007) "Reducing racial bias among health care providers: Lessons from social-cognitive psychology." *General Internal Medicine*, 22,882–887. DOI: 10.1007/ s11606-007-0160-1.

Carpenter, D. A., Kamaka, M. L., & Kaulukukui, C. M. (2011). "An innovative approach to developing a cultural competency curriculum; efforts at the John A. Burns School of Medicine, Department of Native Hawaiian Health." *Hawaii Medical Journal*, *70*(11), 15–19. http://search.proquest.com/docvie w/915629520?accountid=15042.

Castillo, J. J., Goldenhar, L. M., Baker, R. C., Kahn, R. S., & Dewitt, T. G. (2010). "Reflective practice and competencies in global health training: Lesson for serving diverse patient populations." *Journal of Graduate Medical Education*, *2*(3), 449–455. http://search.proquest.com/docview/896832916?accou ntid=15042.

Chen, A. H., Youdelman, M. K., & Brooks, J. (2007). "The legal framework for language access in health-care settings: Title VI and beyond." *Journal of General Internal Medicine*, *22*, 362–7. doi:10.1007/ s11606-007-0366-2.

Collins, J. W., David, R. J., Symons, R., Handler, A., Wall, S. N., & Dwyer, L. (2000). "Low income African American mothers' perception of exposure to racial discrimination and infant birth weight." *Epidemiology*, 11, 337–339.

CSDH (2008). "Closing the gap in a generation: health equity through action on the social determinants of health." *Final Report of the Commission on Social Determinants of Health. Geneva, World Health Organization.*

Corbie-Smith, G., Thomas, S., Williams, M., & Moddy-Ayers, S. (1999). "Attitudes and beliefs of African Americans toward participation in medical research." *Journal of General Internal Medicine.* 14, 537–546. 10.1046/j.1525-1497.1999.07048.x.

Deatrick, J. A., Lipman, T. H., Gennaro, S., Sommers, M., de Leon Siantz, Mary Lou, M.L., Mooney-Doyle, K., & Jemmott, L. S. (2009). "Fostering health equity: Clinical and research training strategies from nursing education." *The Kaohsiung Journal of Medical Sciences, 25*(9), 479–485. http://search.proquest.com/docview/734018431?accountid=15042.

Devieux, J. G., Malow, R. M., Jean-Gilles, M., Samuels, D. M., et al. (2004). "Reducing health disparities through culturally sensitive treatment for HIV+ adults in Haiti." *ABNF Journal, 15*(6), 109–15. http://search.proquest.com/docview/218899384?accountid=15042.

Dohan, D. & Levintova, M. (2007). "Barriers beyond words: Cancer, culture, and translation in a community of Russian speakers." *Journal of General Internal Medicine, 22 Suppl 2,* 300–305. http://search.proquest.com/docview/68431201?accountid=15042.

Fowler, T., Steakley, C., Garcia, R., Kwok, J., & Bennett, M. (2006). "Reducing disparities in the burden of cancer: the role of patient navigators." *PLOS Medicine.* 3(7). 974–976. 10.1371/journal.pmed.0030193.

Fiske, D., Rakfeldt, J., Heffernan, & Rowe, M. (1999). "Outreach workers experiences in a homeless outreach project: Issues of boundaries, ethics and staff safety." *Psychiatric Quarterly.* (70) 3. 231–246.

Gamble, V. (1997). "Under the shadow of Tuskegee: African Americans and health care." *American Journal of Public Health.* (87), 11 1771–1778.

Gaskin, D. J., Headen, A. E, & White-Means, S. I. (2005) "Racial disparities in health and wealth: The effects of slavery and past discrimination." *The Review of Black Political Economy.* Winter–Spring, 95–110.

Gee, G. C. (2002). "A multilevel analysis of the relationship between institutional and individual racial discrimination and health status." *American Journal of Public Health,* 92 (4), 615–623.

Giscombé, C. & Lobel, M. (2005). "Psychological bulletin by the American psychological association explaining disproportionately high rates of adverse birth outcomes among African Americans: The impact of stress, racism, and related factors in pregnancy." *Psychological Bulletin,* 131 (5), 662–683. DOI: 10.1037/0033-2909.131.5.662.

Godfrey, J. R. (2006) "Toward optimal health: Judy Ann Bigby, M/D., discusses the need for cultural competence in the healthcare of women." *Journal of Women's Health.* 15 (5). 480–483.

Gregg, J., & Saha, S. (2007). *Communicative competence: A framework for understanding language barriers in health care.* United States: http://search.proquest.com/docview/68426424?accountid=15042.

Hagen, K. (2005). "Bad blood: the Tuskegee syphilis study and legacy recruitment for experimental AIDS vaccines." *New Directions for Adult and Continuing Education.* (105). 31–41. 10.1002/ace.167.

HealthyPeople.gov (2012). *Leading Health Indicators, LHI 2020 Topics. Social Determinants.* Retrieved April 6, 2012, from http://healthypeople.gov/2020/LHI/socialDeterminants.aspx.

Hines, L. D. (2010). "Preventing HIV: Hearing the voices of African Americans. *Social Justice in Context.* 5(5), 112–129.

Humphreys, M. (2008). *Intensely human: The health of the black soldier in the American Civil War.* Boston: The John Hopkins University Press.

Hunt, P. & Backman, G. (2008). "Health systems and the right to the highest attainable standard of health." *Health and Human Rights,* 10(1), 81–92. http://search.proquest.com/docview/755188855?accountid=15042.

Institute of Medicine (2003). *Unequal treatment: Confronting racial and ethnic disparities in healthcare.* Washington, DC: National Academy of Press.

Irwin, A., Valentine, N., Brown, C, Loewenson, R., Solar, O., Brown, H., & Vega, J. (2006). "The commission on social determinants of health: Tackling the social roots of health inequities." *PLOS Medicine,* 3(6), e106. http://search.proquest.com/docview/68190029?accountid=15042.

Jones, C. P., Jones, C. Y., Perry, G. S., Barclay, G., & Jones, C. A. (2009). "Addressing the social determinants of children's health: A cliff analogy." *Journal of Health Care for the Poor and Underserved, 20*(4), 1–12. http://search.proquest.com/docview/220588673?accountid=15042.

Kaholokula, J. K., Saito, E. E., Mau, M. K., Latimer, R., & Seto, T. B. (2008). "Pacific islanders' perspectives on heart failure management." *Patient Education and Counseling, 70*(2), 281–291. http://search.proquest.com/docview/70210208?accountid=15042.

Kai, J., Beavan, J., Faull, C., Dodson, L., Gill, P., & Beighton, A. (2007). "Professional uncertainty and disempowerment responding to ethnic diversity in health care: A qualitative study." *PLOS Medicine,* 4(11), e323. http://search.proquest.com/docview/69008921?accountid=15042.

Kamaka, M. L., Paloma, D. S., & Maskarinec, G. G. (2011). "Recommendations for medical training: A native hawaiian patient perspective." *Hawaii Medical Journal,* 70(11), 20–24. http://search.proquest.com/docview/915629526?accountid=15042.

Kelly, P. J. (2011). "Exploring the theoretical framework of cultural competency training." *The Journal of Physician Assistant Education: The Official Journal of the Physician Assistant Education Association,* 22(4), 38–43. http://search.proquest.com/docview/920366187?accountid=15042.

Kiger, H. (2003). "Outreach to multiethnic, multicultural, and multilingual women for breast cancer and cervical cancer education and screening." *Family & Community Health.* 26(4), 307–318.

Krieger, N. (1990). "Racial and gender discrimination: Risk factors for high blood pressure." *Social Science and Medicine,* 30, 1273–1281.

Krieger, N., Rowley, D., Hermann, A., Avery, B., & Phillips, M. T. (1993). "Racism, sexism, and social class: Implications for studies of health, disease, and well-being." *American Journal of Preventive Medicine* 9 (6), 82–122.

Lepore, S. & Revenson, T. (2006). "Effects of social stressors on cardiovascular reactivity in Black and White Women." *Ann Behav Med.*, 31(2), 120–127.doi: 10.1207/s15324796abm3102_3.

Laborde, D. J., Brannock, K., Breland-Noble, A., & Parrish, T. (2007). "Pilot test of cooperative learning format for training mental health researchers and black community leaders in partnership skills." *Journal of the National Medical Association,* 99(12), 1359–1368. http://search.proquest.com/docview/70083725?accountid=15042.

Lavizzo-Mourey, R. (2007). "Improving quality of US health care hinges on improving language services." *Journal of General Internal Medicine,* 22, 279–80. doi:10.1007/s11606-007-0382-2.

Lille-Blanton, M. & T. LaVeist. (1996). "Race/ethnicity, the social environment, and health." *Social Science and Medicine,* 43 (12), 83–92.

Marmot, M. (2005). "Social determinants of health inequalities." *The Lancet,* 365(9464), 1099–104. http://search.proquest.com/docview/199002814?accountid=15042.

Marmot, M. (2007). "Achieving health equity: From root causes to fair outcomes." *The Lancet,* 370(9593), 1153–63. http://search.proquest.com/docview/199035765?accountid=15042.

McNeil, J. I. (2003). "A model for cultural competency in the HIV management of African American patients." *Journal of the National Medical Association,* 95(2), 3S–7S. http://search.proquest.com/docview/620033353?accountid=15042.

Metzler, M. (2007). *Social determinants of health: What, how, why, and now.* United States: http://search.proquest.com/docview/68283799?accountid=15042.

Muir, J. A., Schwartz, S. J., & Szapocznik, J. (2004). "A program of research with Hispanic and African American families: Three decades of intervention development and testing influenced by the changing cultural context of Miami." *Journal of Marital and Family Therapy,* 30(3), 285–303. doi:10.1111/j.1752-0606.2004.tb01241.x.

NASW (2012, April 4). *Code of Ethics. Social Justice.* Retrieved from http://www.socialworkers.org/pubs/code/code.asp.

Navarro, V. (1990). "Race or class versus race and class: Mortality differentials in the United States." *Lancet,* 336 (8725), 1238–40.

O'Brien, R. L., Kosoko-Lasaki, O., Cook, C. T., Kissell, J., Peak, F., & Williams, E. H. (2006). "Self-assessment of cultural attitudes and competence of clinical investigators to enhance recruitment and participation of minority populations in research." *Journal of the National Medical Association,* 98(5), 674–682. http://search.proquest.com/docview/621523443?accountid=15042.

Office of Minority Health (2013). "Diabetes and African Americans." Retrieved January 6, 2013, from http://minorityhealth.hhs.gov/templates/content.aspx?ID=3017.

Peate, W. F. & Mullins, J. (2008). "Disaster preparedness training for tribal leaders." *Journal of Occupational Medicine and Toxicology* (London, England), 3, 2-2. http://search.proquest.com/docview/734271065?accountid=15042.

Pietrese, A. & Carter, R. (2007). "An examination of the relationship between general life Stress, racism-related stress, and psychological health among Black men." *Journal of Counseling Psychology*, 54(1), 101–109. DOI: 10.1037/0022-0167.54.1.101.

Robert Wood Johnson Foundation (2012, April 6). "The Blind Side Physician Survey." Retrieved from http://www.rwjf.org/files/research/RWJFPhysiciansSurveyExecutiveSummary.pdf.

Saha, S. & Fernandez, A. (2007). "Language barriers in health care." *Journal of General Internal Medicine*, 22, 281–2. doi:10.1007/s11606-007-0373-3.

Saha, S., Komaromy, M., Koepsell, T. D., & Bindman, A. B. (1999). "Patient-physician racial concordance and the perceived quality and use of health care." *Arch Intern Med.*, 159, 997–1004.

Savitt, T. (2002). *Medicine and Slavery: The Diseases and Health Care of Blacks in Antebellum Virginia*, Urbana: University of Illinois Press, 1978. Issued in paperback, 1981. Reissued in paperback, 2002.

Schyve, P. M. (2007). "Language differences as a barrier to quality and safety in health care: The joint commission perspective." *Journal of General Internal Medicine*, 22, 360–1. doi:10.1007/s11606-007-0365-3.

Shaver, V., Lynch, C & Bermeister, L. (2000). "Knowledge of the Tuskegee study and its impact on the willingness to participate in medical research studies." *Journal of National Medical Association*, 92, 563–572.

Sims, Marion J. 1884. *The Story of My Life*. New York: D. Appleton, 1884.

Sinclair, L. & Kunda Z. (1999). "Reactions to a Black Professional: Motivated Inhibition and Activation of Conflicting Stereotypes." *Journal of Personality and Social Psychology*, 77(5), 885–904.

Smith, D. (2011). "Dirty hands and unclean practices: how medical neglect and the preponderance of stress illustrates how medicine harms rather than helps." *Journal of Black Masculinity*, (2)1, 11–34.

Street, R., Jr., O'Malley, K., Cooper, L., & Haidet, P. (2008). "Understanding concordance in patient-physician relationships: Personal and ethnic dimensions of shared identity." *Annals of Family*, 6(3), 198–205. DOI: 10.1370/afm.821.

Stuber, J., Galea, S., Ahern, J. Blaney, S., & Fuller, C. (2003). "The association between multiple domains of discrimination and self-assessed health: A multilevel analysis of Latinos and Blacks in four low-income New York City neighborhoods." *Health Services Research*, 38,6.

Sulman, J., Kanee, M., Stewart, P., & Savage, D. (2007). "Does difference matter? Diversity and human rights in a hospital workplace." *Social Work in Health Care*, 44(3), 145–159. doi:10.1300/J010v44n03_02.

Thom, D. H. & Tirado, M. D. (2006). "Development and validation of a patient-reported measure of physician cultural competency." *Medical Care Research and Review*, 63(5), 636–655. doi:10.1177/1077558706290946.

Thomas, S. B. & Quinn, S. C. (1991). "The Tuskegee syphilis study, 1932 to 1972: Implications for HIV education and AIDS risk education programs in the black community." *American Journal of Public Health*, 81(11), 1498–505. Retrieved from http://search.proquest.com/docview/215122830?accountid=15042.

US Bureau of the Census (2008). Highlights. Washington, DC.

Uttal, L. (2006). "Organizational cultural competency: Shifting programs for Latino immigrants from a client-centered to a community-based orientation." *American Journal of Community Psychology*, 38(3-4), 251–62. doi:10.1007/s10464-006-9075-y.

Vanderwaal, C., Washington, F., Drumm, R., Terry, Y., Mcbride, D., & Finley-Gordon, R. (2001). "African American injection drug users: tensions and barriers in HIV/AIDS prevention." *Substance use and misuse*. 36(66&7), 735–755. 10.1081/JA-100104088.

Williams D. R., Yu Y., Jackson J.S., & Anderson N.B. (1997). "Racial differences in physical and mental health: Socioeconoomic status, stress, and discrimination." *Journal of Health Psychology*, 2:335–351.

Wise, L., Palmer, J., Cozier, Y., Hunt, M., Stewart, E., & Rosenberg, L. (2007). "Perceived racial discrimination and risk of uterine leiomyomata." *Epidemiology*. 18(6), 747–757.

World Health Organization (2013). "Social determinants of health." Retrieved January 6, 2013, from http://www.who.int/social_determinants/thecommission/finalreport/key_concepts/en/.

Wu, S., Ridgely, M. S., Escarce, J. J., & Morales, L. S. (2007). "Language access services for Latinos with limited English proficiency: Lessons learned from hablamos juntos." *Journal of General Internal Medicine*, 22, 350–355. doi:10.1007/s11606-007-0323-0.

Zuvekas, A., Nolan, L., Tumaylle, C., & Griffin, L. (1999). "Impact of community health workers on access, use of services, and patient knowledge and behavior." *Journal of Ambulatory Care Management*. 22(4), 33–44.

ENDNOTES

1. These include but are not limited to: socioeconomic status, discrimination, housing, physical environment, food security (a household's ability to meet the nutritious needs of the family), child development, culture, social support, health care services, transportation, working conditions, and democratic participation.

2. Health Disparities refers to the differences in health status among distinct segments of the population including differences that occur by gender, race or ethnicity, education or income, disability, or living in various geographic localities. *Health Inequity* refers to inequalities in health (or health care) that are systemic and avoidable and, therefore, considered unfair or unjust resulting in unequal patient treatment and care, typically as a result of health disparities. These two, however, are often used interchangeably.

3. Cultural Competence is defined as processes that promote effective interactions with individuals of all cultures based on curiosity and respect about difference related to language, class, ethnicity (race), and religion. This perspective affirms the dignity of individuals, families, and communities (NASW, 2007).

4. Institutional racism is defined as those policies, practices, or procedures embedded in bureaucratic structures that systematically lead to unequal outcomes for people of color, while individual racism is defined as the negative attitudes one person has about all members of a racial or ethnic group, often resulting in overt individual acts such as name-calling, social exclusion, or violence. Parallel and co-occurring is institutional discrimination defined as prejudicial treatment in organizations based on official policies, overt behaviors or behaviors that may be covert but approved by those with power (Barker, 2003).

5. The Tuskegee Syphilis Study, conducted from 1932 to 1972, was considered ethically unjust because the participants, who were all black men, were deliberately denied the treatment of syphilis in order to study the natural history of syphilis.

THE CITIZEN PA

Integrating the Impact of Social Determinants of Health and
Provider Beliefs into Physician Assistant Training

By Jim Anderson, MPAS, PA-C, ATC, DFAAPA

D espite efforts to identify and address racial and other disparities, inequities continue to mount and even worsen. In 2011, the Executive Summary of the Healthy
People 2010 report notes the continuing and, in some cases, even growing racial
gap in health outcomes of Americans. The cause of these mounting inequities are
frequently linked to social determinants of health, including socioeconomic status,
access to care, provider beliefs and attitudes, cultural competence, systems quality, unconscious bias, racism, income inequality, and related factors.

Medical educator program curriculums (including PA, NP, MD, and DO programs) commonly lack a unified examination of the role of social issues and provider beliefs in sustaining and even increasing racial and other health inequities, despite evidence to prove the
culpability of these issues in the continuance of disease states. Often, this highly critical
information is abandoned in favor of more "clinical" instruction. This missing link in comprehending the complex forces driving these disparities may help to explain their persistence.
This underscores the challenges that PA and other medical educators face to uncover novel
and effective ways to frame and teach future medical providers about health care disparities.

Based on a medical model of curriculum design, PA education is traditionally grounded in
"clinical skills" training. While this bread-and-butter approach to training clinicians has many
positive attributes, it also risks missing the bigger picture when it comes to causes of illness.
For example, the current National Commission on the Certification of Physician Assistants
(NCCPA) Blueprint (NCCPA Blueprint, 2011) and the Accreditation Review Commission
for Education of the Physician Assistant (ARC-PA) competencies (Accreditation Review
Commission on Education for the Physician Assistant Inc., 2006) both feature a narrow set of

skills needed by physician assistants in order to fulfill the education and certification stan-dards. This competency-based criteria is what is driving curriculums, which can too easily exclude examination of social causes of ill health as well as the impact of provider attitudes, beliefs, biases, and stereotypes.

The "Citizen PA," a concept previously discussed in PA literature (Anderson, 2006), provides a road map for an integrated curricular approach to teaching new PAs. Anderson, Bruessow, and Gianola (2010) have described the model as one that fully takes into account the impact of social determinants and provider beliefs on the health of patients. Additionally, the Citizen PA model trains PAs about the interventions to decrease the health impact of these massive but potentially silent forces, which are most certainly "medical" as well as "clinical." This foundation of this concept is that social forces are the primary determinants of health in many populations.

MISSING THE FOREST FOR THE TREES: WHY DISPARITIES PERSIST

As health disparities continue to persist, three overarching themes emerge. First, health care providers lack a comprehensive understanding of why disparities in health and health care exist. The gap in health inequities is not likely to close if providers lack a diagnosis of the problems underlying the disparities, which evidence indicates are commonly socially linked. Second, providers are often unable to acknowledge their own unconscious biases and the role of those biases in health disparities and patient harm. Third, real reduction in disparities will require the medical profession to refocus the training of PAs and other medical providers so that the role of social causes of disease is genuinely integrated into medical education, and not viewed as peripheral.

Social Causes of Disease

The past decade has seen an increasing body of medical literature emphasizing the specific health impacts of social determinants. Pincus (2004) has described the limitations of looking solely to the exam room to solve disparities. He notes that the most effective means for decreasing some disparities in health may occur outside the confines of the exam room, acknowledging the limits of traditionally defined medicine in attacking illness. The tradi-tional biomedical model is limited in that it focuses on a tertiary form of medicine in which clinicians are trained to assess patients on the signs and symptoms they present. Social determinants of health (SDOH) are those health problems directly or indirectly caused by societal inequalities and stressors; thus, they are preventable diseases. Because upward of 20 percent of US mortalities are due to preventable causes (Nolte and McKee, 2012), PA education could benefit from focusing on the role of social forces on many of these disease states.

This is not to say that infectious disease should not be a foundational component of PA education. But to address the unequal care of millions of American patients, socially linked diseases need to be identified, with such integration made central to PA and other medical education.

Implicit Bias

Implicit bias continues to emerge as an area of increased medical study, with a broadening understanding of its implications for clinician-patient interactions. It is important to grasp the conceptual difference between explicit and implicit bias, as research repeatedly indicates that people who do not harbor explicit biases (e.g., open acknowledgement of racial preference) frequently demonstrate measurable implicit and unconscious biases.

Evidence indicates a predictable path that implicit bias takes in humans. This path strongly contrasts with explicit biases, which manifest in outward expressions of partiality. Data show that implicit bias, which indicates an unconscious bias, and racial preference function at similar levels during a lifetime, and is expressed through unconscious thoughts, actions, and motives that are often not recognizable as biased actions to the offender. Explicit bias and racial preference have been shown to work in contrasting ways, with explicit racial preferences decreasing after the age of six. According to this data, implicit bias is much more persistent than explicit bias, and endures over time, despite an often genuine belief in one's own humanity (Anderson, 2012).

To assess human bias, which exists just below the level of conscious awareness, social psychologists at Harvard University developed the Implicit Association Test (IAT) in 1989. One of the most validated research instruments and well-known resources in use to measure unconscious racial understandings and preferences, the IAT features an easy-to-navigate website where users can take a variety of online tests about implicit beliefs and bias. The tests flash pictures of images and ask the user to associate words such as *good* and *bad* with those images. The test measures the speed at which one responds to the answers. At the conclusion of the tests, users receive real-time feedback about their preferences, based on their performance of the IAT.

Banaji (2011) describes two findings essential to the understanding of the role of implicit bias, both of which have been consistent through more than twenty years of research and data collection related to implicit bias and unconscious stereotyping. Both findings have strong implications for PAs as well as for PA educators and preceptors, whose job it is to teach students about the care of patients:

1. When measured on the Implicit Association Test (IAT), more than of 75 percent of white Americans indicate a strong association of white with good, and black with bad.
2. Performance on IAT's race-themed test reliably predicts clinical behaviors of test takers.

Green et al. (2007) and Burgess, van Ryn, Crowley-Matoka, and Malat (2006) both described the emerging consensus within medical communities that implicit biases are pervasive and are predictive of clinical decision making, underscoring the key teaching point that uncon- scious biases are not easily eliminated, but instead must be unlearned and managed in our personal and institutional lives. Burgess et al's (2006) description of the reasons that providers activate implicit bias and stereotypes details the manner in which providers form both conscious and unconscious stereotypes during a clinical encounter. She cites research noting that clinicians use two independent learning and memory systems to guide behaviors, judgments, and stereotype formation. This describes two distinct methods of stereotyping, called automatic stereotyping and goal-modified stereotyping.

Automatic stereotyping occurs when stereotypes are activated unconsciously and without regard to their individual's goals. Goal-modified stereotyping functions much differently. It is a more conscious process and is performed when specific needs of the clinician arise. An example of this would occur in the presence of time constraints, when the provider fills in gaps of information about patients to make complex decisions. Providers are then likely to utilize and call upon information contained in their racial/ethnic stereotypes to guide the interpreting symptoms and subsequent decision making.

Failure to Adequately Address Disparities and Their Causes in Medical Education

Contemporary medical literature is marked by attempts to quantify the health impact of social issues and provider attitudes. One recent example is the work by Lim and Mokdad (2012) in describing the connection between social inequalities and the burden of infec- tious disease. The literature abounds with other pointed illustrations of social causation of illness: Wilper (2009) estimates that lack of health insurance is responsible for the deaths of forty-five thousand Americans annually; Zheng (2012) elucidates the increased death rate of some Americans attributable to income inequality; Brondolo, Love, Pencille, Schoenthaler, and Ogedegbe (2011) write of the role of racism on elevated blood pressure; and Gee (2012) offers a framework for assessing the specific health impacts of racial discrimination. All of this work, as well as research from other historic leaders in this area, repeatedly describes the direct and measurable impact of social factors on the health and well-being of individuals, and continues to build a medical and evidenced-based consensus that moves from asking *if* social issues affect health, to instead investigating the mechanism by which the proven impact occurs.

Yet, the omission of social causes of ill health from academic and research agendas has been cited on several occasions in the literature, describing the perils of focusing only on provider attitudes (i.e., cultural competence) while ignoring the equally important social issues that cause poor health (Jackson, 2011). Shaw and Armin (2011) state, "While a vast array of technologies of CAHC (Culturally Appropriate Health Care) seek to promote the ethical self-fashioning of both physicians and health care systems, few of these transformations hold potential for transforming the larger structures of inequality underlying health disparities." Addressing health inequities will require an increased determination to examine the role of social forces on the illness of populations.

Additionally, discussion of the mechanism of implicit bias and how it occurs is a necessary dialogue in the treatment of patients and can prove useful in promoting a rich classroom discussion. A multi-university research collaboration, Project Implicit is a well-known research tool that started in 1998 as a project between several universities. It is on the Project Implicit website where the Implicit Association Test (IAT) is housed. Ball State University educators Zigmunt-Fillwalk and Clark (2012) have written about their use of the IAT in their continuing education of teachers and students, cautioning users of the IAT to provide context and preparation for the IAT rather than using it as a stand-alone tool. Teal et al. (2010) have described using the IAT as a trigger for medical students' discussion of implicit bias, noting productive small-group discussions resulting in acceptance of having biases as well as increased awareness of strategies to change implicit biases. One of the most fascinating aspects of implicit bias is the strong and validated data from research indicating that increasing a provider's awareness about implicit bias can reduce the activation of implicit biases by clinicians and others (Blatt, LeLacheur, Galinksy, Simmens, and Greenberg, 2010; Burgess, van Ryn, Dovidio, and Saha, 2007; Galinsky and Moskowitz, 2000; Drwecki, Moore, Ward, and Prkachin, 2011; Rudman, Ashmore, and Gary, 2001; Todd, Bodenhausen, Richeson, and Galinsky, 2011).

Perspective-taking is a related clinical technique described as the simple act of placing oneself "in the patient's shoes." Research indicates that when a clinician takes a few moments and considers his or her patient's perspective, implicit bias and stereotyping decrease (Galinsky and Ku, 2004). Blatt et al. (2010) have described the physiology of this practical technique in relating to the activation of neural networks involving emotion and cognition, resulting in the increased empathy on the part of providers who place themselves "in their patient's shoes."

Efforts to reduce health inequities can be summarized in two key observation points of the Citizen PA model (Anderson, 2012):

1. Teaching PA students about improving the health of their patients and communities needs to include detailed discussions of the known health impact of social determinants and provider attitudes.
2. Teaching one without the other fails to adequately prepare the PA student to play a role in closing the gap in health disparities and inequities.

OBSTACLES

Impact of Social Determinants and Provider Attitudes Omitted From Core Competencies

Both the National Commission on Certification of Physician Assistants (NCCPA) and the Accreditation Review Commission on Education for the Physician Assistant (ARC-PA) have an obligation to hold medical education institutions accountable for adequately addressing these issues. Such integration and accountability are necessary to meet the medical needs of all communities, particularly those that have been recipients of unequal treatment and health inequality. Until these accrediting bodies add health disparities as a core competency and health education requirement, the training of these issues will always be secondary in physician assistant education, and many PAs will be ill-equipped to contribute to the elimination of racial and other health disparities.

A clear measure of what is valued as the core educational necessities for PAs can be seen in the National Commission on Certification of Physician Assistants' "Content Blueprint" (NCCPA Blueprint, 2011). This document determines the scope of the national certification examinations for PAs, the foundational test that drives curriculum and program decision making. Physician assistant programs regularly measure their success on pass rates of the NCCPA exam, and the topic scope of the exam plays a crucial role in identifying curriculum decisions of PA schools. Like many programs, the University of Iowa's PA program uses NCCPA pass rates as a recruiting tool, something that is commonplace for PA programs with high pass rates. This underscores the defining influence that the NCCPA exam "Blueprint" has on PA curriculum (University of Iowa NCCPA Examination Performance, 2012).

The NCCPA's description of its Blueprint is absent of a broadened view of the physician assistant's responsibility to engage in activities related to social determinants of health or the impact of provider attitudes and beliefs (NCCPA Blueprint, 2011). The material on NCCPA's certification and recertification exams are organized into two dimensions:

1. Organ systems and the diseases, disorders, and medical assessments that physician assistants encounter within those systems; and
2. The knowledge and skills that physician assistants should exhibit when confronted with those diseases, disorders, and assessments.

Additionally, ARC-PA downplays the medical impact of social determinants and provider beliefs. As one of the four organizations (with the NCCPA and PAEA, then APAP) to create the 2005 Competencies for the Physician Assistant Profession document, the Accreditation Review Commission on Education for the Physician Assistant (ARC-PA) plays a defining role in determining the content that PA programs choose to teach. The competencies document is almost entirely without mention of either "health disparities" or "diversity," noting only that "physician assistants must demonstrate a high level of responsibility, ethical practice, sensitivity to a diverse patient population and adherence to legal and regulatory requirements" (Accreditation Review Commission on Education for the Physician Assistant Inc., 2005). Another limited mention of the general issue of health disparities charges PAs with demonstrating "sensitivity and responsiveness to patients' culture, age, gender, and disability."

A more broadened appeal from ARC-PA was included in its 2010 update of accreditation standards (LeLacheur and Straker, 2011), which notes in section B1.06:

The curriculum *must* include instruction to prepare students to provide medical care to patients from diverse populations.

Even this noteworthy effort to expand the scope of curriculum with the wording "being aware of their own values and avoiding stereotyping" erroneously confuses implicit and explicit bias. Research also shows that implicit bias is not "avoided," but instead is managed by increased awareness and other means. This language is indicative of the lag between PA educational standards and the emerging sophisticated understanding of bias and stereotyping evidenced in recent medical literature.

ANNOTATION: Quality health care education involves an ongoing consideration of the constantly changing healthcare system and the impact of racial, ethnic, and socioeconomic health disparities on health care delivery. Instruction related to medical care and *diversity* prepares students to evaluate their own values and avoid stereotyping. It assists them in becoming aware of differing health beliefs, values, and expectations of patients and other health care professionals that can affect communication, decision making, compliance, and health outcomes.

Mortality Data Summaries Frequently Ignore Social Determinants

Common modern attributions of causes of death also ignore the role of social determinants of health in examples such as this mortality data. The oft-cited 2000 *JAMA* article looking at "actual causes of death" cited the top nine causes of death in 2000, moving from tobacco, diet/inactivity, and alcohol to guns, sexual behavior, and illicit drug use (Mokdad, Marks, Stroup and Gerberding, 2000).

Table 2. Actual Causes of Death in the United States in 1990 and 2000

Actual Cause	No. (%) in 1990*	No. (%) in 2000
Tobacco	400 000 (19)	435 000 (18.1)
Poor diet and physical inactivity	300 000 (14)	400 000 (16.6)
Alcohol consumption	100 000 (5)	85 000 (3.5)
Microbial agents	90 000 (4)	75 000 (3.1)
Toxic agents	60 000 (3)	55 000 (2.3)
Motor vehicle	25 000 (1)	43 000 (1.8)
Firearms	35 000 (2)	29 000 (1.2)
Sexual behavior	30 000 (1)	20 000 (0.8)
Illicit drug use	20 000 (<1)	17 000 (0.7)
Total	**1 060 000** (50)	**1 159 000** (48.2)

*Data are from McGinnis and Foege.[1] The percentages are for all deaths.

None of these categories specifically identify the health impact of social determinants or inequities, even in the face of a growing body of data explicitly identifying health impacts of social issues (Zheng, 2012; Lim, 2012; Brondolo et al., 2011; Gee, 2012).

Health Policy Matters Appear to be Simply Extracurricular

Physician assistant and other health educators have had difficulty finding ways to address social causes of poor health as well as the impact of provider attitudes and implicit bias. The PA education process is deeply grounded in sometimes narrowly defined clinical skills. Traditional definitions of "clinician" often exclude critical and in-depth exploration of social determinants of health, social and public health advocacy, cultural and language sensitivity, and reflection about the role of provider attitudes and beliefs on the health of patients. Laudable efforts to include diversity and disparities into PA school curriculums have failed to yield a centralized integration of identifying and addressing social determinants and clinician beliefs into the causes of illness. Instead, these have continued to be treated as primarily extra-clinical issues.

James Cawley (2007) has noted this historical focus on clinical skill proficiency: "The competency-based PA educational philosophy holds that proficiency in the clinical skills identified as being necessary for future competence in primary care/generalist practice would be the 'gold standard' of PA educational preparation." This "clinical skills" orientation offers little room for addressing growing and consistent evidence that social factors and provider attitudes are major drivers of illness and health inequality.

Teaching PA students about the need to integrate exam room activities with broader policy efforts is key to the "Citizen PA" concept, and there is little evidence that curriculum drivers see this as relevant to PA curriculum. While the ARC-PA/NCCPA/PAEA's competencies describe the role of the "systems-based practice," this appears to primarily address broad issues of quality of care, reimbursement, data, technology, and resource allocation. Missing is specific mention of policy advocacy related to social determinants of health and health inequalities. (ARC-PA, 2005).

This is in contrast to the 2012 competencies for nurse practitioners from the National Organization of Nurse Practitioner Faculties, which include a separate and distinct set of competencies related to policy in addition to the more common systems-based practice competencies called "health delivery system competencies" in the NP document (Nurse Practitioner Core Competencies, 2012). Included in both the policy and health delivery system sections of the NP document are mentions of equity and diversity. Such broadened language could provide needed cover for PA schools interested in advancing the role of the Citizen PA.

RECOMMENDATIONS

1. Humanize the Data

Presenting information about the health impact of social determinants and provider attitudes can uncover a strong distaste for statistics and data in classroom and CME settings. Students are quick to note the numbing effect of data-heavy presentations about social causes of disease, potentially making the issues seem impersonal. By teaching PA students about the interconnectedness of social determinants and provider attitudes, the realms become connected, which is one of the primary principles of the Citizen PA concept. Wrestling with the proven health ravages of inequality in the classroom nurtures an expanded view among future providers of why patients suffer from these inequities.

2. Integrate curriculum modules about social determinants and provider attitudes into PA school curriculum.

To reduce disparities, PA education (as well as training of other health care providers) would benefit from including training about social causes of disease and provider biases. Just as students learn biological processes of disease state, so must they learn the ravages of social inequality and the accompanying stress on the body and its causal link to preventable diseases. Similarly, just as students learn examination skills and diagnostic skills, so must they learn the cognitive skills on how to recognize and work through their own personal biases. These techniques will offer solution-focused approaches that so many PA clinically focused students desire.

As noted earlier, Galinksy (2004) and others have found that by increasing clinician awareness of implicit bias, the activation of biases by clinicians decreases. One classroom-CME presentation tool related to the "just talking about it" research is teaching the 3S-3P mnemonic (Anderson, 2012). In this mnemonic, 3P stands for:

- **Pervasive**–Implicit bias and unconscious stereotyping are pervasive.
- **Predictive**–Implicit bias is predictive of biased clinical decision making.
- **Perspective Taking**–A resource shown to decrease the activation of implicit bias.

3S represents:

- **Standard Work**–Related to Toyota Motor Corporation-style "lean" quality improvement initiatives, standard work provides a framework in which developing awareness of implicit bias is seen as a standardized and core component of being a physician assistant.
- **Small-Ball Data Collection**–Modest data collection efforts can be integrated into the standard work of PAs and can serve as a tool for increased awareness of implicit bias and health inequity. Using techniques from the Disparities Solutions Center "Creating Equity Reports" (2012), increased awareness from such efforts can potentially mitigate and reduce implicit bias.
- **Solution-Focused**–Students increasingly note a desire for solution-focused approaches to learning about health disparities. Driving discussions about implicit bias toward proven solutions can enhance PA student engagement.

Based on the evidence that increased provider awareness of unconscious bias decreases its impact, these exercises can help equip PA students to effectively counter implicit bias in their clinical practice.

One example of a potential model for curriculum design can be viewed at the AAPA site (Heads Up! Health Disparities CME for AAPA Members, 2012). Originally designed as a proposed PA school curriculum module (Heads Up! 2007), the "Heads Up! Implicit Bias, Unconscious Stereotyping and Racial Disparities in Care" category I CME is available to all

AAPA members. This resource represents an example of an easily reproducible module for adding material about social determinants and provider attitudes to an existing PA curriculum.

3. Teach PAs that tackling exam room inequities without addressing social causes of illness will not reduce or eliminate health disparities.

One of the basic features of the Citizen PA model is that not every PA has to do everything (Anderson, 2012). Some PAs may be well-suited to focus on their exam room skills to reduce the impact of social determinants and implicit bias, some may be interested in dealing with policy and systems-based issues, and some may be interested in both. But if the PA and medical profession fail to take both into account, then the health disparities gap is likely to continue to grow.

4. Intensify efforts to revise ARC-PA and NCCPA guidelines to reflect medical evidence about social causes of health inequities.

Until ARC-PA and NCCPA guidelines accurately reflect the now irrefutable evidence about the profound medical impact of social determinants and provider attitudes, integrating these issues into PA curriculum will be most difficult. Without the cover of ARC-PA and NCCPA directives, PA curriculum-makers are unlikely to be motivated to make these kinds of curriculum changes. While both ARC-PA and NCCPA mention social determinants, they do so in ways that imply the non-centrality of these issues. Their current guidelines fail to take into account the proven and significant impact of these issues on the health of patients and communities, and lack meaningful mechanisms to promote integrating these issues into PA program curriculums.

REFERENCES

Accreditation Review Commission on Education for the Physician Assistant Inc. ARC-PA competencies, 2005. Retrieved on April 7, 2012, from http://www.arc-pa.org/documents/CompetenciesFINAL.pdf.

Anderson, J. (2012). "The Citizen PA." *Journal of the American Academy of Physician Assistants*. Retrieved from http://www.jaapa.com/health-disparities-blog/section/2379/.

Anderson, J. (2012). "Should PAs assess and address the impact of implicit bias on patient care?" *JAAPA*, 25(4), 60, 62.

Anderson, J. *Health care disparities. Advance for Physician Assistants,* January 2006. Retrieved on April 7, 2012, from http://nurse-practitioners-and-physician-assistants.advanceweb.com/article/health-care-disparities.aspx?cid=0&ei=vnklr5zzkz2g0ghi0_jkcg&anthem_callback=true.

Anderson, J., Bruessow, D., & Gianola, F. J. (2010). "Can casual use of medical evidence cause harm and erode bioethical values?" *JAAPA,* 23(4), 64–65.

Banaji, M. "The dark, dark side of the mind" (2011). Retrieved on April 2, 2012, from http://onthehuman.org/2011/09/the-dark-dark-side-of-the-mind/

Blatt, B., LeLacheur, S. F., Galinsky, A. D., Simmens, S. J., & Greenberg, L. (2010). "Does perspective-taking increase patient satisfaction in medical encounters?" *Acad Med,* 85(9), 1445–1452.

Brondolo, E., Love, E. E., Pencille, M., Schoenthaler, A., & Ogedegbe, G. (2011). "Racism and hypertension: a review of the empirical evidence and implications for clinical practice." *Am J Hypertens,* 24(5), 518–529.

Burgess, D., van Ryn, M., Crowley-Matoka, M., & Malat, J. (2006). "Understanding the provider contribution to race/ethnicity disparities in pain treatment: insights from dual process models of stereotyping." *Pain Med,* 7(2), 119–134.

Burgess, D., van Ryn, M., Dovidio, J., & Saha, S. (2007). "Reducing racial bias among health care providers: lessons from social-cognitive psychology." *J Gen Intern Med,* 22(6), 882–887.

Cawley, J. "Physician assistant education: an abbreviated history." *Journal of Physician Assistant Education* 2007;18(3):6–15.

Disparities Solutions Center. "Creating equity reports" (2008). Retrieved on April 12, 2012, from http://www2.massgeneral.org/disparitiessolutions/resources.html#creating.

Drwecki, B. B., Moore, C. F., Ward, S. E., & Prkachin, K. M. (2011). "Reducing racial disparities in pain treatment: the role of empathy and perspective-taking." Pain. doi: S0304-3959(10)00747-5 [pii]

Galinsky, A. D., and Ku, G. (2004). "The effects of perspective-taking on prejudice: the moderating role of self-evaluation." *Pers Soc Psychol* Bull, 30(5), 594–604.

Galinsky, A., and Moskowitz, G. (2000). "Perspective-taking: decreasing stereotype expression, stereotype accessibility, and in-group favoritism." *J Pers Soc Psychol,* 78(4), 708–724.

Gee, G. C., Walsemann, K. M., & Brondolo, E. (2012). "A life course perspective on how racism may be related to health inequities." *Am I Public Health,* 102(5), 967–974.

Green, A. R., Carney, D. R., Pallin, D. J., Ngo, L. H., Raymond, K. L., Iezzoni, L. I., & Banaji, M. R. (2007). "Implicit bias among physicians and its prediction of thrombolysis decisions for black and white patients." *J Gen Intern Med,* 22(9), 1231–1238.

Heads Up! Health Disparities CME for AAPA members (2012). Retrieved at http://www.stop-disparities.org/AAPACME.html.

Heads Up! Health Disparities Project. End It. Retrieved on April 7, 2012, from www.stop-disparities.org/endit .

Healthy People 2010 Final Review Executive Summary. 2011. Retrieved on April 7, 2012, from http://www.cdc.gov/nchs/data/hpdata2010/hp2010_final_review_executive_summary.pdf

Implicit Association Test. Harvard University. Retrieved on April 7, 2012, from https://implicit.harvard.edu/implicit/demo/.

Jackson, J. (2011). "Eliminating Disparities: Understanding the Mental Health Connection." Retrieved from http://www.rwjf.org/humancapital/product.jsp?id=72986.

LeLacheur, S. & Straker, H. "Culture, diversity, race, and the standards: Assessing and addressing the hidden curricula." *The Journal of Physician Assistant Education Association.* 2011 Vol 22, No 2. Retrieved at http://www.paeaonline.org/index.php?ht=action/GetDocumentAction/i/127986.

Lim, S. S. & Mokdad, A. H. (2012). "Socioeconomic inequalities and infectious disease burden." *Lancet,* 379(9821), 1080–1081.

Mokdad, A. H., Marks, J. S., Stroup, D. F., & Gerberding, J. L. (2004). "Actual causes of death in the United States" 2000. *JAMA,* 291(10), 1238–1245.

National Association of Nurse Practitioner Faculties. Nurse practitioner core competencies. 2012. Retrieved April 4, 2012, from http://www.nonpf.com/associations/10789/files/NPCoreCompetenciesFinal2012.pdf.

NCCPA Content Blueprint. 2012. Retrieved on April 7, 2012, from http://www.nccpa.net/ExamsContentBPTasks.aspx.

Nolte, E., McKee, & C. Martin (2012). "Measuring the health of nations: Updating an earlier analysis." *Health Affairs,* 27, no.1 (2008):58–71. Retrieved from http://content.healthaffairs.org/content/27/1/58.full.pdf.

Pincus, T. (2004). "Will racial and ethnic disparities in health be resolved primarily outside of standard medical care?" *Ann Intern Med,* 141(3), 224–225.

Rudman, L., Ashmore, R., & Gary, M. (2001). "'Unlearning' automatic biases: the malleability of implicit prejudice and stereotypes." *J Pers Soc Psychol,* 81(5), 856–868.

Shaw, S. J. & Armin, J. (2011). "The ethical self-fashioning of physicians and health care systems in culturally appropriate health care." *Cult Med Psychiatry,* 35(2), 236–261.

Teal, C. R., Shada, R. E., Gill, A. C., Thompson, B. M., Frugé, E., Villarreal, G. B., & Haidet, P. (2010). "When best intentions aren't enough: helping medical students develop strategies for managing bias about patients." *J Gen Intern Med,* 25 Suppl 2, S115–118.

Todd, A. R., Bodenhausen, G. V., Richeson, J. A., & Galinsky, A. D. (2011). "Perspective taking combats automatic expressions of racial bias." *J Pers Soc Psychol.*

University of Iowa NCCPA Examination Performance (2013). Retrieved from http://www.medicine.uiowa.edu/pa/education/

Wilper, A. P., Woolhandler, S., Lasser, K. E., McCormick, D., Bor, D. H., & Himmelstein, D. U. (2009). "Health insurance and mortality in US adults." *Am J Public Health*, 99(12), 2289–2295.

Zheng, H. "Do people die from income inequality of a decade ago?" *Social Science & Medicine* (2012), doi:10.1016.

Zigmunt-Fillwalk, E. & Clark, P. "Using the IAT with teachers to affect change" (2012). Retrieved on April 7, 2012, from http://www.tolerance.org/tdsi/asset/using-iat-teachers-affect-change.

IT TAKES A NETWORK

Building Partnerships to Identify, Access, and Promote Health Disparities Resources

By Patricia Devine, MLS

H ealth inequities are unfair, unjust, and deserve to be addressed urgently by the medical community. Physician assistants are well positioned to take a leadership role in identifying and helping to eliminate the social causes of unequal health, but to do so PAs need the best information available to help make quality, fair, and equitable medical decisions. Medical guidelines and data are powerful and essential tools to use in reversing the burden of disparities and unequal care. While physician assistants do not need a mastery of the complexities of information seeking, they do need to have strategies, networks, and resources to help them identify needed medical information to most effectively and efficiently treat all patients, particularly those who are medically underserved. From developing contacts, to identifying and obtaining information, to evaluating literature and resources, savvy PAs know that it takes a network to ensure that the knowledge they use to drive high-stakes decisions is medically sound.

The tools available for physician assistants that can aid in their practice vary from government and nonprofit research/information databases to the use and knowledge of electronic health records (EHR) and social media. For example, the National Institute of Health's National Library of Medicine has a resource (MedlinePlus.gov) devoted to patient education, including handouts for practitioners' use with their patients. Also, the EHR is a powerful tool that can be used to identify disparities and further address them in clinical practice. And social media is an innovative way for health care providers to reach new groups as well. Exploration has begun to use channels such as Facebook, Twitter, and text messaging to distribute important public health information, especially to teens and young adults.

This chapter is meant to help the typical PA who is driven by a passion for quality care, patient well-being, and the elimination of health disparities to find the best information sources available. It is important to be cognizant of how the effects of low health literacy and providers' lack of knowledge about their patients' diverse backgrounds lend to health inequities. Understanding these factors, as well as learning where to look for information and who to trust, builds a foundation upon which important work can take place.

HEALTH INFORMATION LITERACY

Health information literacy, or the ability to understand basic health information, has an important impact on individual health as well as health disparities. Patients of lower socioeconomic status, and particularly people of color, are disproportionately affected by low health literacy (Gazmararian et al., 1999). Low health literacy (trouble understanding information related to one's health such as illness/disease state, treatment options/adherence, and prevention/healthy lifestyle) is recognized as a barrier to quality patient care and is linked to underutilization of preventive services, reduced medication adherence, less knowledge and understanding of one's own health, poorer management of chronic conditions, and increased risk of hospitalization and re-hospitalization. While these issues may be present in all populations, health literacy disproportionately affects the elderly and racial and ethnic minorities (as it pertains to lower educational attainment in which the two are intimately intertwined), and recent immigrant populations (Health Literacy of America's Adults, 2012). Patients with inadequate health information proficiency may have trouble understanding their health care providers' instructions, taking medication correctly, getting preventive care, and practicing healthier behaviors. Poor health literacy is a critical and often overlooked factor in the nation's health inequities (Sentell and Halpin, 2006).

The US Department of Health and Human Services' Health Resources and Services Administration (HRSA) defines health literacy as "the degree to which individuals have the capacity to obtain, process and understand basic health information needed to make appropriate health decisions and services needed to prevent or treat illness" (http://www.hrsa.gov/publichealth/healthliteracy/healthlitabout.html). Health literacy is recognized as an important part of patient compliance (Shaw, Heubner, Armin, Orzech, Vivian, 2009). A low level of health-related comprehension in patients with chronic conditions is associated with poor management of their health. Becoming more educated in a healthy lifestyle improves a patient's use of health resources and increases the patient's ability to become an active partner in their own health care (Edwards, Wood, Davies and Edwards, 2012). This knowledge can also have a positive effect on preventive health such as a better understanding of a healthy diet and nutrition, increase in physical activity, and compliance with physical checkups (Aihara and Minai, 2011).

Improving health information literacy is a partnership between the patient and the health care provider, and it goes well beyond simply getting a confirmation of the patient's understanding. Trouble comprehending health information (i.e., health literacy) does not equate to trouble reading in general. It is now estimated that roughly 90 percent of Americans have some difficulty grasping and using some aspect of daily health information (Department of Health and Human Services' Office of Disease Prevention and Health Promotion). Thus, it is the provider's responsibility to ensure the patient has a full understanding. Patients need clear communication in order to live a healthy lifestyle and change their behavior.

The best approach to health information literacy is the universal precaution approach, as recommended in a position paper by the American Academy of Physician Assistants (AAPA) titled "Health Literacy: Broadening Definitions, Intensifying Partnerships and Identifying Resources" (2011). Because of the difficulty in identifying those with "low" literacy and the knowledge that 90 percent of Americans are less than proficient in health literacy, AAPA recommends that providers effectively convey the complex medical information to *all* patients. Furthermore, the position paper states "Assigning the responsibility of 'low' health literacy to patients decreases provider accountability, and places the burden of creating such partnerships primarily on the shoulders of the patient." By moving away from these designations and toward a partnership between provider and patient, the responsibility is placed on the provider to find tools and means to improve their patients' understanding.

PROVIDER TOOLS TO IMPROVE HEALTH LITERACY

According to the 2012 National Action Plan to Improve Health Information Literacy, insufficient health literacy is more likely to affect particular populations. These include adults over the age of sixty-five years, racial and ethnic groups other than white, recent refugees and immigrants, people with less than a high school diploma or GED, people with incomes at or below the poverty level, and non-native speakers of English. The plan outlines seven steps to take action on health literacy. While cognizance of populations known to be at high risk for low health literacy can assist the clinician in enhancing communication, AAPA recommends treating all patients with the same level of care, providing all patients with the tools and knowledge to become proficient healthcare consumers. It is important to be aware that labeling patients into certain groups can lead to unconscious stereotyping and the assumption of who does and does not comprehend information based on their age, ethnicity, race, etc. By educating all patients with equal care, providers can aim to eliminate internal biases with respect to health literacy and, ultimately, health care.

The US Department of Health and Human Services' (HHS) web resource, "Health Communication, Health Literacy, and e-Health" (2012), provides an overview as well as tools and resources to understand and improve low health literacy. It includes a guide on how to advocate for health literacy within an organization, utilizing strategies such as making health literacy a part of staff orientations, presenting the issue at staff meetings, and sharing new health literacy resources.

The health services research arm of the HHS, the Agency for Healthcare Research and Quality (AHRQ), provides the "Health Literacy Universal Precautions Toolkit" (2012). Assuming that patients who have low health literacy cannot easily be identified, every patient should be offered resources and treated in a supportive environment. This concept leads to a more patient-partner approach and holds the provider responsible for communication. The Toolkit helps medical practices create an environment where all patients are provided with clear communication and barriers to care are identified and removed.

Other resources on health information literacy include the US Food and Drug Administration's (FDA) "Strategic Plan for Risk Communication" (2012). This document is designed to provide the information needed to ensure all of the FDA's audiences get the information they need to make informed choices. Moreover, its goals include educating FDA reviewers about health information literacy.

The Centers for Disease Control and Prevention's web resource, "Health Literacy: Accurate, Accessible and Actionable Health Information for All" (2012), reports on health literacy activities by state, and provides tools and information to improve health information literacy. Also listed are ways to obtain training in health literacy, steps to develop a plan in the organization, and information on how to evaluate health literacy interventions.

The Institute of Medicine (IOM) of the National Academies issued a position paper, titled "Attributes of a Health Literate Organization," defining a health literate organization as one that "makes it easier for people to navigate, understand, and use information and services to take care of their health" (Brach et al., 2012). This paper states that "addressing health literacy is critical to transforming health care quality" and that "patient-centered, equitable care cannot be achieved if consumers cannot access services or make informed health care decisions." Once again, the position paper advocates for using a universal precautions approach and places responsibility on the health care providers for communicating effectively.

Raising awareness about health literacy and strategizing to improve communication and understanding is an important step in addressing health disparities. Once PAs understand the importance of health literacy, they can then educate their patients appropriately. As frontline health care providers, physician assistants must find ways to improve overall health literacy and help educate patients on healthy living, disease states, treatment options, recovery, and their overall health. This begins by becoming aware of the available health information in order to improve access to information available for patients.

INFORMATION-SEEKING STRATEGIES

PAs experience a compressed educational experience compared with medical school students. This compression may be accompanied by reduced exposure to health information expertise, including lack of interaction with medical librarians. Such a compacted educational interval may also result in a reduced skill level related to searching medical literature, especially in areas such as health disparities that may already be considered esoteric or obscure. This makes it even more advantageous for physician assistants to learn how to create a network of information specialists that are able to "cut to the chase" in obtaining the most reliable, highest quality resources for identifying and eliminating health disparities.

Three specific techniques can guide the PA student toward information well suited to assist them in making the highest quality medical decisions:

1. Know the limits of your knowledge: PA students can enhance the quality of their medical decisions by enhancing the quality of information upon which medical decision are made as well as integrating a career-long effort to learn about use of the medical literature. Medical school programs for MDs often have two complete years of stand-alone training related to accessing and using medical literature in addition to other medical school coursework. With the much shorter didactic period for PA programs, it becomes even more essential to learn to "search smart" to find strong, evidence-based literature efficiently. Accepting medical information that is "good enough" or sub-optimal has high-stakes limitations that potentially impacts patient outcomes.

    Further, all providers have the responsibility to help their patients navigate the complex world of medical information, and learning about how differences of others shape their lives and experiences will help guide PAs to be a better resource for their patients. By understanding provider limitations, such as language barriers or racial differences, PAs can become partners in care with their patients while becoming more proficient in the social factors that hinder good patient care.

2. Improve knowledge of and access to medical resources: By making identification of medical library resources an early and foundational part of the PA student didactic

experience, physician assistant students will form a reliable base on which to build future medical and health knowledge for years to come. The complexities and sophistication of current medical literature coupled with the compressed learning period for PA students make the ability to obtain expert assistance invaluable. Once students graduate, they may not have access to a medical library, but they can continue to have access to information through a variety of ways. For example, some states have information packages available to medical practitioners as part of their state licensing fee. In Washington State, the HEAL-WA program (Health Evidence Resource for Washington State) features resources on diagnosis and therapy, guidelines and evidence, drugs, labs, diagnostic tests, complementary and alternative medicine, prevention and immunization, multicultural information, and patient care management (heal-wa.org). Similar resources are available to PAs in various geographic settings. What's more, any PA can utilize the National Library of Medicine's toll-free number to help them identify what resources may be available to them.

In addition, there is readily available information to aid providers in improving communication, knowledge, and treatment of differing patient populations. For example, HEAL-WA's multicultural information links include the renowned EthnoMed (ethnomed.org), which is Harborview Medical Center's ethnic medicine website, and the respected National Institutes of Health's website RHIN or Refugee Health Information Network (rhin.org). These websites include translated instructions for patients about preparing for tests and examinations, clinically relevant articles on culture and health issues, and resources about emerging refugee populations and public health. These are designed to be a first step to reducing health disparities.

3. Identify (or create) and promote a package of resources: By using an "order-set" approach to information seeking, PAs can save time while increasing the reliability of medical information to which they are exposed. A wide variety of clinician-focused tool kits are available, such as the Texas Department of State Health Services' cardiovascular disease-themed practice management tool kit (Physician Tool Kit, 2012). Similar tools, aimed at PAs and clinicians interested in reducing health disparities, are also readily available. For example, the *Journal of the American Academy of Physician Assistants* (JAAPA) features a health disparities-focused blog (JAAPA Health Disparities Blog, 2012) that includes a regularly updated list of resources and links to practice-based disparities reduction tools. Another example of a vetted tool kit specifically focused on health disparities issues can be found at the "Heads Up!" site created in 2007 by a consortium of PA organizations (stop-disparities.org). The resources page on the site features links to a variety of literature about health inequities, and it is regularly reviewed and updated.

ACCESSING AND UNDERSTANDING HEALTH DISPARITIES RESOURCES

US Government

The Centers for Disease Control and Prevention (CDC) has as its mission "to create the expertise, information, and tools that people and communities need to protect their health—through health promotion, prevention of disease, injury and disability, and preparedness for new health threats" (2102). The CDC's National Center for Chronic Disease Prevention and Health Promotion has a primary concern to achieve health equity by eliminating health disparities (CDC Center for Chronic Disease Prevention, 2012; CDC Promoting Health Equity, 2012). To this end, it provides resources on promoting health equity for community organizations, social determinants of health maps (CDC, Social Determinants of Health Maps, 2012), and other more specific data on particular diseases (CDC, Breast Cancer Rates by Race and Ethnicity, 2012).

The National Network of Libraries of Medicine (NN/LM, 2102) was created to advance the progress of medicine and improve public health by providing all US health professionals with equal access to biomedical information, as well as improving the public's access to information with the purpose to enable patients to make informed decisions about their health. The NN/LM has eight regional offices across the country and can assist health care providers and the public with finding health information. The regional offices also offer training and funding for outreach projects that are designed to serve the needs of underserved populations and include a health information component.

NLM's resources include PubMed (2012) and MedlinePlus (2012). PubMed is a free online index to the biomedical literature that includes some links to full-text content. MedlinePlus, available in English and Spanish, is designed for the healthcare consumer. Other resources for consumers are HIV/AIDS Information (2012) and Clinical Trials (2012). What's more, the NN/LM blog, *Bringing Health Information to the Community*, is a consumer-focused forum that emphasizes health information issues related to underserved communities (2012). These resources not only give providers up-to-date, researched-based information, but also arm them with the tools to direct their patients to becoming active participants in their quest for wellness.

In the Action Plan to Reduce Racial and Ethnic Disparities: A Nation Free of Disparities in Health and Health Care (2012), the **Department of Health and Human Service (HHS)** examines the differences in health outcomes linked with social, economic, and environmental disadvantage and provides a strategy for the action plan to reduce disparities. It is designed to be a complement to the National Stakeholder Strategy for Achieving Health Equity, produced by the **National Partnership for Action to End Health Disparities (NPA)**. The HHS established the NPA in order to mobilize a national and comprehensive strategy to combat health disparities and achieve health equity. The NPA increases awareness of health disparities, works to strengthen leadership, strives to improve health care outcomes for minority and underserved populations, and evaluates and seeks input on data about health disparities. The National Stakeholder Strategy for Achieving Health Equity (2012), produced by the NPA, provides goals and objectives for partnerships and initiatives to improve health disparities. Communities can utilize the plan to determine the best strategy to achieve the goals deemed the most significant for them. These goals may range from increasing health insurance coverage and access to care to increasing the availability and effectiveness of community-based programs for those who are medically disadvantaged, while also using various strategies—such as implementing health disparities data collection and streamlining grant administration for health disparities funding—to achieve these goals.

The HHS **Agency for Healthcare Research and Quality (AHRQ)** is the department's health services research component. The AHRQ focuses on quality improvement and patient safety, effectiveness of care, technology assessment, and healthcare organization and delivery. The Agency is interested in ways to translate knowledge into practice and policy. It produces an annual National Healthcare Quality and Disparities Report that describes progress made and opportunities for improving health care quality and reducing health care disparities. The AHRQ provides state-by-state data on disparities, health care costs, and utilization.

Interprofessional Resources

The Agency for Healthcare Research and Quality has created a **Pharmacy Health Literacy Center** (www.ahrq.gov/pharmhealthlit/). This web-based tool provides pharmacists and pharmacy faculty members with resources and curricular modules. Included are tools for use in pharmacies and guides for training staff members and educating patients. Medication errors are more likely in patients with low health literacy, and this resource addresses what steps can be taken.

Furthermore, **the Health Disparities Toolkit**, which resides on the National Association of County and City Health Officials website (http://www.naccho.org/toolbox/program.cfm?id=24), was created by researchers at the University of Washington School of Nursing. It is a searchable database of summaries of programs and tools used to address health disparities.

Associations and Private/Nonprofit Organizations

The **Pew Internet & American Life Project** (pewinternet.org) is a rich source of data on health disparities. The project is one of the seven created by the Pew Research Center, a nonprofit and non-partisan think tank organization. While the Pew Research Center does not take positions on policy issues, it provides information and data on trends and attitudes shaping the United States and the world. Pew Internet explores and collects public opinion on how the Internet affects individuals, families, and communities, and examines the importance of online information in the lives of the people using it. The website includes data tools to obtain statistics about online activity, including demographic data such as income and race/ethnicity. Statistics are also available about who is looking for health information online, which makes up the majority of Internet users (Pew Internet: Health, 2012).

Focusing on healthcare issues, the **Kaiser Family Foundation** (www.kff.org) provides policy analysis as well as news and information on health policy, in addition to running health information campaigns such as those focusing on HIV/AIDS. A monthly update on health disparities is available on the website and includes health news related to issues that affect underserved racial and ethnic minorities.

REDUCING DISPARITIES THROUGH INFORMATION TECHNOLOGY

Use of the EHR

In recent years, researchers have begun to study the ways in which electronic health record (EHR) systems may impact health disparities. In one study (Samal, Lipsitz, and Hicks, 2012), researchers found that health care providers' use of EHRs resulted in an increased number of African American and Hispanic patients with controlled blood pressure (lower than 140/90). When the EHR also included a Clinical Decision Support system, the number rose. Controlled blood pressure would likely result in fewer cases of cardiovascular disease in those two groups, reducing the racial disparity in the number of those suffering from heart disease.

In another study, an EHR-based tracking system was used to identify women in low income and minority populations who were overdue for screening mammography, noting "Lower mammography screening rates among minority and low income women contribute to increased morbidity and mortality from breast cancer" (Phillips et. al., 2011). Patient navigators then called and wrote reminder letters to patients, resulting in greatly increased adherence rates. Patient navigators, who are trained in cultural sensitivity, can be integrated into medical teams to communicate with providers about patients and identify known barriers. The navigators work with the patients to connect them to resources.

EHRs can also be useful in disease management, providing automated reminders to health care providers. One study showed a decrease in gaps in care for osteoporosis between white patients and those of other ethnic groups (Navarro, Greene, Burchette, Funahashi, and Dell, 2011). The EHR is able to identify a lack in care for patients with certain characteristics and continue to send reminders until the deficit is resolved and care is adequate.

The patient portal into the EHR is an additional tool that can be used to reduce disparities (Gibbons, 2011). The electronic system allows providers to give patients access to an electronic copy of their health information (containing diagnostic test results, problem lists, medication lists, medication allergies, discharge summaries, and procedures) (Eligible Hospital and CAH Meaningful Use Table, 2012). A portal can be used to increase patients' participation and engagement in their care. For instance, seeing a trend in improved lab results over the past year can help motivate a patent to continue with lifestyle changes that initially led to improved health. Patients can also communicate with health care providers through the portal and follow links to culturally and linguistically appropriate guidelines and recommendations for managing their chronic conditions. Thus, improving access to information increases patients' engagement in their own health care.

Including a patient education module within the EHR, such as MedlinePlus Connect from the National Institute of Health's National Library of Medicine (MedlinePlus Connect, 2012), is another way to increase patient engagement. MedlinePlus Connect, which is a free service, allows health organizations to provide patient-appropriate educational information using the ICD-9 classification system, SNOMED CT, and Problem List subset codes. (MedlinePlus Connect will be upgraded to support ICD-10 when it becomes the standard.) Based on the codes entered, MedlinePlus Connect returns patient-appropriate information, which comes from the MedlinePlus.gov database. Available resources include information on health and wellness issues, diseases and conditions, and drug information. Also included are links to patient organizations, support groups, and clinical trials. MedlinePlus is an authoritative, high quality, and free health information resource. MedlinePlus Connect uses existing coding for diagnoses, medications, and lab tests within the EHR.

The Health Information Technology for Economic and Clinical Health (HITECH) Act of 2009 created what is determined as "meaningful use" or a set of criteria that enables healthcare providers and practices to gain government incentive by meeting certain standards. Providing medical records to patients is included in meaningful use criteria. Also included is a requirement to record race and ethnicity. This data can be studied and utilized to further demonstrate health disparities and treatment inequities. Once an organization is aware of where the gaps are, steps can be taken to close the gaps and overcome the inequities. Collecting this data offers a "key opportunity to mitigate health disparities" (Sequist, 2011).

To stay current with newly published research about health disparities and EHR, set up a saved search in PubMed to be run periodically using the Medical Subject Heading or MeSH. MeSH is a controlled vocabulary of biomedical terms that describes the main concepts of journal articles in the MEDLINE database. Using MeSH terms such as electronic health records, health care disparities, health care disparities/statistics and numerical data, ethnic groups, ethnic groups/statistics and numerical data, data collection, and patient advocacy make the retrieval of articles more relevant. (Use the Search Builder accessible from the Advanced Search button on the home page of PubMed.gov. See the MeSH database for more information, accessible from the PubMed home page.)

Social Media Resources

The Internet is a powerful tool for patients to find information about their health. According to Pew Internet, 80 percent of Internet users in the United States, or 59 percent of US adults, look online for health information (Pew Internet Health, 2012). Although adults in households with incomes higher than $75,000 use the Internet more frequently (95 percent), those in household with incomes of $30,000 or less also go online (57 percent). Those in the higher income group are more likely to look for health information online (87 percent), but 72 percent of Internet users in the lower income group are likely to look for health information online (Pew Internet Profiles of Information Seekers, 2012). The medical community should not overlook this significant source for patients and healthcare consumers who seek medical information. Clinicians can benefit from understanding their patients' information-seeking behaviors and can help direct them to authoritative sources. Even for patients who are not online themselves, peer-to-peer information gathering plays a big role in obtaining health information, and much of that information is likely to come from online sources.

In this age of electronic information, social media has become an important and influential medium to communicate with and inform patients with regard to taking ownership of their health. Public health departments have begun to use Twitter to communicate with groups they may not be reaching otherwise. People with low health literacy may miss important public health alerts, and this is another way to reach audiences more likely to have health disparities (Thackery, Neiger, Smith, and Van Wagenen, 2012; and Vance, Howe and Dellavalle, 2009).

Another tactic that organizations can employ to engage healthcare consumers who may not be otherwise connected to good sources of information is to host Twitter Chats. A Twitter Chat is a prearranged discussion during which those involved are all online at the same time to discuss a particular topic. By using a hashtag to note the subject of the discussion, participants can link with one another on the same topic. Typically, these chats are directed by a moderator and sometimes include a guest "presenter." There is often a blog used to announce the Twitter Chat and keep a record of the transcript afterward. In addition, Twitter Chats are publicized via tweets, with lots of retweeting to attract new participants. A calendar of health-related Twitter Chats (Symplur Health Tweet Chats, 2012) is maintained by Symplur.com, which also includes a list of hashtags used on Twitter to discuss diseases (Symplur Disease Hashtags, 2012).

Automated text messaging is also a way to reach underserved audiences when more than 85 percent of Americans have cell phones, and 72 percent of them receive text messages (www.text4baby.org). Text4Baby is a project of the Healthy Mothers, Healthy Babies Coalition, which consists of the American College of Obstetricians and Gynecologists, the March of Dimes, the American Academy of Pediatrics, the American Nurses Association, the National Congress of Parents and Teachers, and the US Public Health Service. The goal of the coalition is to improve the quality and reach of public and professional education related to prenatal and infant care. Text4Baby is available in English and Spanish and sends health information and resources in text-length format to expectant mothers.

Patients depend on providers for guidance in finding authoritative sources. Thus, providers can benefit from understanding where patients are getting health information. And by becoming familiar with the health information available on the Internet, including social media resources, a provider can influence a patient's online choices and, hopefully, their health choices as well.

CONCLUSION

Physician assistants are uniquely positioned to be able to influence and help reduce health disparities. With a long history of serving the needs of underserved communities, PA practice is built on the foundation of leveling the playing field for patients, and providing the care that all patients deserve but that some seldom obtain. By becoming familiar with the definitions and data, using the tools provided, and partnering with other medical professionals and librarians, PAs can make a difference.

With the compressed PA education and uniquely collaborative MD-PA practice model comes a special understanding of the value of building and sustaining a network of interprofessional colleagues. It's this foundational utilization of built networks that can enhance PAs' ability to find the resources they need to address health disparities in a meaningful way. With the help of physician assistants across the country driven by a desire to provide equitable care for all patients, as well as to identify and integrate the social forces that make people ill, this nation can begin to heal its health disparities and end the unfair suffering of so many patients.

REFERENCES

AAPA Health Disparities Workgroup (blog). *Journal of the American Academy of Physician Assistants.* Retrieved on May 5, 2012, from http://www.jaapa.com/health-disparities-blog/section/2379.

About Health Literacy. Retrieved on May 5, 2012, from http://www.hrsa.gov/publichealth/healthliteracy/healthlitabout.html.

AHRQ Pharmacy Health Literacy Center. Retrieved on May 5, 2012, from http://www.ahrq.gov/pharmhealthlit.

Aihara, Y. & Minai, J. (2011). "Barriers and catalysts of nutrition literacy among elderly Japanese people." *Health Promot Int,* 26(4), 421–431.

Brach, C., Dreyer, B., Schyve, P., Hernandez, L., Baur, C., Lemerise, A., & Parker, R. (January 2012). "Attributes of a health literate organization." Retrieved from Institute of Medicine website: http://iom.edu/~/media/Files/Perspectives-Files/2012/Discussion-Papers/BPH_HLit_Attributes.pdf.

Bringing Health Information to the Community. Retrieved on May 5, 2012, from http://nnlm.gov/bhic/.

Centers for Disease Control (CDC). Retrieved on May 5, 2012, from http://www.cdc.gov/.

Centers for Disease Control (CDC). *Breast Cancer Rates by Race and Ethnicity.* Retrieved on May 5, 2012, from http://www.cdc.gov/ cancer/breast/statistics/race.htm.

Centers for Disease Control (CDC). *Center for Chronic Disease Prevention.* Retrieved on May 5, 2012, from http://www.cdc.gov/ chronicdisease/healthequity.

Centers for Disease Control (CDC). *Promoting Health Equity.* Retrieved on May 5, 2012, from http://www.cdc.gov/nccdphp/dach/chhep/pdf/SDOHworkbook.pdf.

Centers for Disease Control (CDC). *Social Determinants of Health Maps.* Retrieved on May 5, 2012, from http://www.cdc.gov/ dhdsp/maps/social_determinants_maps.htm.

Christopher Gibbons, M. (2011). "Use of health information technology among racial and ethnic underserved communities." *Perspect Health Inf Manag,* 8, 1f.

Clinical Trials. Retrieved on May 5, 2012, from http://clinicaltrials.gov/.

Edwards, M., Wood, F., Davies, M., & Edwards, A. (2012). "The development of health literacy in patients with a long-term health condition: the health literacy pathway model." *BMC Public Health,* 12, 130.

Eligible Hospital and CAH Meaningful Use Table. Retrieved on May 5, 2012, from http://www.cms.gov/Regulations-and-Guidance/Legislation/EHRIncentivePrograms/downloads//Hosp_CAH_MU-TOC.pdf.

Gazmararian, J. A., Baker, D. W., Williams, M. V., Parker, R. M., Scott, T. L., Green, D. C., Fehrenbach, S. N., Ren, J., & Koplan, J. P. (1999). "Health literacy among Medicare enrollees in a managed care organization." *JAMA, 281*(6), 545–551.

Health Communication, Health Literacy, and e-Health. Retrieved on May 5, 2012, from http://www.health.gov/communication/literacy/Default.asp.

Health Disparities Toolkit. Retrieved on May 5, 2012, from http://www.naccho.org/toolbox/program.cfm?id=24&display_name.

Health Literacy: Accurate, Accessible and Actionable Health Information for All. Retrieved on May 5, 2012, from http://www.cdc.gov/healthliteracy.

Health Literacy: Broadening Definitions, Intensifying Partnerships and Identifying. (2011). American Academy of Physician Assistants. Retrieved from http://www.aapa.org/uploadedFiles/content/About_AAPA/Governance/Resource_Items/32-HealthLiteracy.pdf.

Health Literacy of America's Adults. Retrieved on May 5, 2012, from http://nces.ed.gov/pubs2006/2006483.pdf.

Health Literacy Universal Precautions Toolkit. Retrieved on May 5, 2012, from http://www.ahrq.gov/qual/literacy/.

HHS Action Plan to Reduce Racial and Ethnic Health Disparities. Retrieved on May 5, 2012, from http://minorityhealth.hhs.gov/npa/files/Plans/HHS/HHS_Plan_complete.pdf.

HIV/AIDS Information. Retrieved on May 5, 2012, from http://sis.nlm.nih.gov/hiv.html.

Journal of the American Academy of Physician Assistants (JAAPA) Health Disparities (blog). Retrieved on May 5, 2012, from http://www.jaapa.com/health-disparities-blog/section/2379/.

MedlinePlus. Retrieved on May 5, 2012, from http://www.nlm.nih.gov/medlineplus/.

MedlinePlus Connect. Retrieved on May 5, 2012, from http://www.nlm.nih.gov/medlineplus/connect/overview.html.

National Action Plan to Improve Health Literacy. Retrieved on May 5, 2012, from http://www.health.gov/communication/HLActionPlan/pdf/Health_Literacy_Action_Plan.pdf.

National Healthcare Disparities Report. Retrieved on May 5, 2012, from http://www.ahrq.gov/qual/nhdr11/nhdr11.pdf.

National Network of Libraries of Medicine (NN/LM). Retrieved on May 5, 2012, http://nnlm.gov/.

National Partnership for Action. Retrieved on May 5, 2012, from http://minorityhealth.hhs.gov/npa/.

National Stakeholder Strategy for Achieving Health Equity. Retrieved on May 5, 2012, from http://minorityhealth.hhs.gov/npa/templates/content.aspx?lvl=1&lvlid=33&ID=286.

Navarro, R. A., Greene, D. F., Burchette, R., Funahashi, T., & Dell, R. (2011). "Minimizing disparities in osteoporosis care of minorities with an electronic medical record care plan." *Clin Orthop Relat Res, 469(7)*, 1931–1935.

Pew Internet: Health. Retrieved on May 5, 2012, from http://www.pewinternet.org/Commentary/2011/November/Pew-Internet-Health.aspx.

Pew Internet Profiles of Information Seekers. Retrieved on May 5, 2012, from http://www.pewinternet.org/Reports/2011/HealthTopics/Part-2/Higherincome-adults.aspx.

Phillips, C. E., Rothstein, J. D., Beaver, K., Sherman, B. J., Freund, K. M., & Battaglia, T. A. (2011). "Patient navigation to increase mammography screening among inner city women." *J Gen Intern Med, 26(2)*, 123–129.

Physician Tool Kit. Retrieved on May 5, 2012, from http://www.dshs.state.tx.us/wellness/toolkit.shtm.

PubMed. Retrieved on May 5, 2012, from http://www.ncbi.nlm.nih.gov/pubmed/.

Samal, L., Lipsitz, S. R., & Hicks, L. S. (2012). "Impact of electronic health records on racial and ethnic disparities in blood pressure control at US primary care visits." *Arch Intern Med* (Vol. 172, pp. 75–76). United States.

Sentell, T. L. & Halpin, H. A. (2006). "Importance of adult literacy in understanding health disparities." *J Gen Intern Med, 21(8)*, 862–866.

Sequist, T. D. (2011). "Health information technology and disparities in quality of care." *J Gen Intern Med, 26(10)*, 1084–1085.

Shaw, S. J., Huebner, C., Armin, J., Orzech, K., & Vivian, J. (2009). "The role of culture in health literacy and chronic disease screening and management." *J Immigr Minor Health*, 11(6), 460–467.

Strategic Plan for Risk Communication. Retrieved on May 5, 2012, from http://www.fda.gov/AboutFDA/ReportsManualsForms/Reports/ucm183673.htm.

Symplur Healthcare Tweet Chats. Retrieved on May 5, 2012, from http://www.symplur.com/healthcare-hashtags/tweet-chats/].

Symplur Disease Hashtags. Retrieved on May 5, 2012, from http://www.symplur.com/healthcare-hashtags/diseases.

Thackeray, R., Neiger, B. L., Smith, A. K., & Van Wagenen, S. B. (2012). "Adoption and use of social media among public health departments." *BMC Public Health*, 12, 242.

Vance, K., Howe, W., & Dellavalle, R. P. (2009). "Social internet sites as a source of public health information." *Dermatol Clin*, 27(2), 133–136.

III

THE ROLE OF PROVIDER INTERACTION AS A SOCIAL DETERMINANT OF HEALTH

ADDRESSING HEALTH DISPARITIES IN PRIMARY CARE

Adapting Community-based Approaches to the Primary Care Setting

By Cherise B. Harrington, Ph.D., MPH and James F. Cawley, MPH, PA-C, DHL (hc)

BACKGROUND

Health disparities include not only differences in the incidence, prevalence, mortality, and morbidity of disease, but also include differences in access to care and care quality. These differences can be based on both non-modifiable and modifiable characteristics such as age, gender, race, ethnicity, income, education, health insurance, and geographic location, among others (R. Cooper et al., 2000; Mensah, Mokdad, Ford, Greenlund, & Croft, 2005; Schultz et al., 2005; Shaya, Gu, & Saunders, 2006). Disparities linked to race/ethnicity and socioeconomic statuses are the most detrimental and affect large portions of the population. Research shows that these disparities exist regardless of insurance status, income, age, and disease severity (Nelson, 2002). Among the leading causes of death in the United States (i.e., heart disease and cancer), disparities between racial/ethnic groups are the most striking. Cardiovascular disease incidence and mortality are higher among African Americans, American Indians, and Asian or Pacific Islander groups compared with Caucasians (R. Cooper, et al., 2000; Mensah & Brown, 2007; Mensah, et al., 2005). And compared with Whites, African Americans have higher incidence and mortality rates for most cancer sites (American Cancer Society).

Addressing health inequities between differing populations is a major challenge, evidenced by its continued presence as a national priority for the previous several decades as seen in the Healthy People reports (US Department of Health and Human Services, 2011). Aside from individual behavior change to decrease risk factors for the most pressing, costly, and individually devastating illnesses and diseases, or assuring that groups have equal access to both preventative and curative health care, the most promising method of intervention is ensuring that when health care resources are available and accessed, they are evidenced-based, free from bias, timely, and equitable.

There is no easy answer for the broad question, "Why do health disparities exist?" A complex set of factors synergistically occurs that influence how, why, and to whom disease affects and the type and quality of care that one receives. In the difficulty of addressing and decreasing health disparities, it is important to note that both individual and organizational—as well as modifiable and non-modifiable—factors contribute to the problem. While this chapter will not explore the historical, biological, socioeconomic, and environmental themes that occur in explaining health disparities, it will attempt to briefly note contributing factors, how disparities can manifest with regard to primary care, and offer a brief review of strategies to address them. Primary care is key in the effort to decrease health disparities, and research has shown that higher quality primary care is associated with reduced racial and ethnic disparities (Shi, Green, & Kazakova, 2004; Starfield, Shi & Macinko, 2005).

CONTRIBUTING FACTORS TO HEALTH DISPARITIES

Individual factors that can contribute to a health disparity include personal health behavior choices that may differentially affect health such as diet, weight, level of physical activity, healthy eating, and the likelihood of attaining preventive health care services or chronic disease screening. There are, however, other less personally mediated elements that contribute to health disparities, including problems of access (typically most affected by socioeconomic status), social and environmental factors, and personal biases and racial discrimination.

Access and Socioeconomic Factors

Certain barriers often related to socioeconomic conditions decrease the utilization of preventive services and medical treatments among racial and ethnic minorities. One example is the lack of health insurance or being underinsured. Latinos and Blacks are uninsured at higher rates compared with Whites (Lurie & Dubowitz, 2007), partly due to high rates of employment-based health insurance. While health insurance does not guarantee that one has access to care or quality care, it does increase the likelihood that one has a "medical home," which is linked to improved health outcomes (Homer, 2009).

Even among the insured, however, disparities continue to exist. Across multiple diseases, individuals of lower economic status have poorer health outcomes related to not only the disease, but subsequent health care as well (Braverman, 2006). Racial and ethnic minorities and those of lower economic status are less likely to utilize services, establish a medical home, or receive quality of care compared with advantaged non-minorities (Lurie & Dubowitz, 2007). Although "access" with respect to health care typically denotes insurance, it can also incorporate many factors that prevent patients from accessing medical care, including the hours of operation and location of the clinic, mode of transportation for the patient, and language barriers (e.g., lack of translation resources).

Social and Environmental Factors

Working in concert with issues of access, social and environmental factors are important considerations for primary care professionals because they both directly and indirectly affect health and disease (Gee & Payne-Sturges, 2004). There are implications on health behaviors that are directly related to social and environmental factors, including the availability of nutritious foods and physical activities. For example, healthy eating is only possible with access to a healthy menu that includes non-processed foods and fresh fruits and vegetables, which is made easier in communities with health food stores or farmers markets. Furthermore, diets are socialized, as we develop our acquired tastes to certain foods as early as two and three years of age, and eating tends to be a social process throughout one's life. Individuals must have exposure to healthy eating as well as a social support to maintain a healthy diet (Bril, Hombessa-Nkounkou, Bouville, & Ocampo, 2001; Drewnowski, 1997).

Additionally, many low-income communities have environmental exposures that can affect health and disease (Gee & Payne-Sturges, 2004). Environmental exposures can include, for example, those related to increased rates of asthma and other respiratory diseases. Asthma prevalence in the United States has continued to increase over the past ten years, up to a rate of 8.4 percent in 2010 (Akinbami, Moorman, Bailey, & al.). Increased prevalence and poorer asthma outcomes in children is linked to race and class. This may be due, in part, to pollution in more urban areas, but much evidence shows the greatest predictor is that of stress pertaining to one's surrounding environment (Clarke & Calam, 2012; Yonas, Lange, & Celedón, 2012). African American children are twice as likely as white children to have asthma (CDC., 2012). What's more, characteristics of the "built environment"—or a human-made environment designed for the community's action and interaction—vary from accessibility to parks and adequate sidewalks to the degree of neighborhood violence or air quality, all of which may hinder many outdoor activities and, with it, opportunities for physical activity necessary for good health and well-being. Having a more thorough understanding of a community's overall environment and resources (or lack of) and how they affect health can result in more realistic health behavior-change conversations between health care professionals and their patients.

Personal Bias or Racial Discrimination

In addition to the historical, social, and environmental factors that contribute to health disparities, a difficult but important topic is how personal bias or racial discrimination about a group can affect that group's care. Biases may not be intentional or even apparent to most, particularly those who hold them, but they do unfortunately and undeniably exist (Schulman, Berlin, Harless W, & al., 1999; van Ryn & Burke, 2000). A substantial body of research has shown that across physicians and health care facilities, certain groups receive differential treatment attributed to their race or ethnicity. This has been seen in pain-care experiences, documented in acute, chronic, cancer and palliative pain,[1] and surgical outcomes (Ayanian, 2008). While most of the research in this area focuses on when and what types of treatment are recommended and prescribed, there is also research showing differential perception of personal interactions between racially discordant patient and physician pairs (Blanchard, Nayar, & Lurie, 2007). Ethnic minorities, who are most likely to not share the same race/ethnicity with their caregiver, negatively rate their interactions with non-racially concordant health professionals more so than Whites (Carrasquillo, Orav, Brennan, & HR., 1999; K. Collins et al.; T. Collins, Clark, Petersen, & Kressin, 2002; Cooper-Patrick, Gallo, & Gonzales, 1999; LA. Cooper & Roter, 2003; Gross, Zyzanski, Borawski, Cebul, & KC., 1998; Malat, 2001; Saha, Komaromy, Koepsell, & Bindman, 1999). And research shows that when a medical encounter is viewed negatively (e.g., disrespectful), it may influence one's likelihood to seek health care services in the future, result in a delay of care, decrease the likelihood of following physician recommendations, and result in a decrease in chronic disease screening (Blanchard & Lurie, 2004). This literature highlights how vital the perception of the medical encounter has on health outcomes.

---

1 (Anderson, Green, & Payne, 2009; Green et al., 2003) K.O.</author><author>Green, C.R.</author><author>Payne, R.</author></authors></contributors><titles><title>Racial and ethnic disparities in pain: causes and consequences of unequal care</title><secondary-title>J Pain</secondary-title></titles><periodical><full-title>J Pain</full-title></periodical><pages>1187-1204</pages><volume>10</volume><number>12</number><dates><year>2009</year></dates><urls></urls></record></Cite></EndNote>, cardiovascular disease diagnosis and treatment (Wyatt et al., 2003).

IMPROVING HEALTH CARE QUALITY FOR RACIAL/ETHNIC MINORITIES

There exists a fairly large body of work that focuses on strategies for improving health care quality and equality for racial and ethnic minorities. The Institute of Medicine report, *Unequal treatment: Confronting racial and ethnic disparities in health care*, provides a comprehensive review of health care disparities and offers several recommendations to eliminate them. The recommendations include steering clear of fragmented insurance plans that are based on socioeconomic status, stabilizing relationships between the patient and provider in publically funded care plans, and increasing the number of racial and ethnic minorities in the health workforce (Nelson, 2002). The report also specifically addresses the role of academic medicine and notes that patient care can be improved through better reporting of the race/ethnicity of patients, cross-cultural education for health care professionals, and an increase in focused research that investigates ways to identify sources of disparities and efficacious interventions (JR. Betancourt, 2006). Other recommendations include approaches to improve the health care setting by assessing criteria for the development and testing of interventions or programs to address disparities in health care.

Health Care Settings

A 2006 review discusses several promising quality-improvement strategies implemented in the primary care setting that may aid in addressing health disparities (Beach et al., 2006). While based on small sample sizes, the helpful methods included: 1) provider education; 2) using a system that bypasses the physician and directly offers preventive services to patients; and 3) remote simultaneous translation (Beach, et al., 2006). These strategies can be especially useful for small primary care practices that often have limited resources to devote to addressing issues of health disparities (Weinick, Byron, Han, French, & Scholle, 2010).

The good news in the battle to decrease health disparities is that there are strategies that can be broadly employed to address the inequities in health care settings, including cultural competence education. Betancourt et al. describes establishing a framework that addresses barriers and competence within the organizational, structural, and clinical settings to improve conditions and quality of care for racial/ethnic minorities (JR. Betancourt, Green, Carrillo, & Ananeh-Firempong, 2003). This cultural competence framework includes the recruitment of more racially/ethnically diverse professionals into the health field, interpreter services and language-appropriate health education materials, and provider education on culture, including differing cultures within the United States (JR. Betancourt, et al., 2003). One of the challenges, however, is that some strategies may be disease-specific, such as clinical practice guidelines, which often draw more interest among physicians, researchers, and funding agencies to support thorough investigations of these particular issues, thereby removing funding from the examination of social-related issues.

Strategies for Effective Interventions

Another tactic to combat health disparities is the identification of strategies that influence the effectiveness of interventions designed to reduce health care disparities (LA Cooper, Hill, & Powe, 2002; Jones, Trivedi, & Ayanian, 2010). Among these are both contextual and organizational factors. The contextual factors focus on accountability and aligning incentive (Jones, et al., 2010). This means that for efforts designed to address health disparities to be effective, there must be a method for evaluating outcomes. The outcomes, then, are used to determine whether problems persist, if goals are being met, assigning accountability for those unmet goals, and subsequent incentives for improvements.

Organizational factors stress commitment, population health focus, solutions that are informed by data, and a comprehensive approach to issues (Jones, et al., 2010). This means that the health care professional and practice should first establish a commitment to introduce strategies to address disparities in the health care setting through an allocation of resources. This commitment is further emphasized by focusing on a population or public health problem affecting the community being served (best accomplished through community involvement). Additionally, adopting and implementing practices that are evidence-based offers the best opportunity to achieve success for these tailored programs/interventions. And lastly, efforts should be comprehensive and multifaceted, attempting to intervene across multiple levels of patient/community care, health and/or environment (note: socioecological framework) (McLeroy, Bibeau, Steckler, & Glanz, 1988; Stokols, 1996b).

MODELS FOR ADDRESSING HEALTH DISPARITIES IN PRIMARY CARE

There are several conceptual frameworks that can aid in addressing health disparities in primary care and serve as a model for practice. The social ecological framework (SEF) is useful in this endeavor, because it both functions from the premise that since the etiology of health and disease is multidimensional, preventive and curative care should similarly be multifaceted, and also that it examines issues as they intersect with personal and environmental factors. Another model for practice is the community-oriented primary care model, which illustrates how theory and practice merge to address the challenge of provider time limitations while providing complete and thorough care to patients (especially among underserved populations) through a team approach that considers the resources and health needs of the community being served.

Social Ecological Model

Employing a community-based approach to primary care requires understanding of the social ecology of health and its impact on behavior-change efforts. By emphasizing the multidimensional influences on health, including environmental, cultural, social, and psychological factors, health care providers and their patients are better served (Sallis, Owen, & Fisher, 2008). This model targets the various levels and factors on health-related behavior (McLeroy, et al., 1988) and functions from four basic assumptions: 1) behavior is influenced by multiple levels; 2) influence occurs within and between levels; 3) targeting behavior change with a multidimensional approach is more effective than a single-factor approach, and; 4) interventions are most effective when behaviorally specific. Individuals and communities are complex, multidimensional, and multilayered. Lives are inundated with complex networks of individuals, social networks, organizations, and social norms. The social ecological health paradigm is particularly useful in conceptualizing the how social and environmental factors synergistically influence health. Thus, understanding how environmental and social factors impact disease is an important educational tool to inform providers and trainees on how to decrease health disparities.

Promoting health behavior changes should first acknowledge the relationship between the social environment and negative health-related behavior and then include interventions at the following multiple levels: intrapersonal, interpersonal, organizational, community, and/or social policy (McLeroy, et al., 1988; Sallis, et al., 2008; Stokols, 1996a). At the intrapersonal level, educational efforts are typically taken to alter the knowledge, beliefs, and intentions of the individual to promote behavior change, where the benefits of social support and improved communication are utilized at the interpersonal level. The organizational level of the model targets altering the social and physical environment (such as where people tend to congregate) to reinforce behavior-change efforts. And community-level interventions will employ communities or towns to collectively influence behavior on a larger scale (e.g., media efforts, community organizing efforts, new walking trails, etc.). At the macro level, the influence of social policy targets the larger society with approaches to promote a broad level behavior change (e.g., healthy school lunches). When the social ecological model is used to promote changes in health behaviors simultaneously across multiple levels, the potential for success is exponentially improved through continued and multifaceted reinforcements.

In the primary care setting, intervening on each of these levels may not be directly applicable; however, adapting this model into recommendations for the patients may be promising. The success of an effort of this type hinges on a thorough understanding of the resources and challenges for both the individual patient and a community. Only then can providers successfully partner with other community organizations to meet their patients' needs.

Community-Oriented Primary Care

Community-oriented primary care (COPC) is a multifaceted approach to primary care, originating from a combination of epidemiology, primary care, preventive medicine, health promotion, and, to some extent, public health (Longlett, Kruse, & Wesley, 2001; Wright, 1993). COPC is a process by which one defines and characterizes the demographics and resources of a community, takes that data and identifies a priority health need or problem, thoroughly assess the epidemiology of the health problem, plans an intervention or program, implements and evaluates the successes and failures of the program, and continually revisits this process to ensure that the most pressing community need is being addressed. Developed in the 1950s by Sidney Kark, this approach was first seen in South Africa where it was used successfully to improve the health status of an entire community. In the United States, the approach has shown its usefulness, especially with poor and underserved populations, resulting in an endorsement by the Institution of Medicine (IOM) for the principles of COPC to be disseminated through medical settings and educational institutions in order to strengthen the US primary care system. At a conference convened by the IOM, an operational definition was developed that included three implementation requirements, establishing that primary care should: 1) provide "... accessible, comprehensive, coordinated, continuous-over-time, and accountable health care services"; 2) assume responsibility for the health of a defined community; and 3) define and characterize the community being served, know the communities' pressing health problems, employ methods to address the priority health problem, and evaluate the progress and effectiveness of methods employed (Longlett, et al., 2001).

There are challenges to this approach (Longlett, et al., 2001). Overall, many physicians view the model as intuitive in theory, but difficult to practice. First, the dissemination of this approach has been hindered by its potential for limited or difficult sustainability. The COPC model requires a commitment and resources, which may be problematic for some practices. The adoption and/or implementation of this model is a team approach. The practice must dedicate resources to monitoring the health needs of a given community, developing practices/programs to attend to those health needs, implementing those practices/programs, and evaluating the results. When implemented, however, this model has shown remarkable success and impact on health outcomes (Longlett, et al., 2001). This model could be successfully implemented by utilizing the time of nurses, physician assistants, or program managers employed in primary care practices. Additionally, the utilization of this model has the potential to balance the disparities in the healthcare system by establishing a system that is more accountable and relevant to the population (Wright, 1993).

CONCLUSIONS

The primary care physician, along with other providers such as nurse practitioners and physician assistants, are key players in addressing and preventing health disparities. Based on the literature and review of conceptual and practice-based models, there are several strategies that should be implemented to address health disparities in the primary care setting. First and simplest is cultural competence training for any health care professional with patient interaction. This training should be specific to the population being served in the clinic. Cultural competence programs have proliferated in US medical schools in response to increasing national diversity as well as mandates from accrediting bodies. Cultural competence training is increasingly a standard component of health professions' educational curriculum, yet PA and NP schools are lacking adequate training (Furman & Dent, 2004). This instruction is necessary as evidence suggests perception of the interaction between patient and health care professional is key to patient satisfaction, but more critically, it is related to health outcomes and future treatment outcomes. Also, improving the interaction between the patient and provider is the key to patients establishing a "medical home." Research has shown improved health outcomes among those with a medical home and that racial/ethnic minorities are less likely to have one (Homer, 2009).

Secondly, employ approaches that promote relationships with community stakeholders. This allows for dialogue and cross-learning regarding community health needs, barriers and challenges to care-seeking, and it may influence participation and, eventually, establish trust with a particular health professional. Additionally, there may be community organizations that could be useful partners in efforts to assist patients with health care access and healthy behavior (e.g., faith-based organized transportation to clinics, free access to neighborhood school exercise equipment, or a community garden).

Next, it is vital to implement evaluation measures. To address and/or eliminate disparities in health care or to evaluate efforts implemented to reduce health care disparities, quality and consistent data is needed (Moy, Arispe, Holmes, & Andrews, 2005). One study found that racial and economic data is often not collected, inconsistently collected, or collected in ways that differ from standards and did not allow for reliable assessments or comparisons across groups (Moy, et al., 2005). A possible remedy for these data gaps includes federal efforts and standardizations of electronic medical records (EMR).

Equally important is to routinely monitor this evaluation data and employ accountability processes. This allows for health care facilities to observe who and what they are treating as well as track the successes or failures of medical interventions and programs. This data also could highlight barriers to care and adherences previously unidentified that could be addressed. The use of EMR and consistent improved tracking of patients' health information better enables needs-assessment efforts to ensure that individuals and communities are getting the resources that they need.

Primary care providers and clinics dedicated to addressing health disparities have various resources at their disposal. But continued research is needed to identify innovative, efficacious, cost-effective, and clinic-friendly strategies that address health disparities. A potential future direction is to investigate adapting the principles of the Chronic Care Model for preventive care to enhance service delivery (Glasgow, Orleans, Wagner, Curry, & Solberg, 2001). Also, the expanded use of health (e.g., use of mobile technology to improve health outcomes) is showing promise in underserved populations.

In reducing health inequities, research should seek to utilize a multimethod, multidimensional strategy composed of theory-driven hypothesis development, key formative work, and intervention development and testing to intervene on key social determinants of chronic health. The focus of needed research should be to identify barriers to engaging in life-saving health behaviors, and developing approaches to overcome those barriers. This involves developing interventions to target the cognitive, social, psychological, and behavioral factors that impact chronic illness health disparities using community- and worksite-based approaches. Primary care providers are instrumental in developing these strategies that will benefit the community at large.

Adapting community-based approaches into the primary care setting is a promising approach. Community-based participatory research [CBPR] involves reaching individuals where they live, work, play, worship, and seek care. CBPR approaches engage communities in a partnership to adapt programs/interventions to fit the needs and characteristics of the target community. These approaches work by establishing connections with local leaders, partnering to identify the most pressing health problems, developing goals and strategies, and tailoring interventions based on the unique needs and interests of the community. While potentially time-consuming, this method offers big rewards because with community buy-in/partnership, there is an increased likelihood for sustainability. With dedication and innovation, principles of community-based approaches could be adapted into primary settings as a strategy to address health disparities.

Awareness and comprehension of social determinants of health is instrumental to the preventive and curative care of a patient. Once contributing factors to health disparities are identified, the health care community (with providers at the helm) can contribute innovative and useful community-based conceptual and practice-based strategies to address health disparities in the clinic. Primary care is the link to all care in the US healthcare system and the gateway to improved health in US societies. Establishing a commitment to addressing health disparities in the primary care setting is imperative to decreasing the devastating health disparity trends.

REFERENCES

Akinbami, J., Moorman, J., Bailey, C., et al. Trends in Asthma Prevalence, Health Care Use, and Mortality in the United States, 2001–2010. *MCHS Data Brief, No. 94, USDHHS. CDC, May 2012.*

American Cancer Society. *Cancer Facts & Figures 2009.* Atlanta: American Cancer Society; 2009.

Anderson, K. O., Green, C. R., & Payne, R. (2009). Racial and ethnic disparities in pain: causes and consequences of unequal care. *J Pain, 10*(12), 1187–1204.

Ayanian, J. (2008). Determinants of racial and ethnic disparities in surgical care. *World J Surg, 32*(4), 509–515.

Beach, M., Gary, T., Price, E., Robinson, K., Gozu, A., Palacio, A., et al. (2006). Improving health care quality for racial/ethnic minorities: a systematic review of the best evidence regarding provider and organization interventions. *BMC Public Health, 6*(104).

Betancourt, J. (2006). Eliminating racial and ethnic disparities in health care: what is the role of academic medicine? *Acad Med, 81*(9), 788–792.

Betancourt, J., Green, A., Carrillo, J., & Ananeh-Firempong, O. (2003). Defining cultural competence: a practical framework for addressing racial/ethnic disparities in health and health care. *Public Health Rep, 118*(4), 293–302.

Blanchard, J. & Lurie, N. (2004). R-E-S-P-E-C-T: patient reports of disrespect in the health care setting and its impact on care. *J Fam Pract, 53*(9), 721–730.

Blanchard, J., Nayar, S., & Lurie, N. (2007). Patient-provider and patient-staff racial concordance and perceptions of mistreatment in the health care setting. *J Gen Intern Med, 22*(8), 1184–189.

Braverman, P. (2006). Health disparities and health equity: Concepts and measurement. *Annual Review and Public Health, 27*, 167–194.

Bril, B., Hombessa-Nkounkou, E., Bouville, J., & Ocampo, C. (2001). From Milk to Adult Diet: A comparative study on the socialization of food. *Food and Foodways, 9*(3–4), 155–186.

Carrasquillo, O., Orav, E., Brennan, T., & H. R., B. (1999). Impact of language barriers on patient satisfaction in an emergency department. *J Gen Intern Med, 14*, 82–87.

CDC. (2012). Asthma's Impact on the Nation. *http://www.cdc.gov/asthma impacts_nation/?s_cid=w_c_CustomImageWidget_frm_001.*

Clarke, S. & Calam, R. (2012). The effectivenss of psychosocial interventions designed to improve health-related quality of life (HRQOL) amongst asthmatic children and their families: A systematic review. *Qual Life Res, 21*(5), 747–764.

Collins, K., Hughes, D., Doty, M., Ives, B., Edwards, J., & Tenney, K. Diverse Communities, Common Concerns: Assessing Health Care Quality for Minority Americans. Findings from The Commonwealth Fund 2001 Health Care Quality Survey. *New York: The Commonwealth Fund; 2002.*

Collins, T., Clark, J., Petersen, L., & Kressin, N. (2002). Racial differences in how patients perceive physician communication regarding cardiac testing. *Med Care, 40*(suppl 1), 127–134.

Cooper-Patrick, L., Gallo, J., & Gonzales, J. (1999). Race, gender, and partnership in the patient-physician relationship. *JAMA, 282*, 583–589.

Cooper, L., Hill, M., & Powe, N. (2002). Designing and evaluating interventions to eliminate racial and ethnic disparities in health care. *J Gen Intern Med, 17*(6), 477–486.

Cooper, L., & Roter, D. (2003). Patient-Provider Communication. The Effect of Race and Ethnicity on Process and Outcomes of Healthcare. In: Smedley BD, Stith AY, Nelson AR, editors. Unequal Treatment: Confronting Racial and Ethnic Disparities in Healthcare. *Washington, DC: National Academy Press*, 552–593.

Cooper, R., Cutler, J., Desvigne-Nickens, P., Fortmann, S., Friedman, L., Havlik, R., et al. (2000). Trends and Disparities in Coronary Heart Disease, Stroke, and Other Cardiovascular Diseases in the United States: Findings of the National Conference on Cardiovascular Disease Prevention. *Circulation, 102*, 3137–3147.

Drewnowski, A. (1997). Taste Preferences and food intake. *Annual Review of Nutrition, 17*, 237–253.

Furman, G. & Dent, M. M. Cultural Competency in Medical Education: A Guidebook for Schools. Department of Health and Human Services; 2004. Seamless learning: incorporating cultural competency into the curriculum.

Gee, G. & Payne-Sturges, D. (2004). Environmental Health Disparities: A Framework Integrating Psychosocial and Environmental Concepts. *Environmental Health Perspectives, 112*(17), 1645–1653.

Glasgow, R., Orleans, C., Wagner, E., Curry, S., & Solberg, L. (2001). Does the chronic care model also serve as a template for improving prevention? *Milbank Quarterly, 79*(4), 579–612.

Green, C., Anderson, K., Baker, T., Campbell, L., Decker, S., Fillingim, R., et al. (2003). The unequal burden of pain: confronting racial and ethnic disparities in pain. *Pain Med, 4*(3), 277–294.

Gross, D., Zyzanski, S., Borawski, E., Cebul, R., & KC., S. (1998). Patient satisfaction with time spent with their physician. *J Fam Pract, 47*, 133–137.

Homer, C. (2009). Health disparities and the primary care medical home: Could it be that simple? *Acad Pedia, 9*, 203–205.

Jones, R., Trivedi, A., & Ayanian, J. (2010). Factors influencing the effectiveness of interventions to reduce racial and ethnic disparities in health care. *Soc Sci Med, 70*(3), 337–341.

Longlett, S., Kruse, J., & Wesley, R. (2001). Community-oriented primary care: Historical perspectiv. *J Am Board Fam Pract, 14*, 54–63.

Lurie, N., & Dubowitz, T. (2007). Health Disparities and Access to Health. *JAMA, 297*(10), 1118–1121.

Malat, J. (2001). Social distance and patients' rating of healthcare providers. *J Health Soc Behav, 42*, 360–372.

McLeroy, K. R., Bibeau, D., Steckler, A., & Glanz, K. (1988). An ecological perspective on health promotion programs. *Health education quarterly, 15*(4), 351–377.

Mensah, G. & Brown, D. (2007). An Overview of Cardiovascular Disease Burden in the United States. *Health Affairs, 26*(1), 38–48.

Mensah, G., Mokdad, A., Ford, E., Greenlund, K., & Croft, J. (2005). State of Disparities in Cardiovascular Health in the United States. *Circulation, 111*, 1233–1241.

Moy, E., Arispe, I., Holmes, J., & Andrews, R. (2005). Preparing the national healthcare disparities report: gaps in data for assessing racial, ethnic, and socioeconomic disparities in health care. *Med Care, 43*(3 Suppl), I9–16.

Nelson, A. (2002). Unequal Treatment: Confronting racial and ethnic disparities in health care. *Journal of the National Medical Association, 94*(8), 666–668.

Saha, S., Komaromy, M., Koepsell, T., & Bindman, A. (1999). Patient-physician racial concordance and the perceived quality and use of health care. *Arch Intern Med, 159*, 997–1004.

Sallis, J., Owen, N., & Fisher, E. (2008). *Chapter 20: Ecological Models of Health Behavior.* San Francisco: Jossey-Bass.

Schulman, K., Berlin, J., Harless W., et al. (1999). The effect of race and sex on physicians' recommendations for cardiac catheterization. *N Engl J Med, 340*, 618–626.

Schultz, A., Kannan, S., Dvonch, T., Israel, B., Allen, A., James, S., et al. (2005). Social and Physical Environments and Disparities in Risk for Cardiovascular Disease: The Health Environments Partnership Conceptual Model. *Environmental Health Perspectives, 113*(12), 1817–1825.

Shaya, F. T., Gu, A., & Saunders, E. (2006). Addressing cardiovascular disparities through community interventions. *Ethnicity & disease, 16*(1), 138–144.

Shi, L., Green, L., & Kazakova, S. (2004). Primary care experience and racial disparities in self-reported health status. *J Am Board Fam Pract, 17*(6), 443–452.

Starfield, B., Shi, L., & Macinko, J. (2005). Contribution of primary care to health systems and health. *The Milbank Quarterly.* 83 (2), 457–502.

Stokols, D. (1996a). Translating social ecological theory into guidelines for community health promotion. *American Journal of Health promotion: AJHP, 10*(4), 282–298.

Stokols, D. (1996b). Translating social ecological theory into guidelines for community health promotion. *AJHP, 10*(4), 282–298.

U.S. Department of Health and Human Services. (2011). Healthy People 2020. *http://www.healthypeople.gov/2020/default.aspx.*

van Ryn, M. & Burke, J. (2000). The effect of patient race and socio-economic status on physicians' perceptions of patients. *Soc Sci Med, 50*, 813–828.

Weinick, R., Byron, S., Han, E., French, J., & Scholle, S. (2010). Reducing disparities and improving quality: understanding the needs of small primary care practices. *Ethn Dis, 20*(1), 58–63.

Wright, R. (1993). Community-oriented primary care: The cornerstone of health care reform. *JAMA, 269*(19), 2544–2547.

Wyatt, S., Williams, D., Rosie, C., Henderson, F., Walker, E., & Winters, K. (2003). Racism and cardiovascular disease in African Americans. *Am J Med Sci, 325*(6), 315–331.

Yonas, M., Lange, N., & Celedón, J. (2012). Psychosocial stress and asthma morbidity. *Curr Opin Allergy Clin Immunol, 12*(2), 202–210.

CHANGING THE COURSE OF MEDICINE

Learning to Put Prevention First

By J. Leocadia Conlon, PA-C, MPH

The current medical model in the United States is designed to address acute medical issues. In the words of John R. Paul, professor of preventative medicine at the Yale School of Medicine, in 1942: "Disease is the motivating force which stirs the clinician into action, and we can never be as excited about health as we can about disease." But with the rising cost of health care, limited resources, and increasing health care disparities, the current model needs to be adjusted, and infrastructure needs to be implemented to support the clinician's necessary role in disease prevention.

Prevention has three components: screening, interventions, and health promotion. Screening includes tests such as a colonoscopy for screening of colorectal cancer and mammography for breast cancer screening, as well as blood work for diabetes and high cholesterol screening. Interventions include limiting exposure to environmental hazards such as providing clean water, particularly where an individual has little control, and delivering clinical interventions such as immunizations. Health promotion focuses on behaviors where the individual has more control, such as smoking and sedentary lifestyles. Clinicians play a vital role in all three components to improve patient wellness and prevent disease. This is best stated from the President's Commission on Health Needs of the Nation in 1952, which noted that an individual can only be fully responsible for their health with the proper education, support, and professional services (Breslow, 1999). This is an important thought to consider in discussing health prevention in the context of social inequalities and social justice, and to disabuse the notion that individuals alone are responsible for their health behaviors.

Current trends in health and well-being in the United States demand that we focus more attention on preventing chronic disease. The US Department of Health and Human Services estimates that 40 percent of deaths in the United States are caused by modifiable behavior patterns, with tobacco use leading the way of preventable causes of death. According to the Centers for Disease Control and Prevention (CDC), preventable conditions of obesity and cardiovascular disease account for more than 75 percent of the national expenditure on health care. Obesity in the United States continues to increase, as every state reported an obesity prevalence of at least 20 percent, according to the CDC's obesity trends data for 2010. Among children, rising prevalence of obesity will result in the current generation of children leading sicker and shorter lives than their parents.

It is has been well established that many of these poor health trends disproportionately affect different groups within the population. In 2011, the CDC released its first periodic Health Disparities and Inequalities Report (CHDIR). The report shows that people of lower socioeconomic status and with lower levels of education have increased risk for mortality, morbidity, younger age of death, and unhealthy behaviors. Diabetes, a leading cause of mortality in the United States, shows racial differences with the age-adjusted incidence of diabetes per 1,000 in the population aged 18–79 years: 8.5 among whites, 11.7 among blacks, and 13.1 among Hispanics. In terms of modifiable risk factors for chronic disease, such as obesity and smoking, the report reflects the following: The prevalence of obesity is higher among blacks and Mexican-Americans than among whites, and these differences persist even after controlling for differences in family incomes as well as diet and exercise (CDC, 2011).

Prevention practices to reduce these health trends remain narrow from a national perspective. For example, although smoking is the leading cause of preventable death in the United States, the overall percentage of smokers who receive smoking cessation interventions and successfully quit is extremely low. A 2010 CDC National Health Interview Survey (NHIS) found that of 68.8 percent of current smokers who stated they wanted to completely stop smoking, only 48.3 percent reported that a health care professional in the past year had given them advice regarding smoking cessation. Also, 31.7 percent used counseling and/or FDA-approved medication to quit, but only 6.2 percent were successful. In relation to disparities, a separate evaluation of a community-based tobacco dependence treatment program showed that patients of lower socioeconomic status were less likely to quit smoking and received fewer resources and support than people of higher socioeconomic status (Sheffer, 2012). The current trends show that a concerted effort is needed to promote and support prevention practices as well as address barriers to prevention that contribute to disparities and inequality in health.

OVERCOMING BARRIERS TO PREVENTION

There are many barriers to putting prevention into practice. These include a lack of reimbursement for prevention services, limited access to care, unclear clinical roles in prevention, lack of provider knowledge about prevention interventions, insufficient time per clinic visit, lack of infrastructure for delivering prevention, and lack of provider understanding of and patient control over social and environmental factors. These commonly affect minority and lower-income populations to a much greater extent, but a few programs on the government level have been implemented to address and overcome these barriers for all Americans.

Costs and Access to Care

The Patient Protection and Affordable Care Act of 2010 (PPACA) has reformed and implemented many healthcare policies that aim to promote health prevention and wellness. It has made health prevention and promotion the key focus of a national strategy to reduce incidence of preventable disease, disability, and death in the United States. Four policies that have already gone into place are: (1) Reduction of insurance abuses by implementing a "rate review authority" to control rising insurance premium costs and prohibiting pre-existing condition clauses for children—soon to be expanded to adults; (2) Decrease in patient costs by mandating that prevention services—as recommended by the US Preventive Services Task Force—are covered without cost-sharing for the patient; (3) Strengthening of Medicare by reforming prescription coverage and ensuring affordable prescriptions for Medicare beneficiaries, and; (4) Increase in access of affordable health care by extending age of child-benefit coverage under the parent's insurance plan, which has helped narrow the gap of the largest number of uninsured Americans who are between the ages of nineteen and twenty-nine years (HHS, 2012).

The provision that would make the largest impact on access to care and controlling costs—the mandate that all Americans must have health insurance—has yet to come into effect. Once implemented in 2014, the individual mandate intends to control costs for the public in two significant ways. As people with expensive medical conditions enroll for insurance (particularly those with pre-existing conditions who are finally allowed coverage), insurance premiums are projected to soar while insurance companies search for ways to cover their consumers. With the enrollment of all individuals, including healthy patients, insurance rates can remain low and affordable to everyone, as the balance of cost is equaled out. Additionally, those without insurance often visit emergency rooms where the cost is incurred on insured patients and taxpayers. By instituting the individual mandate, all citizens will have affordable health insurance (http://www.kramerandkramer.com/files/2012/07/k2.pdf).

Despite the debates, health reform has already been put into action with a major focus on prevention at the national, state, and local levels throughout the country. Federal agencies, such as the Centers for Medicare and Medicaid Services (CMS), are engaging providers in prevention through quality initiatives. Launched in 2001, the quality initiatives include a value-driven health care model for provider reimbursement. This incentive will support providers who place an emphasis on preventive care and the coordination of care to improve health outcomes (CMS, 2012). CMS activities will inevitably influence other private-payer insurances. This practice has already begun with some payers such as Hawaii Medical Service Association (HMSA), the Blue Cross Blue Shield provider of Hawaii that launched a Pay For Quality Program in 2011. A major focus of the Pay for Quality Program is prevention and screening (HMSA, 2010). These are all examples of policies implemented to motivate and encourage clinicians to utilize and adhere to prevention guidelines and overcome barriers related to cost and access to care.

Clinicians Roles in Prevention and Promotion

The aforementioned Pay for Quality Programs may contribute to a misunderstanding of the roles that different clinicians have in prevention, which is often considered the province of the primary care provider. The most effective way to reduce the chronic medical problems plaguing the nation is for all providers to take ownership in the delivery of preventative care, recognize different opportunities for prevention, and appreciate that the message needs to be a constant one. Considering that there are different levels of prevention and that there is a place for prevention at every stage in a patient's life span, preventative care should be on the mind of every provider in every clinic, including the specialty setting.

All levels of prevention have a value in health outcomes. Primary prevention focuses on improving and maintaining health and protection from disease. This includes immunization, taking aspirin to reduce risk for heart disease, healthy diet and exercise, and tobacco cessation. Secondary prevention occurs when disease is identified in the early asymptomatic stage in efforts to reverse or suspend the advancement of disease. Tertiary prevention concentrates on reducing the risk of serious and/or long-term complications in patients with known disease. This would also apply to a patient who may initially present with a serious complication of a disease; prevention then would seek to limit the chances of an exacerbation once the acute complication is controlled.

Different tools and approaches are needed when addressing different levels of disease prevention. Clinicians need to incorporate prevention into their practice and recognize opportunities that can easily be missed. For example, when a woman presents for a well woman exam, a pap smear may be performed to screen for cervical cancer. The screening alone, however, is not adequate for cervical cancer prevention. A discussion about reducing risk factors for HPV and smoking cessation should also be a part of preventive strategy for cervical cancer. Likewise, if a patient follows up with their specialist for chronic disease management and that clinician does not also address general health maintenance and recommended screening and interventions, it is a lost opportunity to prevent another medical condition.

Every practice setting should be able to at least incorporate a simple check of basic screening tests and prevention questions. Even if it turns out that a certain screening test is not indicated, it should still be considered so that decisions can appropriately be made. In some cases, the treatments prescribed by a specialist require more vigilance for prevention. For example, some chemotherapies for cancer patients increase their risk for heart disease. The specialist prescribing the chemotherapy should discuss recommendations for the prevention of heart disease. In terms of health promotion, basic questions related to diet and physical activity have a role to play in every specialty setting. Repeated messaging sends an important signal to patients about the importance of taking action to maintain good health and well-being.

OVERCOMING SOCIAL DETERMINING BARRIERS TO PREVENTION

In health care we emphasize patient education and invest in many tools to help patients understand their health and healthy behaviors. Research has given attention to health literacy when addressing health behaviors. Health literacy is the degree to which a person can obtain, process, and understand health information. It is well documented that people with low health literacy have poor health outcomes, but this is only part of the story. Increasing a patient's level of health literacy does not necessarily influence their behavior or address the social factors that influence their behavior. A computer kiosk using audio and video to improve health literacy in diabetes by explaining key concepts in diabetes management and prevention of complications showed little change in health outcomes, despite increased patient understanding measured by the perceived susceptibility to complications of diabetes (Gerber, 2005). Therefore, in the age of new online applications and handheld technologies, providers need to be aware of not just providing patients with proper education, but also proper support.

Furthermore, provider awareness regarding societal inequalities surrounding those with lower health literacy is essential. For example, a study of elderly patients who were deemed to have low health literacy were more likely than their more literate counterpart (40 percent vs. 12 percent) to have received help with understanding drug labels or with filling out medical forms. They were, however, less likely to receive "tangible support" with such assistance as transportation to a medical office for an appointment or someone to help them with meals

(Shoou-Yih D. Lee, 2006). A paradigm shift is needed from solely focusing on what the patient understands about health, to what the provider understands about the patient.

Clinicians first need to recognize what they do not understand about their patients. Current population trends show the current health care workforce does not match the increasing racial and ethnic representation of the US population. In this setting, cultural competency of the provider is a significant concern. A clinician needs to understand the social and cultural environment in which a patient lives and be sensitive to their culture and beliefs. As they strive to become culturally aware, clinicians should become familiar with the community in which their patient population lives. Even a provider with the best intentions can miss the mark on effectively communicating with their patient and gaining their trust. For example, when counseling on proper nutrition and healthy eating habits, a provider must be sensitive to not offend one's culture by saying "those foods are all bad." This simple response may give the patient the perception their culture is bad, the food their mother and grandmother cooked was bad, and the way he or she was raised was wrong. If the patient interprets this as rejection, the provider will have a difficult time changing health behaviors. Clinicians need to be aware of the population they serve to target reasonable preventative health options within that community. They need to know the cultural feelings, beliefs, and everyday challenges of the communities in which they practice.

Culture is just one aspect of social determinants that influence patient health and health behaviors. Social determinants relate to the circumstances in which people are born, grow, live, work, and age. These circumstances are shaped by socioeconomic status, education level, and cultural practices, beliefs, and values. Social determinants are not equal to behavior, but rather can be the cause of certain behaviors. The degree to which social determinants affect health is evident in the aforementioned data that show an association between education, social economic status, and mortality rates.

Social determinants of health are a major cause of health inequities. While only individuals can take action and responsibility for behaviors such as diet, alcohol intake, exercise, and smoking, they can only do so in the context of the social factors that affect their everyday life (e.g., daily living conditions, financial resources, and access to social support). Therefore, significant improvements in health and prevention can be made by addressing social determinants and unmet social needs.

In 2011, the Robert Wood Johnson Foundation released a summary of findings from a survey of one thousand physicians where 4 in 5 physicians believed that unmet social needs are directly leading to a worsening of health nationally. Only 1 in 5 felt confident that they had the ability to address a patient's unmet social needs, and 3 in 4 identified a need for the healthcare system to cover costs associated with connecting patients to services that would meet their social needs (RWJ, 2011).

Most clinic settings lack the infrastructure and resources to address social factors when advising patients on prevention and healthy lifestyle changes. Many of the challenges faced by patients in their daily lives can be quite extreme. A recent article in *The New Yorker* magazine titled "The Hot Spotters" underscored many of these situations and the lack of resources in the healthcare system to help patients overcome social barriers. The article highlighted a community physician who mapped out the areas of greatest health disparities in one city based on ER admission data. He then focused his practice on these areas and became involved in his patients' daily lives, with frequent home visits and phone calls just to lend them social support (Gawande, 2011). One provider, however, cannot sustain this model for a larger number of patients. Interdisciplinary patient care teams and an infrastructure to support them will be an important approach in addressing social determinants of health and aiding the change of health behaviors.

Clinicians should also think outside the box when practicing prevention and considering interdisciplinary teams. Using patients as intermediaries is one way to deliver health promotion and address social needs. There are several models of patient support groups, or patient-to-patient support systems, that can be duplicated. This can be as simple as keeping a list of patients who agree to have another patient contact them for support or convening patient support groups in your practice setting. Providers can also gather information to refer patients to community resources such as community recreational centers. The YMCA is one example of a community center implementing health programs in a nationwide effort to improve health. Reliance on individual-focused interventions alone is ineffective.

Health prevention is most effective if delivered before a patient becomes ill or shows signs of chronic disease (i.e., primary prevention or primary care). To do this, we must meet people where they live, work, and play. Providers can partner with workplace wellness and community wellness initiatives to promote prevention before a patient presents with disease and/or disease complications. This can function while having limited infringements on a provider's time as clinicians can simply serve as a consultant and/or an outlying supporter. In fact, populations are best served by others who are more closely related to their community. For example, a Harvard Medical School affiliate founded "The Family Van." Started in 1992, The Family Van is a mobile resource with health screening and health promotion services delivered by community health educators, dieticians, and counselors who travel into neighborhoods where they have personal connections and are trusted members of the community. They do not provider diagnostic or treatment service. Several tools such as automated blood pressure cuffs and kits for rapid testing of cholesterol and blood sugar make it possible to provide screening services and offer advice on healthy lifestyles from someone who is a member of their community and viewed as a friend. This program empowers clients by allowing them to access prevention services and make decisions regarding their own health and well-being within their own community. An evaluation of the program showed an increase in health-seeking behavior among participants. It is also important to note that most clients who participated in the services were insured, indicating that a lack of health insurance is not the only factor preventing access to health care (Hill, 2012). When considering health disparities in prevention medicine, partnering with an innovative organization such as The

Family Van will allow for the extension of prevention and health promotion services in many communities.

Several resources exist within the public health system to provide prevention services and carry out health promotion activities that address many social determinants of health. Traditionally, however, the public health and primary care clinical settings have not collaborated. Public health focuses on population health while primary care focuses on individual health. Yet, by recognizing that both groups share a common goal of promoting the health and well-being of all people makes this an opportunity for integration. Identifying this need, the CDC and the Health Resources and Services Administration (HRSA) requested the Institute of Medicine (IOM) to explore integration between the two fields with the goal to improve population health. An expert committee convened and published a report in March 2012 with recommendations for fostering an environment in which to merge primary care and public health. This report is a significant step and has identified a need for mutual awareness, cooperation, collaboration, and partnership in order to promote better health and well-being, particularly in underserved communities, and reduce the burden of chronic disease (IOM, 2012). The current model of our healthcare system is not sustainable, and therefore, new models of resource sharing and integration are imperative. Partnering with community and/or public health resources is a vital component of prevention.

THE DIRECTION OF PA EDUCATION AND MEDICAL TRAINING

The concepts of social determinant of health, population health, and health promotion have traditionally been limited to public health education programs. But to prepare the new generation of health care professionals, some of these concepts need to be added to traditional nonpublic health curriculums.

In 1993 the Pew Health Professions Commission challenged medical professional schools to educate students in new competencies in response to evolving health care needs in the United States. In 1998 it specified competencies to include the incorporation of the multiple determinants of health in clinical care. In response, some schools adopted the problem-based learning (PBL) curricula versus the traditional lecture-based learning (LBL) curricula. The PBL allows for the integration of knowledge to include humanities, sociology, and social psychology (James A. Van Rhee, et al., 2003).

As most medical schools are headed in this direction, physician assistant and nurse practitioner schools need to consider similar integration to keep up with twenty-first century medical needs. Recognizing that all health professional programs have extensive rigorous curricula, the goal would not be to add an entire public health curriculum to the degree program. Rather, the goal would be to incorporate many of the concepts needed to provide future health professionals with the tools and knowledge necessary to carry out prevention and health promotion.

Further, there is a need to train health professionals to identify themselves as community leaders and advocates. One of the main factors driving prevention practices and health behaviors among patients are those outside the confines of the clinic setting. Providers need to be able to reach out within their community to understand social and cultural barriers and to find resources to improve the health of their community. Mentors will have to show students examples of how they can connect with their community, understanding that there is as high a regard for promoting health and well-being as there is for treating illness. This can be done by connecting students with organizations and practices that are sharing resources and participating in models of health promotion similar to some of the examples cited throughout this chapter.

Additionally, students should be given instruction in research. This includes performing a needs assessment of the health problems in their community to determine services and resources needed to promote health. It includes instruction on how to review the literature and evidence behind screening and prevention guidelines in order to help patients make the best decisions regarding their health and well-being.

Finally, health professional programs should be taking great efforts to increase diversity within the population of their profession. Bureau of the Census data from 2010 show that the Hispanic population accounts for more than 16 percent of the US population, and African Americans account for approximately 12 percent of the population (census, 2010). Yet, data from the American Academy of Physician Assistants (AAPA) census show that Hispanics only make up 5.2 percent of the PA workforce and African Americans only 6 percent (AAPA, 2010). Similar trends are reported in the physician population with Hispanics accounting for less than 6 percent of all physicians, and the African American population just over 6 percent (AAMC, 2010).

CONCLUSION

Prevention is complex, and screening and prevention guidelines are not always clear. There is not a "one size fits all" model when practicing patient-focused care. Many providers believe they lack the expertise of certain prevention interventions and/or lack the time and infrastructure needed for support. The reality, however, is that current health trends in the nation are poor. It is time for all clinicians to become motivated about and engage in the complexities of prevention in the same way that we engage in the complexities of medical treatment.

Many policies have been implemented to overcome several barriers to prevention. Overcoming the greatest barriers related to social determinants of health begins simply with clinicians knowing the patients and the communities in which they serve. Providers have a responsibility to understand their patients in the context of their social and cultural environments. A speaker presented a talk comparing the late Steve Jobs and the success of Apple to patient-centered health care. She noted that the success of Jobs could be attributed to the fact that he never lost sight of his end user. He studied his audience and he knew his audience. He did not force his users to adapt to the system, but instead created something that worked best for them. This practical model is where prevention begins; know your community, know your patient.

REFERENCES

AAMC. (2010). Association of American Medical Colleges Center for Workforce Studies. https://www.aamc.org/download/150584/data/physician_shortages_factsheet.pdf.

AAPA. (2010). *Physician Assistant Census*. Alexandria: American Academy of Physician Assistants.

Breslow, L. (1999). "From Disease Prevention to Health Promotion." *JAMA, 281* (11), 1030–1033.

CDC. (2011). *CDC Health Disparities and Inequality Report* (CHDIR). MMWR Supplement, 60, 1–116.

Census. (2010). *2010 US Census*. US Bureau of the Census. Washington, DC: US Census Bureau.

CMS. (2012). *Roadmap for Implementing Value Driven Healthcare in the Traditional Medicare-Fee-for-Service Program*. Centers for Medicare and Medicaid Services. Baltimore: US Department of Health and Human Services.

Gawande, A. (2011, January). "The Hot Spotters." *The New Yorker*.

Gerber, B. L. (2005). "Implementation and evaluation of a low-literacy diabetes education computer multimedia application." *Diabetes Care, 28* (7), 1574–1580.

HHS. (2012). *Affordable Care Act, title IV*. US Department of Health and Human Services. Washington, DC: healthcare.gov.

Hill, Z. B.-W. (2012). "Knowledgable Neighbors: A Mobile Clinic for Disease Prevention and Screening in Underserved Communities." *American Journal of Public Health*, 102, 406–410.

HMSA. (2010). Hawaii Medical Service Association (HMSA), Quality Improvement Program Evaluation. Honolulu: HMSA.

IOM. (2012). *Primary Care and Public Health. Exploring Inegration to Improve Population Health*. Washington, DC: National Academies of Science.

James A. Van Rhee, M. P.-C., C. Sonia Wardley, M., Cynthia A. Hutchinson, P.-C., E. Brooks Applegate, P., Eric H. Vangsnes, M. P.-C., Jeanette M. Meyer, M. et al. (2003). "Problem-based Learning in Physician Assistant Education: Establishing a basis for a comparative study." *Journal of Physician Assistant Education*, 14 (4), 242–248.

RWJ. (2011). *Health Care's Blind Side. The Overlooked Connection between Social Needs and Good Health*. Robert Wood Johnson Foundation. Princeton: Fenton.

Sheffer C. E., S. M. (2012). "Socioeconomic Disparities in Community-Based Treatment of Tobacco Dependence." *American Journal of Public Health*, 102 (3), e8–e16.

Shoou-Yih D. Lee, P. J. (2006). "Health Literacy, Social Support, and Health: Survey of Medicare Enrollees." *Journal of Applied Gerontology*, 25 (4), 324–37.

PROVIDER PERCEPTIONS AND THE REALITIES OF SOCIAL FACTORS THAT DETERMINE HUMAN HEALTH

By Daniel S. Goldberg, JD, PhD

t is an open secret that acute care services have a relatively minor impact on health and its distribution. Public health professionals are generally quite familiar with the overwhelming body of epidemiologic evidence suggesting that social and economic conditions, rather than access to acute care services, are the prime determinants of health and its distribution in human societies in *both* the Global North and the Global South (Venkatapuram, Marmot, and Bell 2010; Commission on Social Determinants of Health, 2008). Health care providers, on the other hand, are much less likely to be aware of the weight of this evidence, even if the idea of the social determinants of health is not wholly foreign. This is not simply anecdotal. There is excellent empirical evidence suggesting that the very idea of health in the United States is conceptualized largely in terms of access to health care services (Goldberg, 2012; Robert and Booske, 2011). In other words, health and its absence are generally thought of in the United States as a function of access to health care. Those who enjoy such access are generally likely to be healthy, those who lack it are generally likely to be unhealthy, and the contrapositive of each. Therefore, the challenge of understanding what health care providers can do about the social determinants of health inevitably begins with educating health care providers on the quality and the weight of the evidence showing that acute care services are minor determinants of population health and health inequities.

HISTORY

The lesson, such as it is, typically begins with history. A key figure in anchoring the under-standing of social determinants of health is physician and anthropologist Rudolf Virchow. It is instructive to consider that Virchow is both the father of cellular pathology and the father of social medicine. Interestingly, every accredited physician assistant school in the United States requires courses in pathology; yet, none of them require courses in social medicine, and it is presumed that only a small number even offer instruction in social medicine. (Medical schools have, in fact, embraced the idea that social factors are critical in patient care and outcome, and they now require incoming students to have coursework that demonstrates an understanding and proficiency of the social world.) Whatever the true figure in the latter category, there is no doubt that the proportion in the former category is dramatically larger.

Virchow wrote one of the modern classics in both public health and social medicine in his 1848 report, *On a Typhus Epidemic in Upper Silesia*. He was interested not simply in document-ing the epidemic itself, but also in scrutinizing the distribution of the disease—both in who was more likely to contract typhus and also who experienced more severe outcomes from typhus within the affected general population. Virchow noticed that the same subgroup of miners satisfied both criteria, realizing that the principal reasons for this disparity were the insalubrious conditions in which the miners lived and, especially, those in which they worked. Thus, he noted, the true remedy for the inequitable distribution and severity of the typhus epidemic was not merely the treatment of the sick, but rather the amelioration of the social and economic conditions in which the miners lived and worked. "There cannot be any doubt that such a typhoid epidemic was only possible under these conditions and that ultimately they were the result of the poverty and underdevelopment of Upper Silesia. I am convinced that if you changed these conditions, the epidemic would not recur," Virchow stated (Taylor and Rieger, 1985, p. 551). These kinds of considerations led Virchow to propose a concept of medical practice directed not simply at the pathogens that caused active typhus, but at the macrosocial structures of class, income, education, and occupation among others—the accumulated social disadvantages—that rendered the miners so vulnerable to disease and to premature death. This was his idea of social medicine.

The lessons from history continue with discussion of the McKeown thesis. McKeown, trained as both a physician and a demographer, meticulously documented that virtually all of the major diseases in nineteenth-century Great Britain were in substantial decline well before the first effective chemotherapeutics were manufactured (McKeown, 1979; McKeown, Record, and Turner, 1975; McKeown and Record, 1962; McKeown and Brown, 1955). The con-clusion, then, was that modern allopathic medicine had very little to do with the dramatic increases in life expectancy in Great Britain in the nineteenth and early twentieth centuries (Szreter, 2004). Medical historian Gerald Grob noted exactly the same phenomenon during the same period in the United States, observing that the evidence suggesting that American allopathic medicine played a significant role in decreasing morbidities and mortality during these one hundred forty years was "extraordinarily weak" (Grob, 2002, p. 181).

If the historical evidence is suggestive, the contemporary evidence is overwhelming to the point of being unassailable. One of the most compelling examples stems from the Whitehall studies, which are without a doubt some of the most important epidemiologic studies of the twentieth century. The studies showed a pronounced gradient in health corresponding in lockstep fashion with employment grade among British civil servants over long periods of time. Because all of the subjects enjoyed access to health care services under the British National Health Service, it follows that such access simply could not be a primary cause of the stark health inequalities the investigators documented. Moreover, the research team noted that in the stratus with the highest mortality rates (and the lowest employment grade), even combining the effects of risk factors such as smoking and high cholesterol did not explain more than one-third of the mortality burden for members (Adelman, 2008).

Many health care providers and Americans, in general, are stunned at the possibility that behavioral risk factors may not account for large proportions of the disease footprint in the United States today. In other words, most Americans believe that poor health is typically and largely caused by one's poor health habits. Recent reanalyses of the Whitehall data suggest the original analyses were limited methodologically in the 1970s and 1980s and that newer, more sophisticated measures show that those risky behaviors, in fact, accounted for more than the originally calculated two-thirds of the mortality burden. As much as 75 percent of the total mortality burden in the highest mortality stratus in the Whitehall studies actually can be attributed to risky health behaviors (Stringhini et al., 2010).

One important point, however, is the way in which social and economic conditions structure a gradient in risky health behaviors. Even the evidence suggests that behaviors are highly significant determinants of health and its distribution in human populations by demonstrating a link between income inequality and the distribution of such behaviors shown to impact unequal health outcomes. Although the distribution of such behaviors accounts for much of the distribution of health, it is important to note that even after controlling for such behaviors and income levels, those of marginalized groups continue to have poorer health outcomes. This is directly linked to the stress response that marginalized groups experience at significantly higher rates secondary to discrimination, whether real or perceived, compared with non-marginalized groups.

SOCIAL CONDITIONS AS THE FUNDAMENTAL CAUSE OF DISEASE

Why is it that behaviors themselves track along a social gradient? After all, there is compelling evidence that risky health behaviors such as smoking (Woolf et al., 2011; Jarvis and Wardle, 2006), promiscuity (Akers, Muhammad, and Corbie-Smith, 2010), and poor nutrition (Woolf et al. 2011; Ogden 2009) are disproportionately concentrated among the least well-off. One possible explanation is that the least well-off are simply ignorant of the health risks that attend such behaviors. If so, the obvious remedy is to educate members of these communities, to arm them with superior knowledge needed to avoid risky health behaviors in the first place.

And yet, if the root cause of the inequitable distribution of risky behaviors is ignorance, one would expect that the relatively large amount of resources and attention devoted to health education and health promotion would have some level of impact on the distribution of these negative health-related behaviors, and hence on health outcomes themselves. Abundant evidence demonstrates that this is not so (Jarvis and Wardle, 2006; Raphael et al., 2003; Ebrahim and Davey Smith, 2001). As the editor in chief of the *American Journal of Health Promotion* noted recently:

> Three decades ago, we thought that education was enough. We thought all we had to do was help people understand the health risks of tobacco, junk food, alcohol and drugs, and the health benefits of exercise, nutritious foods, stress management, and proactive medical self-care. We thought people would use this knowledge to transform their lives. Three decades of research and practical experience have shown us that education is not enough, in fact, it may not be very important at all (O'Donnell, 2011).

Two possible inferences could be drawn from the fact that intensive efforts at health education and promotion have been largely ineffective. First, the different types of health education initiatives deployed have been insufficient; second, health education of any kind is unlikely to have a large effect in decreasing risky health behaviors and compressing the inequalities in those behaviors. These, of course, are not incompatible. The second possibility, however, calls into question the idea that educating individuals, families, and/or communities on health risks and the means to avoid them is likely to be effective in improving population health and compressing gross health inequities. (Even if health education is unlikely to produce positive effects on health and its distribution, it might still behoove providers to discern and execute more as opposed to less effective models and techniques of health education.)

One of the best evidence-based frameworks for understanding reality is Link and Phelan's fundamental cause theory (Phelan, Link, and Tehranifar, 2010; Link and Phelan, 1995). Link and Phelan argue that social conditions are fundamental causes of disease. A fundamental cause of disease involves access to resources that can be used to avoid risks or to minimize the consequences of disease once it occurs (Link and Phelan, 1995). Furthermore, in the causal pathways of disease, fundamental causes are logically prior to risk factors. Risk factors are best understood as intervening mechanisms in those pathways. The evidence for this is that fundamental causes endure while risk factors can change. Link and Phelan point out that even if public health efforts did eliminate intervening risk factors, fundamental causes will create new ones (Link and Phelan, 1995). For example, in Europe during the middle to late nineteenth century, socioeconomic status was a major determinant of who had access to sanitation and clean water, which determined overall health outcomes for differing populations. As the scope of sewerage expanded, thus improving sanitary conditions in poorer areas, this mechanism diminished as both an overall cause of poor health and of health inequalities. The relationship between socioeconomic status (SES) and disease, however, remains extremely robust in the Global North (i.e., developed world) at present, and other risk factors (smoking, poor nutrition, etc.) have become primary intervening mechanisms through which SES determines health and its distribution (Link and Phelan, 1995).

The takeaway here is the idea that risk factors such as health behaviors are not fundamental causes of disease, but are rather themselves shaped by more distal, upstream factors such as SES, education, and occupation. Social epidemiologist Hilary Graham puts the point succinctly, "[U]nequal social positions carry with them unequal probabilities of being exposed to health hazards along the environment/risk factors/illness pathway" (Graham, 2004, p. 113). There are powerful and obvious reasons why the least well-off might be more vulnerable to the experiences of deprivation than those higher up the social hierarchy (Woolf and Braveman, 2011; Woolf et. al, 2011). Misery and despair create stressful conditions, which have an impact on the physiology of the human condition, influencing pernicious behaviors such as smoking and promiscuity (Voigt, 2010; Akers, Muhammad, and Corbie-Smith, 2010). Without denying the existence of human agency, even in the face of adverse social and economic conditions, there is abundant support that undermines the presumption that poorer communities in the United States are disproportionately more likely to engage in high-risk health behaviors because they are unaware of the nature of the risks.

THE "JUST WORLD" THEORY

Moreover, lurking beneath the surface of this presumption is the soft bigotry of the "just world" theory, a theory that is both historically and presently dominant in US society (Puhl and Heuer, 2010; Scott, 2008). Put simply, the "just world" theory posits that generally people deserve what they get and get what they deserve (Goldberg, 2011). This theory has a particularly pointed result when applied to health, for it implies that sick people are sick because of acts they committed or omitted. Put differently, sick people are responsible for their illness.

There remains two problems with the "just world" theory. First, the extent to which it can explain much about population health is dubious given the evidence surveyed above regarding the extent to which upstream macrosocial conditions structure the range of choices available to individuals and communities. One example that often helps illuminate this problem is recited in the Final Report of the World Health Organization's Commission on Social Determinants of Health: a baby born tomorrow in Sierra Leone has an average life expectancy of forty-five years, while a baby born tomorrow in Sweden has an average life expectancy of eighty-one. It is inconceivable that there is anything an unborn child could be responsible for that would justify a difference of nearly forty years of life. And it is just as inconceivable that the entire populations of unborn children's parents in Sierra Leone and Sweden, respectively, could have committed or omitted acts sufficient to justify the size of this gap.

Second, to the extent it has merit, the "just world" theory unfortunately fails to take into account the impact of stigma as an urgent public health problem. Stigma is pernicious. It erodes social capital, alienates individuals and communities, and is independently correlated with adverse health outcomes (i.e., it is bad for one's health) (Link and Phelan, 2006; Burris, 2002). Additionally, because those populations more at risk for perilous behaviors are most likely to be stigmatized, it also means that the burden of such stigma generally tracks social inequities: the least well-off are most likely to be stigmatized, a dilemma that is ethically intolerable.

CASTING OFF PROVIDER PERCEPTIONS: WHAT CAN PROVIDERS DO?

The remaining task in this chapter is to assess the implications of all of these findings for the health care provider. Specifically, what can the practitioner do about the social determinants of health? Perhaps the best way to answer this question is through an example. It is common knowledge that type 2 diabetes (or diabetes mellitus type 2, "DM2") is a growing health problem both in the United States and across the globe. There are, of course, stark inequities in prevalence and outcomes for DM2 in the United States. For example, the community with the highest rates of DM2 prevalence in the world is the Tohono O'odham Indians of the southwestern United States, a community that also experiences a number of social disadvantages including high rates of poverty and unemployment as well as low educational attainment (Tohono O'odham Community Action, 2011). Not coincidentally, the Tohono O'odham have also experienced centuries of racism, discrimination, oppression, and colonialism. The connection between these two classes of phenomena has important implications for health care providers involved in caring for members of this population or of any other disadvantaged group.

Management of DM2 is extraordinarily complex. It involves a regimen of constant testing, frequent consultation with a number of health care providers and allied health professionals, close scrutiny of diet on a daily basis, a shifting matrix of drugs and medical interventions, and an enormous expenditure of time, energy, and resources. Unsurprisingly, health literacy is a major determinant of outcomes in DM2 (Schillinger et al, 2002). The key point, then, is that proper control of glucose level and long-term management of type 2 diabetes is highly dependent on resources of exactly the kind that Link and Phelan indicate are fundamental causes of disease. It is, therefore, equally unsurprising that some commentators have pointed out that poverty and material deprivation are properly considered the primary determinants of DM2 and its distribution in the United States, if not across the globe (Dinca-Panaitescu et al., 2012; Chaufan, Davis, and Constantino, 2011; Raphael et al., 2011).

How can the health care provider incorporate this understanding into the care of their patients with type 2 diabetes? Providers frequently report significant frustration with the care and management of patients with DM2 (Wens et al., 2005; Larme and Pugh, 1998). Providers lament at what they perceive as their patients' unwillingness to take the steps needed to maintain tight glucose control. Their frustration is in some sense understandable, but the shadow of the "just world" theory and the individualism of American political culture are also perceptible here. Especially in resource-poor settings, many patients with DM2 will have difficulty managing their illness and meeting all of the various demands that the illness places on themselves, their providers, and their caregivers. Even a basic understanding of the ways in which accumulated disadvantage and material deprivation conspire to diminish the resources needed to adequately manage DM2 suggests a very different outlook and mind-set regarding "non-adherent" patients with DM2 than the kinds of blame and stigma that are so readily facilitated by a slavish focus on individual responsibility.

The patient who seemingly refuses to exercise may in fact have little time and opportunity to do so if they must commute two hours to and from work every day, live in a dangerous neighborhood that affords little opportunity for safe outdoor recreation, and must manage the care of a number of dependents while dealing with the persistent stress and stigma of discrimination. These demographic characteristics describe a specific patient that obviously does not apply to everyone; but across the *population* of DM2 patients, patients experiencing the slings and arrows of these or other (compound) social disadvantages are disproportionately prevalent. The probability that any individual DM2 patient or group of DM2 patients is living in conditions that may dramatically affect their capacity to effectively control their DM2 will, of course, vary depending on the community and geography of the health care provider's catchment area. Providers should be aware of the enormous challenges many of their patients face—particularly within underserved communities of rural setting, urban setting, or predominately racial/ethnic minorities—in managing the complex and persistent demands of their diabetes.

It is these social disadvantages, these inequities, these devastating histories of structural racism and subjugation that constitute fundamental causes of disease. Although the social epidemiologic evidence is compelling on the social determinants of health, some health care providers remain skeptical to its overall impact; however, those providers who come to understand this notion often report feelings of great frustration and even despair. If, indeed, these macrosocial structural factors are the fundamental causes of disease, and dyadic treatment relationships obviously leave these factors untouched, then emphasis on the social determinants of health can seem to suggest that efforts to deliver high-quality health care services are relatively unimportant.

Yet, the fact that macrosocial variables are fundamental causes of disease does not imply that the provision of health care is of no value. The existence of a robust, trusting primary care relationship does produce better outcomes (Starfield, 2011; Kunitz, 2006), even if the overall effect size of health care services on health and its distribution remains small relative to other variables such as income, occupation, and education. Furthermore, it is essential that providers understand that the sole measure of value is most certainly not health outcomes. There is enormous moral significance to the healing relationship itself, to the fact of illness and the intense vulnerability it brings to the sick person, and to the literal profession of medicine and healing. Edmund Pellegrino instructs that the concept of "profession" is of great moral importance:

> The word profession comes from the Latin word, *profiteri*, which means to declare aloud. But how do we declare aloud? When you come to a physician, his question is, How can I help you? Implied in that question is his promise, the promise to help. Thus, in the presence of one vulnerable human being who is ill we have another human being who promises to help, to heal, to restore the balance insofar as scientific knowledge will allow (Pellegrino, 2006, p. 67).

Providers should not underestimate the meaning of the healing relationship and the immense importance it can and does have in the lived experiences of illness among people and communities. This type of importance is a category apart from the epidemiologically driven emphases on outcomes and their distribution. While both are of vital significance, the corrosive effects of stigma are self-evidently adverse to the creation and sustenance of trusting and continuous treatment relationships with primary care providers. Without an understanding of the ways in which social and economic conditions heavily structure the range of choices available to one's patients, the American beliefs in "just world" theory and individualism make it much more likely that people with preventable illness such as diabetes will be stigmatized by health care providers.

The point is not remotely that health care providers set out to demonize their patients; it is quite the contrary, in fact. But managing the care of patients with complex, demanding illnesses such as DM2 is difficult for providers under the best of circumstances, and the frequency with which especially disadvantaged patients may not adhere to treatment regimens understandably results in frustration on the part of providers. Given that the American predilections for the idea of individualism are cultural tropes, it is not difficult to understand how, even assuming the best of intentions on the part of providers, people with preventable disease may end up feeling blamed and shamed for their illness and the course it takes. No matter how uncomfortable it may be to acknowledge, the fact of the matter is that patients do, in fact, report significant experiences of stigma in encounters with health care providers (Broom and Whittaker, 2004; Hopper, 1981).

So, what does the example of DM2 reveal in answer to the question of "what can health care providers do about the social determinants of health?" First, an understanding of the ways in which social and economic conditions shape the lived experiences of illness can have a dramatic impact on the individual patient-provider relationship. Enhanced comprehension of precisely how the accumulated burdens of social disadvantages converge to restrict the choices and options available to marginalized people and groups can go a long way toward facilitating greater empathy and trust between provider and patient. This is not simply a moral good insofar as it strengthens primary care relationships; there is increasing evidence that trust is actually good for one's health, especially for people dealing with complex chronic illnesses who are simultaneously members of traditionally marginalized, disadvantaged, or oppressed groups.

Second, a greater understanding of the extent to which social and economic conditions are fundamental causes of disease could conceivably help with the amelioration of disease stigma. This is of particular importance because it is a tenable answer to the question health care providers often voice in context of the social determinants of health: "But what can *I* do?" An individual provider can make every effort to avoid stigmatizing people who seem to have difficulty adhering to a given treatment regimen. Although stigma is without question a social phenomenon, unlike other social determinants of health, it is one in which individuals arguably enjoy greater agency. Stigma occurs when in-groups mark out-groups as deviant on the basis of an identifiable demographic characteristic. This definition shows that stigma is inextricably linked to power gradients because without power and privilege, the in-group literally could not exist as an in-group and would lack the capacity to mark another group of people as an out-group. By virtue of their position, and also because of their education, income, and occupational status, health care providers and especially physicians are unquestionably privileged relative to most of their patients, and even more so with regard to patients who belong to disadvantaged and marginalized groups. Providers, therefore, have some measure of power and agency they can exercise in resisting the tendency to shame, blame, and stigmatize patients who show difficulty in managing their complex illnesses.

It is in some sense ironic that education on the distinctions between health and medicine leads along a circuitous route to the conclusion that enhanced understanding of the impact of social and economic conditions on health can have a profound influence on the nature of the provider-patient relationship itself. It is, of course, true that the individual health care provider cannot, by prescribing a treatment regimen, change entrenched power structures or ameliorate material deprivation and its inequitable distribution. But one should not overlook the soteriological significance of the health care provider, the social role of the providers as the collective savior of the sick and vulnerable person (Goldberg, 2012). In the United States, sick people traditionally invest a great deal of hope in their providers, and this investiture is nothing if not powerful. Greater understanding of the social determinants of health can enhance the provider-patient relationship, build and sustain trust, and provide a path to the diminution of disease stigma, all of which are significantly impactful factors in the improvement of health care and overall health of society.

REFERENCES

Adelman, L. (creater and executive producer). (2008). *Unnatural Causes: Is inequality making us sick?* Motion picture. US: California Newsreel.

Akers, A. Y., Muhammad, M. R., & Corbie-Smith, G. (2011). "'When you got nothing to do, you do somebody': A community's perceptions of neighborhood effects on adolescent sexual behaviors." *Social Science and Medicine,* 72(1), 91–99.

Broom D. & Whittaker, A. (2004). "Controlling diabetes, controlling diabetics: moral language in the management of diabetes type 2." *Social Science & Medicine,* 58(11): 2371–2382.

Burris, S. (2002). "Disease stigma in U.S. public health law." *Journal of Law, Medicine and Ethics,* 30(2), 179–190.

Chaufan C., Davis M., & Constantino S. (2011). "The twin epidemics of poverty and diabetes: understanding diabetes disparities in a low-income Latino and immigrant neighborhood." *Journal of Community Health,* 36(6): 1032–1043.

Dinca-Panaitescu, M. et al. (2012). "The dynamics of the relationship between diabetes incidence and low income: Longitudinal results from Canada's National Population Health Survey." *Maturitas,* 72(3): 229–235.

Ebrahim, S. & Smith, G. D. (2001). "Exporting failure: Coronary heart disease and stroke in developing countries." *International Journal of Epidemiology,* 30(2), 201–205.

Goldberg, D. S. (2012). "The difficulties of enhancing public understanding of the social determinants of health in the US: A commentary on Pesce et al." (2011). *Social Science and Medicine*, 74(8), 1139–1142.

Goldberg, D. S. (2011). "What kind of people: Obesity stigma and inequities." *American Journal of Medicine*, 124(8): 788.

Graham, H. (2004). "Social determinants and their unequal distribution: clarifying policy understandings." *The Milbank Quarterly*, 82(1), 101–24.

Grob, G. N. (2002). *The deadly truth: a history of disease in America*. Cambridge, MA: Harvard University Press.

Hopper, S. (1981). "Diabetes as a stigmatized condition: the case of low-income clinic patients in the United States." *Social Science & Medicine*, 15B(1): 11–19.

Jarvis, J. M. & Wardle, J. (2006). "Social patterning of individual case behaviours: The case of cigarette smoking." In M. Marmot and R. G. Wilkinson, eds. *Social Determinants of Health* (2d ed.) (pp. 224–237). New York, NY: Oxford University Press.

Kunitz, S. (2006). *The health of populations: General theories and particular realities*. New York, NY: Oxford University Press.

Larme, A. C. & Pugh, J. A. (1998). "Attitudes of primary care providers toward diabetes: barriers to guideline implementation." *Diabetes Care*, 21(9): 1391–1396.

Link, B. G. & Phelan, J. C. (2006). "Stigma and its public health implications." *Lancet*, 367, 528–529.

Link, B. G. & Phelan, J. C. (1995). "Social conditions as fundamental causes of disease." *Journal of Health and Social Behavior, Spec. Issue*, 80–94.

McKeown, T. (1979). *The role of medicine: Dream, mirage, or nemesis?* Princeton, NJ: Princeton University.

McKeown, T., Record, R. G., & Turner, R. D. (1975). "An interpretation of the decline of mortality in England and Wales during the twentieth century." *Population Studies*, 29, 391–422.

McKeown, T. & Record, R. G. (1962). "Reasons for the decline in mortality in England and Wales during the nineteenth century." *Population Studies*, 16, 94–122.

McKeown T. & Brown, R. G. (1955). "Medical evidence related to English population changes in the eighteenth century." *Population Studies* 9, 119–141.

O'Donnell, M. P. (2011). *2012 Conference Theme*. Retrieved from http://healthpromotionconference.com.

Ogden, C. L. (2009). "Disparities in obesity prevalence in the United States: black women at risk." *American Journal of Clinical Nutrition*, 89(4), 1001–1002.

Pellegrino, E. (2006). "Toward a reconstruction of medical morality." *American Journal of Bioethics*, 6(2): 65–71.

Phelan, J. C., Link, B. G., & Tehranifar, P. (2010). "Social conditions as fundamental causes of health inequalities: theory, evidence, and policy implications." *Journal of Health and Social Behavior, 51 Supp.,* S28–S40.

Puhl, R. M. & Heuer, C. (2010). "Obesity stigma: Important considerations for public health." *American Journal of Public Health,* 100(6), 1019–1028.

Raphael, D. et al. (2011). "A toxic combination of poor social policies and programmes, unfair economic arrangements and bad politics: the experiences of poor Canadians with Type 2 diabetes." *Critical Public Health,* 22(2): 127–145.

Raphael, D. et al. (2003). "The social determinants of the incidence and management of type 2 diabetes mellitus: are we prepared to rethink our questions and redirect our research activities?" *Leadership in Health Services,* 16(3), 10–20.

Robert, S. A. & Booske, B. C (2011). "US opinions on health determinants and social policy as health policy." *American Journal of Public Health,* 101(9), 1655–1663.

Schillinger, D. et al. (2002). "Association of health literacy with diabetes outcomes." *Journal of the American Medical Association,* 288(4): 475–482.

Scott, C. (2008). "Belief in a just world: A case study in public health ethics." *The Hastings Center Report,* 38(1), 16–19.

Starfield, B. (2011). "Politics, primary healthcare and health: was Virchow right?" *Journal of Epidemiology & Community Health,* 65(8): 653–655.

Stringhini, S. et al. (2010). "Association of socioeconomic position with health behaviors and mortality." *Journal of the American Medical Association,* 303(12): 1159–1166.

Szreter, S. (2004). *Health and wealth: Studies in history and policy.* Rochester, NY: University of Rochester.

Taylor, R. & Rieger, A. (1985). "Medicine as social science: Rudolf Virchow on the typhus epidemic in Upper Silesia." *International Journal of Health Services,* 15(4), 547–559.

Tohono O'odham Community Action. (2011). *Community Action.* Retrieved from http://www.tocaonline.org/TOCAnalysis/Entries/2011/10/1_Community_Context_The_Tohono_Oodham_Nation.html.

Venkatapuram, S., Bell, R., & Marmot, M. (2010). "The right to sutures: Social epidemiology, human rights, and social justice." *Health and Human Rights,* 12(2), 3–16.

Voigt, K. (2010). "Smoking and social justice." *Public Health Ethics,* 3(2), 91–106.

Wens, J. et al. (2005). "GPs' perspectives of type 2 diabetes patients' adherence to treatment: A qualitative analysis of barriers and solutions." *BMC Family Practice,* 6(1): 20.

Woolf, S. & Braveman, P. (2011). "Where health disparities begin: The role of social and economic determinants—and why current policies may make matters worse." *Health Affairs,* 30(10): 1852–1859.

Woolf, S. H. et al. (2011). "Citizen-centered health promotion: building collaborations to facilitate healthy living." *American Journal of Preventive Medicine, 40*(Supp. 1), S38–S47.

World Health Organization Commission on Social Determinants of Health. (2008). *Closing the gap in a generation: Health equity through action on the social determinants of health.* Retrieved from http://www.who.int/social_determinants/thecommission/finalreport/en/index.html.

THE ROLE OF THE HEALTH PRACTITIONER BIAS IN HEALTH DISPARITIES

Accepting It and Addressing It

By Susan LeLacheur, DrPH, PA-C

HEALTH DISPARITIES AND THE CLINICIAN'S ROLE

The existence of racial and ethnic disparities in health care and the effects of these disparities on health outcomes are well documented (Smedley et al., 2002, Sue and Dhindsa, 2006). This occurs despite the fact that we know "race" and ethnicity are poorly defined and have no real biologic salience. In fact, the human genome project has now clearly shown that there is generally far more genetic variation within a given race than between races (Yudel and DeSalle, 2002). The reasons for disparities are complex and overlapping, but the actions of health care practitioners are the piece of the causation of health disparities on which clinicians and clinicians in training must focus. Clinicians and clinical students want the best for their patients, yet bias and stereotyping on the part of the health practitioner plays some part in contributing to health disparities (Smedley et al., 2002). The exact mechanisms by which this occurs, and the extent of its contribution to the larger problem, are less clear. That said, bias and stereotyping are factors involved in racial and ethnic health disparities over which clinicians can, and must, exert some control. This chapter will explore our understanding of unconscious bias and review some methods by which it may be modified. A more complete discussion of the data regarding health disparities is detailed in *Unequal Treatment* (Smedley et al., 2002) as well as Dr. Jacobson's chapter on health care statistics. These resources describe a large body of data supporting the existence of and various factors involved in health care disparities.

Of note, some studies have demonstrated that these disparities persist regardless of the race of the physician. Chen et al. (2001) examined Medicare patients and looked for differences between black and white physicians. In a retrospective study of data on 35,676 white and 4,039 black patients with acute myocardial infarction who were treated by 17,550 white and 588 black physicians, they found that black patients had lower rates of cardiac catheterization than white patients, regardless of whether their attending physician was white (rate of catheterization, 38.4 percent vs. 45.7 percent; P<0.001) or black (38.2 percent vs. 49.6 percent; P<0.001) (Chen et al., 2001). That said, there is much evidence to suggest the race and ethnicity of the provider plays a huge role in the care they receive. Patients of color are more likely to build relationships of trust with someone who looks like them, thus improving patient outcomes (Cooper and Powe, 2004).

The IOM report delineates three ways in which the individual clinician can affect disparate care: bias (or prejudice) against minorities; greater clinical uncertainty when interacting with minority patients; and beliefs (or stereotypes) held by a provider about the behavior or health of minorities (Smedley et al., 2002). In examining the specific impact of clinician bias, as with examining the effect of health care disparities, there are few good studies, but there appears to be an increasing focus on this area.

One notable study was done by Schulman et al. (1999). Physicians (N=720) at two national meetings were shown videotaped scenarios in which standardized patients of different ages (middle-aged and old), genders, and races (black and white) all played the same role of a patient with a history strongly consistent with coronary artery disease (CAD). Each physician subject viewed one of eight scenarios and made diagnostic and treatment decisions based on the video portrayal. They found that white patients were recommended to have surgery at an odds ration of 1.67 when compared with black patients when both age groups and genders were combined. This number, based solely on clinician perceptions of identical cases, is remarkably similar to the odds ratios found in the literature looking at actual differences in care for patients with CAD as documented in large multicenter trials.

A few clinically based studies have looked specifically at clinician recommendations and disparities by race. In the context of a large national cardiac database, Maynard and colleagues reviewed data for 202 blacks and 13,105 whites from July 1974 to May 1980 at fifteen clinics. The retrospective study found that surgery was recommended for 46.5 percent of Blacks and 50.7 percent of Whites, despite a higher proportion of Class III or IV angina and unstable angina in Blacks. Of note in this study, for patients to whom medical therapy rather than surgery was recommended, only 1 percent of Blacks received surgery, while 11 percent of Whites did so. It is possible that this indicates white patients overuse surgery when available (opting for surgery when medical treatment was recommended), while black patients do not (Maynard, Fisher, Passamani, and Pullum, 1986); however, it is difficult to determine the cause of discrepancy in a retrospective study.

In another assessment of clinician bias in cardiac care, LaVeist, Arthur, Morgan, Plantholt, and Rubinstein (2003) examined the differences in rates of specialist referrals for more than two thousand cardiac patients at three hospitals in Baltimore, Maryland, using data from the Cardiac Longitudinal Access Study. In multivariate logistic regression, they found that black patients (N=1,220) were twice as likely (OR 2.06) *not* to be referred to a cardiac specialist or for cardiac catheterization (OR 2.40) than white patients (N=1,403) after controlling for age, gender, and insurance status (LaVeist et al., 2003). As with many of the other studies discussed, LaVeist and colleagues relied on retrospective data from patient records.

In another retrospective study of 217 emergency department patients in Atlanta, Georgia, researchers found that white patients were significantly more likely than black patients to receive analgesia (Todd, Deaton, D'Adamo, and Goe, 2000). A separate study used national hospital data (N =65,557) to explore the use of analgesics in emergency departments nation-wide for three conditions: migraine, back pain, and long bone fracture (Tamayo-Sarver, Hinze, Cydulka, and Baker, 2003). Unlike Todd et al., they found no significant difference in analgesia for fracture or in the overall use of analgesia for the other two conditions. They did, however, find statistically significant differences in the dispensation of opioids for migraine and back pain between black and white patients (p <0.01) (Tamayo-Sarver et al., 2003).

Additional evidence that clinician bias is likely a factor in several other areas is reviewed in the IOM report with large-scale studies showing that African American patients are less likely to be evaluated appropriately for kidney transplantation, receive antiretroviral therapy for HIV infection, or receive mental health services (Smedley, Stith, and Nelson, 2002). In the IOM report, some portion of the provider contribution to disparities is attributed to clinical uncertainty, stereotyping, and bias. Clinical uncertainty will always exist to some extent, and it is addressed in a general way through the diligent use of appropriate practice guidelines and "best practices." Stereotyping and bias are more deep-seated, unconscious actions and remain difficult to address.

Michelle van Ryn is a leader in researching provider perceptions. She and her colleagues examined data for a large cohort of cardiac patients in New York State for association be-tween the perceptions of physicians and their recommendations for their patients. Using multivariate analysis, after controlling for physician characteristics, clinical variables and insurance status, they found that only physician *perception* of the patient level of education (which was perceived significantly lower for Blacks than for Whites) was an independent predictor of physician recommendation for coronary artery bypass graft in appropriate pa-tients (OR 3.28 (1.24–8.73), p .001) (van Ryn, Burgess, Malat, and Griffin, 2006). This is the first study to directly relate the differing physician perceptions of black and white patients to physician behaviors. If clinicians behave differently toward patients according to their race or socioeconomic status, it may be because of overt discrimination or, more often, because of an unconscious discrimination based on race (or class) in our society at large.

Van Ryn's work is based on the idea that physician assumptions regarding patients are, in part, causative of differential treatment of minority patients and the disparities in their health (van Ryn, 2002; van Ryn and Fu, 2003). This idea is echoed in the work of the IOM: "[W]hile the relationship between race or ethnicity and treatment decisions is complex and may also be influenced by gender, providers' perceptions and attitudes toward patients are influenced by patient race or ethnicity, often in subtle ways" (Smedley et al., 2002). While some part of this may be overt in individual cases, research on the cognitive processes involved in bias and stereotyping indicates that a significant portion of it is below the level of consciousness and difficult both to measure and to influence. The unconscious influences affecting disparate patient care explains how, given the fact that most clinicians and clinical students have the best intentions with regard to the patients they treat, inequalities in care persist. Extensive research in stereotyping and bias, spanning much of the past century, has led to new understanding of the nature of these factors.

THE NATURE OF STEREOTYPING AND BIAS

The term "stereotype" was coined by journalist Walter Lippman in 1922 when he altered the concept of the term from its original designation (in the late 1700s) in reference to a printing plate made to duplicate a particular page multiple times. He used it to signify the tendency of people to form mental images or "frames" based on preconceptions of members of a particular group in society as being alike in certain ways (Hamilton, Stroessner, and Driscoll, 1994). There was an explosion of interest in understanding the nature and operation of stereotypes and prejudice after World War II, much of it looking at the content of stereotypes and the motivations behind their development and application. Adorno and colleagues (1950), for instance, described particularly prejudiced individuals who displayed a controlling personality type in *The Authoritarian Personality*, with the control being their motivation.

Stereotypes are a form of human categorization used to make judgments about the people one encounters. They may range from the fairly innocuous, such as the notion that a blue-collar worker is more likely to bowl than to play golf, to the more detrimental, such as the idea that a black man is more violent in nature. In either case, stereotyping is a presumption based on unsubstantiated associations of unrelated traits. Stereotypes frequently result in prejudice or an irrational bias against another, usually because the individual's membership in a particular group is considered as being different from one's own.

Stereotypes come into play when people of different cultures interact and affect the attitudes and behaviors of both parties in their interaction. In the clinical setting, practitioners are under time pressure and must make rapid judgments with regard to diagnosis and treatment decisions. We all stereotype, but it is essential that clinicians develop an awareness of the process as well as tools to modulate stereotyping in clinical practice.

Characteristics of stereotypic thinking, according to Harding, Kutner, Proshansky, and Chein (1954), include:

1. A tendency to attribute traits to all members of a group (neglecting the reality that within-group differences far exceed between-group differences [Yudel and DeSalle, 2002]);
2. Group membership is sufficient to explain a trait; and
3. A tendency to evade conflicting or contradictory evidence.

Stereotypes influence what information is processed, sometimes the information most conforming to the stereotype, but sometimes information that is incongruent, depending on other cognitive demands. Stereotypes also influence how information is interpreted in either nature or quality. For example, what is seen as assertive in a man might be seen as aggressive in a woman. And what might be seen as playful behavior when performed by a white child might be seen as threatening when performed by a black child. Stereotypes will also influence interactions with members of another group. Hamilton et al. found that when person A behaves toward person B according to their stereotype, person B will often reciprocate, reinforcing the stereotype (1994). For example, a clinician who holds a negative stereotype about black people will spend less time in the interaction, make less eye contact and not speak as clearly. Detecting that they are not being treated as well as they wish, the patient will respond by becoming irritated and argumentative, thus confirming the stereotype.

The connection between stereotype and prejudice is clear, but the distinction is equally important. A stereotype is a preconception while prejudice refers more to the application of that preconception either in attitude, belief, or behavior. Within psychology, social cognitive approaches have led to a shift in research from looking at the content and development of stereotypes to measuring processes involved in their activation and application (Hamilton et al., 1994). The study of prejudice has had a major place in the psychological, sociological, and anthropological literature over much of the past century. This work has frequently focused on stereotypes and their nature, the developmental and cognitive processes involved, and their application to interpersonal interactions. A stereotype can lead to prejudice either toward or against members of the group it is supposed to define, depending on whether the stereotype is positive or negative. Prejudice, in this context, is defined as an unreasoning preference or objection, a bias. This change in research focus has also led to changes in the approach to prejudice reduction (Monteith, 1994).

TESTING IMPLICIT BIAS AND STEREOTYPING

Much of the more recent work has focused on ways to measure various aspects of stereo-types. Explicit measurements are done by self-report and, thus, subject to self-report bias or the tendency to answer in a way that will highlight oneself in a more positive light. People can only report attitudes and behaviors of which they are aware and may paint a somewhat idealized version of even these attitudes and behaviors. While self-report measures of preju-dice are intended to be nonreactive to allow people to feel comfortable in giving honest answers, many have questioned the ability of any self-report instrument to obtain accurate results. More subtle methods have been used to evaluate racial bias since the 1980s, focus-ing on subconscious rather than conscious responses. Results of these subconscious tests, exemplified by the Implicit Association Test (IAT), are often at odds with explicit surveys.

The IAT was developed in 1998 by Greenwald and colleagues when they completed a set of experiments using pictures and words on a computer screen (Greenwald, McGhee, and Schwartz, 1998). This test works by flashing two sets of words and/or images on the screen that are either stereotype congruent or stereotype dissonant. The subject is asked to identify and correctly match the words/images irrespective of stereotypes, and the speed of response is measured. A more rapid response is found when the brain can easily merge two stimuli, and a slower response occurs when the two stimuli are more difficult to associate. For example, in matching images to either the term "intelligence" or a non-related term such as "carnivore," a picture of Albert Einstein will elicit a quick response time in pairing it to "intelligence," as the brain can identify the association easily, while the term "carnivore" is obviously not congruent with an image of Einstein. Yet, matching another valid image such as one of an elephant to the word "intelligence" would likely elicit a slower response time, particularly with the term "carnivore" as a distractor. Elephants are highly intelligent herbivores, but a number of things (such as the size of the animal or the distracting term) might divert the test taker briefly from the correct pairing. And, in occasional cases, the test taker might actually pair the word incorrectly.

Stereotypes have been evaluated in this way using the IAT for race (black/white), gender, and sexual orientation among other characteristics. When a stereotype is flashed on the screen and is associated with one of these characteristics, most subjects cognitively recog-nize the stereotype as invalid, but the brain takes longer to respond to the correct match. Hence, individuals are influenced, albeit subconsciously, by these stereotypes, and snap judg-ments in the form of impressions or actions can be made based on subconscious thought. (Examples of this procedure can be found at https://implicit.harvard.edu/.)

Research by Green et al. ties implicit bias and stereotyping directly to clinician decision making. All internal medicine and emergency medicine residents in three Boston-area hos-pitals were invited to participate (and offered ten dollars) in a twenty-minute, anonymous, web-based survey. After eliminating those with prior knowledge of this testing, 220 medical residents completed the randomized vignette in which a black or white patient was pictured. After completing the vignette, three black-white IAT tests (race, racial attitude, and racial stereotyping) were administered as well as a questionnaire to measure explicit bias. Using multiple regression, explicit responses and IAT scores were compared with treatment decisions. Interaction between IAT and treatment decisions was significant such that as anti-black IAT scores increased, decisions to treat a black patient decreased (p=0.009)(Green et al., 2007). This supports research indicating that implicit—but not explicit—bias influences behavior as well as the relationship, described in van Ryn's work, between unconscious bias and clinician decision making. The study, however, was small and subject to selection bias given the poor participation rate and high proportion of excluded participants.

Several studies have looked at ways of reducing unconscious bias, as measured by the IAT as well as through explicit measures. One strategy for prejudice reduction that has long been pursued is that of exposing people to positive role models from the group that is the target of prejudice. Dasgupta and Greenwald (2001) explored this technique, both in the positive and the negative, using the IAT. Exposure to positive and negative role models influenced IAT scores both immediately after exposure to the role model and twenty-four hours later, offering significant possibilities for potentially durable change in implicit attitudes. The effect was only seen in implicit—and again, not explicit—measures, indicating an effect on unconscious bias with little effect on conscious bias.

PERSPECTIVE-TAKING AND ITS EFFECT ON BIAS AND STEREOTYPING

While there is evidence that the expression of stereotypes can be controlled (Dasgupta and Greenwald, 2001), it seems that attempts to consciously suppress stereotypes actually backfire, increasing consciousness of the stereotype (Burgess et al., 2004; Galinsky and Moskowitz, 2000). Galinsky and colleagues have demonstrated in a series of studies that a simple alternative, perspective-taking, shows far more success in removing both stereotypical behavior and thinking (Galinsky et al., 2003; Galinsky, 1999; Galinsky and Ku, 2004; Galinsky and Moskowitz, 2000). Perspective-taking consists simply of an instruction to put oneself "in the shoes" of the person with whom one is interacting and to consider how that person might presume the situation. There is a great deal of overlap between perspective-taking and sympathy, but researchers are attempting to differentiate between the effect of sympathy, or understanding the feelings of another, and perspective-taking, or understanding the thoughts of another.

In a series of three experiments, Galinsky and Moskowitz (2000) have taken this work a step further in providing some evidence that perspective-taking can reduce stereotype expression and even the cognitive accessibility of the stereotype, while conscious attempts to reduce stereotyping only serve to make the stereotype more accessible. In a study of thirty-seven undergraduates, subjects were randomized to perspective-taking, stereotype suppression, or control prior to completing a writing task. Instructions for perspective-taking were to put themselves in the pictured individual's "shoes, seeing the world through their eyes," while suppression subjects were instructed that "previous research has demonstrated that thoughts and impressions are constantly influenced by stereotypic preconceptions, and therefore, you should actively try to avoid thinking about the photographed target in such a manner." Participants were asked to take about five minutes to write a narrative about a photograph of an elderly man sitting on a bench near a newspaper. They were then given a mathematical filler task for fifteen minutes and then a word task in which they were asked to simply identify words versus nonwords (nonsense groupings of letters) as they were flashed on a computer screen. Half of the actual words were stereotypic of the elderly (lonely, depressed, dependent, stubborn, forgetful, and traditional), and the other half were non-stereotypic words matched for valance and length (jumpy, scheming, cowardly, envious, and deceptive). The rapidity of response in identifying theses terms as an actual word versus a nonword was measured.

The essays were evaluated by two raters, each using a nine-point scale for level of stereo-typing. Because inter-rater reliability was high (r(37) 0.84), ratings were averaged and ANOVA performed by group. Both suppressors and perspective-takers wrote less stereotypic essays than controls (M = 5.4 and 4.4, respectively, as compared with controls M= 6.8), as shown in ANOVA scores with a statistically significant difference between the two intervention groups and controls (F(1,34) 10.2, $p<0.003$). This means that both suppressing the stereotype and taking the perspective of the man in the picture resulted in a less consciously stereotypical portrayal of the man in the picture relative to the control group. On the other hand, hypoth-esizing that both control and perspective-takers would respond more slowly to stereotypical words than suppressors, a preplanned ANOVA of reaction times showed this to be the case (F(1,34 5.8, $p<0.02$). The suppression group responded most quickly to stereotypical words (M = 451ms) as contrasted with perspective-takers (M = 529ms) and control (M = 510ms). Thus, stereotype suppression actually results in quicker impulse to unconsciously stereotype.

In a second experiment to explore the effect of perspective-taking as compared with sup-pression when it involved the idea of self-other overlap, or how much we compare/distance ourselves from the "other," these two strategies were further evaluated. Eighty-two paid undergraduates were told they would be participating in a series of unrelated tasks and randomized to control, perspective-taking or suppression groups. First, they were given a list of ninety traits and asked how closely the traits described themselves on a seven-point Likert scale. They then completed the essay task, using the same photograph described previously. After fifteen minutes of filler tasks, subjects were given the same list of traits as used in the first task and asked to ascribe them to the elderly. Results of stereotypicality of the essay were similar to those in the first experiment. Comparing the two intervention groups to the controls were both explicitly less stereotypical in their essays (F(2. 79) 9.0, p<0.01). Looking at the degree of overlap between self-ascribed traits and traits ascribed to the elderly, perspective-takers showed more overlap between self and the elderly in both positive and negative traits (ANOVA F(1,79) 6.8, p 0.01) when compared with the other two groups (Galinsky and Moskowitz, 2000). Similar to the idea that if one is told not to think about a white bear, it is almost impossible to keep the thought out of one's mind, subjects told not to think of a stereotype were successful in suppressing its conscious expression, but could not keep the stereotype out of their minds.

Perspective-taking was found to offer a potential mechanism for influencing behavior of clinicians in a way that improves the patient's perception of the clinical interaction in a series of experiments done by Blatt et al. (2010). Three studies were performed—two with cohorts of third-year medical students and one with a cohort of physician assistant students—to test perspective-taking in a simulated (standardized patient) interaction. The first medical student study (N=245) and the PA study (N=105) were done concurrently, but the PA study utilized only African American standardized patients. In the third study, a baseline evaluation was done for a pre-existing propensity for perspective-taking. In all three studies, a simple perspective-taking intervention, telling the students to consider the patient's point of view, seeing the world through their eyes and walking in their shoes, was compared with a control group that received no such instructions (p <0.01 all studies). In all three, a small but positive effect was found on patients' assessments of the interaction with the perspective-taking students as compared with the controls. Of note, the effect size was highest for the PA student group (0.31) and for those in the final medical student study who had the highest baseline perspective-taking tendency (0.25). It is unknown whether the PA group had a higher perspective-taking tendency or if the African American patients were more positively affected by the intervention. That said, prior work showing stereotype reduction with perspective-taking along with these data bolster the potential for this technique, a simple suggestion to take the patient's point of view in the context of the clinical interaction.

Along similar lines, Beach et al. explored the effects of patient-centeredness or a constellation of factors, including empathy and responsiveness to the values and needs of the patient, that overlaps with perspective-taking. They found that students displaying higher scores on a patient-centered attitude survey performed better in interactions with African American standardized patients (SPs), while scores for the same students with European-American SPs were not significantly better than other students with lower patient-centeredness scores. One hundred seventy-seven students were surveyed using a nine-question questionnaire on patient-centeredness. The group was then divided at the median into patient-centered and those not patient-centered. Patient-centered students scored higher on every section of the SP evaluation when interacting with the African American patients: a mean of 2 points on interpersonal skills (p .010); 2.7 points on history taking (p 0.003); 5 points on physical exam (p insignificant at 0.311); and 3.4 points on counseling (p .002). These results led authors to conclude that patient-centeredness is more important in improving the care of African American patients, who are typically marginalized as the "other" from the student/provider in charge of their care, often leading to reports of feeling less engaged with their provider. This might lead to a reduction in health disparities (M. C. Beach et al., 2007).

Patient centeredness and perspective-taking likely work in the same way to help overcome a perception of "difference" or "otherness" between patient and clinician. Clinician bias and stereotyping is but one component of the multiple and complex interaction of factors contributing to the perpetuation of health care disparities. It is, however, one area in which the individual clinician can exert some control and make some positive change. A few simple steps can be recommended for all clinicians and clinical students:

1. Evaluate and acknowledge your own subconscious bias toward various groups of patients using the Implicit Association Test (https://implicit.harvard.edu).
2. Encourage self-awareness and evaluation of the cognitive forces that conspire to maximize versus minimize bias and stereotyping.
3. Utilize perspective-taking and other patient-centered approaches in patient interactions.

Each individual clinician can only change his or her own practice directly and, at that, only to a limited extent. Yet, each of us becomes a model and a teacher for others. The barriers between people of different races and ethnicities will continue to blur, but until they disappear, we will have to act individually to do our best to keep them out of our medical decision-making processes.

REFERENCES

Adorno, T. W., Frenkel-Brunswik, E., Levinson, D. J., & Sanford, R. N. *The Authoritarian Personality.* Oxford, England: Harpers. (1950).

Bargh, J. A., Chen, M., & Burrows, L. (1996). "Automaticity of social behavior: Direct effects of trait construct and stereotype activation on action." *Journal of Personality and Social Psychology,* 71(2), 230–244.

Blatt, B., LeLacheur, S. F., Galinsky, A. D., Simmens, S. J., & Greenberg, L. (2010) "Does Perspective-Taking Increase Patient Satisfaction in Medical Encounters?" *Academic Medicine.* 85(9):1445–52.

"Why do providers contribute to disparities and what can be done about it?" *Journal of General Internal Medicine,* 19(11), 1154–1159.

Chen, J., Rathore, S. S., Radford, M. J., Wang, Y., & Krumholz, H. M. (2001). "Racial differences in the use of cardiac catheterization after acute myocardial infarction. [comment]." *New England Journal of Medicine,* 344(19), 1443–1449.

Cooper, L. A. & Powe, N. R. "Disparities in Patient Experiences, Health Care Processes, and Outcomes: The Role of Patient-Provider Racial, Ethnic, and Language Concordance." *The Commonwealth Fund,* July 2004.

Dasgupta, N. & Greenwald, A. G. (2001). "On the malleability of automatic attitudes: combating automatic prejudice with images of admired and disliked individuals." [comment]. *Journal of Personality & Social Psychology,* 81(5), 800–814.

Devine, P. (1989). "Stereotypes and prejudice: Their automatic and controlled components." *Journal of Personality and Social Psychology,* 56, 5–18.

Dovidio, J. F., Kawakami, K., Johnson, C., & Howard, A. (1997). "On the nature of prejudice: Automatic and controlled processes." *Journal of Exerimental Social Psychology,* 33, 510–540.

Erikson, E. H. (1985). "Pseudospeciation in the nuclear age." *Political Psychology,* 6(2), 213–217.

Fazio R. H. & Dunton, B. C. (1997). "Categorization by race: The impact and controlled components of racial prejudice." *Journal of Exerimental Social Psychology,* 33, 451–470.

Galinsky, A., Martorana, P., & Ku, G. (2003). "To control or not to control stereotypes: Separating the implicit and explicit processes of perspective-taking and suppression." [References]. In Forgas, Joseph P (ed.), Williams, Kipling D. (ed.) et al. (2003) *Social judgments: Implicit and explicit processes* (pp. 343–363). New York, NY: Cambridge University Press.

Galinsky, A. D. (1999). *Perspective-taking: Debiasing social thought. (stereotyping).* US: Princeton U.

Galinsky, A. D. & Ku, G. (2004). "The Effects of Perspective-Taking on Prejudice: The Moderating Role of Self-Evaluation." *Personality & Social Psychology Bulletin,* 30(5), 594–604.

Galinsky, A. D. & Moskowitz, G. B. (2000). "Perspective-taking: Decreasing stereotype expression, stereotype accessibility, and in-group favoritism." *Journal of Personality & Social Psychology,* 78(4), 708–724.

Green, A. R., Carney, D. R., Pallin, D. J., Ngo, L. H., Raymond, K. L., Iezzoni, L. I., et al. (2007). "Implicit Bias among Physicians and its Prediction of Thrombolysis Decisions for Black and White Patients." *Journal of General Internal Medicine,* 22(9), 1231–1238.

Greenwald, A., McGhee, D., & Schwartz, J. (1998). "Measuring Individual Differences in Implicit Cognition: The Implicit Association Test." *Journal of Personality and Social Psychology,* 74(6), 1464–1480.

Hamilton, D., Stroessner, S., & Driscoll, D. (1994). "Social cognition and the study of stereotyping." In Devine, P. G., Hamilton, D. L., Ostrom, T. M. (ed.), *Social Cognition: Impact on Psychology* (pp. 292–321). San Diego: Academic Press.

Harding J., Kutner B., Proshansky, H., & Chein, I. (1954). "Prejudice and ethnic relations." In Fiske, S. T., Gilbert, D. T., Lindzey, G. (ed.), *Handbook of Social Psychology* (Vol. 2, pp. 1021–1061). Cambrige MA: Addison-Wesley.

LaVeist, T. A., Arthur, M., Morgan, A., Plantholt, S., & Rubinstein, M. (2003). "Explaining racial differences in receipt of coronary angiography: the role of physician referral and physician specialty." *Medical Care Research & Review,* 60(4), 453–467; discussion 496–508.

Lepore, L. & Brown, R. (1997). "Category and stereoptype activation: Is prejudice inevitable." *Journal of Personality and Social Psychology,* 72(2), 275–287.

Maynard, C., Fisher, L. D., Passamani, E. R., & Pullum, T. (1986). "Blacks in the coronary artery surgery study (CASS): race and clinical decision making." *Am J Public Health,* 76(12), 1446–1448.

Monteith, M. J., Zuwerink, J. R., & Devine, P. G. (1994). "Prejudice and prejudice reduction: Classic challenges, contemporary approaches." In Devine, P. G., Hamilton, D. L., Ostrom, T. M. (ed.), *Social Cognition: Impact on Social Psychology* (pp. 324–346). San Diego: Academic Press.

Schulman, K. A., Berlin, J. A., Harless, W., Kerner, J. F., Sistrunk, S., Gersh, B. J. et al. (1999). "The effect of race and sex on physicians' recommendations for cardiac catheterization." [comments] [published erratum appears in *N Engl J Med* 1999 Apr 8;340(14):1130]. *N Engl J Med,* 340(8), 618–626.

Smedley, B., Stith, A., & Nelson, A. (2002). *Unequal Treatment: Confronting Racial and Ethnic Disparities in Health Care.* Washington, DC: National Academy Press.

Sue, S. & Dhindsa, M. K. (2006). "Ethnic and racial health disparities research: issues and problems." *Health Education & Behavior,* 33(4), 459–469.

Tamayo-Sarver, J. H., Hinze, S. W., Cydulka, R. K., & Baker, D. W. (2003). "Racial and ethnic disparities in emergency department analgesic prescription." *American Journal of Public Health,* 93(12), 2067–2073.

Todd, K. H., Deaton, C., D'Adamo, A. P., & Goe, L. (2000). "Ethnicity and analgesic practice." [comment]. *Annals of Emergency Medicine,* 35(1), 11–16.

van Ryn, M. (2002). "Research on the provider contribution to race/ethnicity disparities in medical care." *Medical Care,* 40(1 Suppl), 140–151.

van Ryn, M., Burgess, D., Malat, J., & Griffin, J. (2006). "Physicians' perceptions of patients' social and behavioral characteristics and race disparities in treatment recommendations for men with coronary artery disease." *American Journal of Public Health,* 96(2), 351–357.

van Ryn, M. & Fu, S. S. (2003). "Paved with good intentions: do public health and human service providers contribute to racial/ethnic disparities in health?" *American Journal of Public Health,* 93(2), 248–255.

von Hippel, W., Sekaquaptewa, D., & Vargas, P. (1997). "The linguistic intergroup bias as an implicit indicator of prejudice." *Journal of Experimental Social Psychology,* 33(5), 490–509.

Yudell, M. & DeSalle, R. (ed.) (2002). *The Genomic Revolution: Unveiling the Unity of Life.* Washington, DC: John Henry Press.

IV

AN EXAMINATION OF SPECIFIC MENTAL AND PHYSICAL CIRCUMSTANCES OF INEQUITIES IN HEALTH CARE STATUS FOR PARTICULAR POPULATIONS

REDUCING ORAL HEALTH DISPARITIES

The Important Role of Physician Assistants

By Anita Duhl Glicken, MSW

INTRODUCTION TO THE PROBLEM

In February 2007, the *Washington Post* carried a news story that quickly went viral across the country. Twelve-year-old Diamonte Driver had died of an apparent toothache; an eighty-dollar tooth extraction may have prevented his untimely death. The article further noted that this might have been avoided if his mother had been insured, if his family had not recently lost their Medicaid coverage, if dentists who accept Medicaid were not difficult to find, and if his mother had not been distracted by her attempts to find a dentist willing to treat his younger brother who had six rotting teeth (Otto, 2007). Unfortunately, Diamonte's toothache did not receive attention until the abscessed tooth had already transmitted bacteria to his brain, and despite two operations and a long hospital stay, he died in the shadow of the nation's capital.

Diamonte's story brought renewed attention to a public health crisis that had been described nearly a decade earlier in the surgeon general's report, *Oral Health in America* (National Institute of Dental and Craniofacial Research [NIDCR], 2000), and the subsequent *Call to Action* (NIDCR, 2003), which labeled the nation's poor oral health as a "silent epidemic" calling attention to the fact that dental caries is "the single most common chronic childhood disease." Years earlier, in the 1980s and 1990s, the Institute of Medicine argued that basic dental services should be broadly available and covered by a national health insurance plan. In fact, as early as 1926, Gies noted that "Certain common and simple disorders of the teeth may involve prompt or insidious development of serious and possibly fatal ailments in other parts of the body." Yet, despite multiple initiatives designed to address this issue over several decades and emerging science that clearly documents the importance of the oral-systemic connection, our current educational programs, financing systems, and treatment services continue to operate in siloed and fragmented ways, perpetuating one of the most significant sources of health care inequities in the United States. Drawing from evidence cited in the 2011 report, *Improving Access to Oral Health for Vulnerable and Underserved Populations*, this chapter describes strategies to enhance physician assistants' oral health care for their patients, thereby improving overall patient health and reducing health disparities (Institute of Medicine [IOM], 2011).

The Cost of Dental Disease

The cost of health care in the United States has been steadily increasing over the past decade, with the cost of medical spending far outstripping the growth in dental expenditures. The overall cost of health care expenditures in 2012 has been estimated at $2.8 trillion (Centers for Medicare & Medicaid Services [CMS], 2013), and disbursements for dental services constituted approximately 5 percent of this amount, or $102.2 billion. Despite the seemingly small fraction of medical costs, dental expenses are burgeoning. This cost is primarily due to estimates related to direct services provided by dentists in typical practice settings. In other words, these costs do not likely account for efforts to improve the general oral health of patients (IOM, 2011).

Social Determinants of Oral Health: Disparities in Dental Care

It is clear that underserved populations experience disproportionate barriers to oral health access and care. They are deprived of essential services that could significantly reduce oral disease and promote overall health and well-being. Recently, the Institute of Medicine and National Research Council's Committee on Oral Health Access to Services suggested several barriers to oral health, such as geographic factors, that cut across demographic lines and affect a variety of populations. Disenfranchised minorities, however, are disproportionately affected at higher rates when compared with their white counterparts, illustrating the race-based reality of inequities (IOM, 2011). The factors that influence these inequities, deemed as social determinants of health, are described by the World Health Organization as a combination of structural forces—e.g., the distribution of power, wealth, goods, services, and daily living conditions—that affect the health of an individual or population (World Health Organization [WHO], 2008).

One major social determinant affecting health is an individual's availability or absence of health insurance. Lack of dental coverage, in particular, is a significant cause of health care disparities in the United States, thus causing an unsettling inequity in the dental health/ condition between those who have and those who do not have dental health insurance coverage. The National Association of Dental Plans, which provides coverage to 90 percent of the 166 million Americans who have dental care plans, estimated that 130 million US adults and children lacked dental coverage in 2009 (National Association of Dental Plans [NADP], 2009), a rate of more than 40 percent in adults aged 21–64 (Liu, Probst, Martin, Wang, & Salina, 2007). And yet this overall number fails to highlight the severity of the problem in older adults, where approximately 70 percent of those sixty-five and older lack any kind of dental coverage (Manski & Brown, 2008).

No matter the dental coverage, poor children overall are less likely to receive dental care. Roughly 1 of every 3 near-poor children had not visited a dentist in the prior year compared with 1 in 5 children who were not low income (Kaiser Family Foundation [KFF], 2012). And while adults and youths have shown a decrease in dental caries, children 2–5 years of age actually have shown an increase in caries in their primary teeth (Dye et al., 2007). Fifty-one percent of children 6–11 years of age have had dental caries in their primary teeth and 21 percent have experienced dental caries in their permanent teeth (Dye et al., 2007). This is consistent with data that show poorer children also have twice as many untreated caries in their primary teeth (Dye et al., 2007) and are also only half as likely to have received dental sealants (Centers for Disease Control and Prevention [CDC], 2011). Poor children are not only more likely than their higher-income counterparts to have dental caries, but the extent and severity of the decay are greater. In other words, dental coverage is lacking in those who cannot afford it; without coverage, the care is limited and disease is greater. It is estimated that half of poor children age 2–11 have decay in their primary teeth, compared with one-third of children in families with income levels at or above the federal poverty level (NIDCR, 2014; CDC, 2011).

The burden of poor oral health extends beyond the pain and suffering of the child; an additional measure of this income-related disparity is that children in low-income families have twelve times as many restricted activity days in comparison with children from families in higher socioeconomic groups (NIDCR, 2000). Poor oral health amounts to increased absence from school and time off work for the parents. Psychological issues such as depression often result from difficulties with speech, learning, and eating, leading to increased problems with productivity. In the surgeon general's report, he highlighted the fact that fifty-one million school hours are missed annually due to dental-related illness (NIDCR, 2000). Additionally, adults lose more than 164 million work hours each year due to problems with their teeth, which leads to a whole host of other calamities for the employee as well as the employer, industry, and economy, potentially resulting in lost wages and decreased productivity (Gift, Reisine & Larach, 1992).

Access to oral health care in the United States is closely tied to socioeconomic status and the individual's access to dental coverage. The ability to pay for private insurance and out-of-pocket expenses enables individuals and their families to access comprehensive dental care. On the other hand, for those who lack dental insurance or the financial means to pay for dental care, options are quite limited. Access is further compromised by the fact that many public programs such as Medicaid and the Children's Health Insurance Program (CHIP) provide low reimbursement to providers, which discourages them from participating as care providers to lower income populations (KFF, 2012).

Several studies have documented how access and utilization of care both appear linked to dental coverage. There is greater utilization of care by those that purchase dental coverage. As noted in the recent Institute of Medicine report, *Improving Access to Oral Health Care for Vulnerable and Underserved Populations*, it is unclear "if more coverage leads to greater use or greater demand leads to the purchase of dental coverage (and then greater use)" (IOM, 2011). The report goes on to state, however, that the link between the two is clear. Several studies report that uninsured children have significantly more unmet needs of oral health care than children with dental coverage, estimated to be at least twice the need for care (Fox, Moore, Davis, & Heintzelman, 2003; McBroome, Damiano, & Willard, 2005; Mofidi, Slifkin, Freeman, & Silberman, 2002; Wang, Norton, & Rozier, 2007). Still other studies have shown that when children are enrolled in a public program and provided access to dental care, they are significantly less likely to continue to have unmet dental needs, such as were the results that Klein et al. (2007) found in a study of adolescents who were enrolled in CHIP. Similarly, Kenney (2007) discovered that in a population of children who needed special health care services, enrolling in CHIP improved their access to general health care as well as dental care. Thus, the inference can be made (referring to the IOM report) that more coverage leads to greater use as opposed to the antithesis, and so an otherwise inconspicuous health care disparity is illuminated.

Additionally, a lack of knowledge about oral health remains a pervasive problem across all segments. Studies demonstrate low oral health literacy in categories related to low general health and communication skills (Neuhauser, 2010; Rozier et al., 2011). This lack of knowledge and understanding is a significant social determinant of health that inhibits the use of strategies that can prevent oral disease, including the utilization of fluoride in public water systems, toothpastes, mouth rinses, and varnishes. Also, dental sealants can prevent caries on the surface of the teeth; however, despite their effectiveness, sealants are also underutilized (Ahovou-Saloranta, Hiiri, Norblad, Worthington, & Makela, 2008). Like fluoridation, sealants can be provided through a community-based program, such as school-based programs that target high-risk populations. But without the general health knowledge, parents are often ineffective at maintaining healthy habits as they are ill informed of the benefits to their child's health.

It is noteworthy that racial/ethnic disparities in oral health access, care, and overall status of health are also evident. These disparities relate to a variety of social factors that include a lack of available dentists in communities primarily inhabited by racial and ethnic minorities. African Americans, American Indians, and Alaskan Natives have been noted to have poorer oral health throughout their lives as compared with the general US population (The Office of Minority Health [OMH], 2010). Additional barriers to oral health include a lack of access to fluoridated water, a lack of continuity in Indian Health Service dental programs, and geographic challenges to affordable care. Similarly, Latino populations receive less dental care compared with white populations. Several authors have noted that differences appear independent of dental coverage, income, education, and attitudes toward prevention (Dietrich, Culler, Garcia, & Crenshaw, 2008).

The above examples illustrate the significant impact that oral disease has on overall health as well as the significant disparities that occur in the nation's most vulnerable populations, including children, ethnic minorities, and older adults. These social determinants affect oral health and contribute to the complexity of attempts to improve the overall health of the US population. Recognizing that these determinants of health will require significant changes in the nation's social and physical environment requires that health practitioners, health educators, and lawmakers think more broadly about the policies needed to bridge these social determinants with emerging science and practice to effectively reduce oral health disparities.

IMPROVING ORAL HEALTH: THE PHYSICIAN ASSISTANT ROLE IN PROMOTING ORAL HEALTH

Improving oral health requires a comprehensive effort on the part of providers, policy makers, payers, and patients. While community-based programs are important in preventing oral disease, personal health behaviors are critical to maintaining good oral health. Primary health professionals play an essential role in promoting oral health in their patients. Over the past few years, considerable attention has been given to educating the non-dental health care workforce in its evolving role in prevention, diagnosis, and treatment of oral disease. Primary care clinicians, including physician assistants, are uniquely positioned to recognize early oral disease and refer to dentists and other oral health providers.

The Bureau of Labor Statistics identified the PA profession as the seventh fastest-growing occupation between 2012 and 2022 (BLS, 2013). Given that approximately half of PAs work in family or general medicine, they often have repeated contacts with patients over time. As trusted agents of behavioral change counseling, PAs provide counseling, participatory guidance, and prevention strategies to a wide variety of patient populations. PAs are valued care providers to HPSAs (Health Professional Shortage Areas)—typically composed of urban and rural communities—often treating medically underserved communities of low-income and minority populations (Everett, Schumacher, Wright, & Smith, 2009). Given that these populations are also known to be those with the greatest unmet needs in terms of oral health care, physician assistants can serve as an important resource in addressing oral health prevention and disease management.

Unfortunately, although data on oral health literacy are scarce, it does appear that the public's knowledge about oral health may be low, in part due to a lack of knowledge on the part of health care professionals, including dental and non-dental providers. Very little is known about oral health education in physician assistant education programs. In 2009, a survey of PA program directors indicated "over 75% believed that dental disease prevention should be addressed in PA education, yet only 21% of programs actually did so" (Jacques et al., 2010). Over the past two years, the profession has begun to address this issue in PA education and practice. The Physician Assistant Initiative in Oral Health has engaged the profession in both a dialogue and creation of shared goals to improve access to preventive health care by increasing physician assistant delivery of oral health services.

Fortunately, readily accessible tools are available to assist providers in enhancing their knowledge of oral health and disease. The Society of Teachers of Family Medicine (STFM) has released its third version of Smiles for Life, a national oral health curriculum for improving oral health training (http://www.smilesforlifeoralhealth.org). Dentists, physicians, and educators developed the curriculum, which has dual portals of entry for educators and providers. The curriculum, free to users, is profession neutral and offers a common knowledge base on oral health, thereby improving health literacy across the health professions. The curriculum consists of CME-approved modules and has been endorsed by the American Academy of Physician Assistants and the Physician Assistant Education Association. Individual modules discuss issues of oral health prevention and disease throughout the life cycle, address skills for risk assessment and examination, and instruct on patient counseling and the needs of specific populations. The curriculum provides practical education such as the application of fluoride varnish during the primary care visit where, in many states, it is now required as a prerequisite for reimbursement. The National Interprofessional Initiative on Oral Health website (www.niioh.org) also includes many resources and tools for health professionals and educators, including a link to the award-winning documentary produced last year by the NCCPA Health Foundation titled *Joining the Fight for Oral Health*. The video provides an introduction to the importance of oral health as viewed through the lens of physician assistants, patients, and other health professionals.

Physician assistants are on the front and back ends of the disease process. In addition to working with patients on prevention of disease, physician assistants and other health professionals can also support patients in disease management through strategies that employ caries risk-assessment models. These models identify patients deemed to have higher than average risks for dental disease and who may need to be encouraged to visit their oral health provider more frequently to reduce carcinogenic bacteria.

Physician assistants have long been recognized as change agents in the American healthcare system. As those who promote levers for change within their communities and in daily practice, they are in a position to promote oral health. PAs provide primary health care across the patient lifespan, and consequently have significant opportunities to be involved in educating their patients, practices, and communities about oral health and its importance to overall health.

WHAT CAN PHYSICIAN ASSISTANTS DO?

Providing quality oral health care to your patients begins with education to improve health literacy. This may start with educating patients on simple health and dietary habits. Developing good eating habits, such as avoiding sugar-rich foods and high sugar carbonated drinks, help reduce oral disease (WHO, 2014). Eating fruits and vegetables may protect against oral cancer and consuming sufficient levels of folic acid helps reduce the risks of cleft lip and palate (NIDCR, 2000). Avoiding tobacco and excessive alcohol use can also reduce the risk of oral cancers, as they have also been shown to work together as carcinogens (NIDCR, 2000). Truman et al. (2002) noted that tobacco use and excessive alcohol consumption account for 90 percent of all oral cancers. Tobacco use is also associated with periodontal disease, oral candidiasis in HIV-positive individuals, and the recurrence of oral cancer (Gelskey, 1999; Palacio, 1997). Several studies have shown that personal oral hygiene including brushing with a fluoridated toothbrush, flossing, and using mouth rinses also reduce the risk of dental caries and gingival inflammation (Deery et al., 2004; Walsh et al., 2010). This health information understanding is vital to patients and is best obtained through a well-informed health professional.

In addition to becoming an oral health advocate, PAs can work to build collaboration with oral health providers in the community and build a network of oral health providers who accept Medicaid and other public insurance programs. This includes creating processes that encourage bidirectional referral and monitoring of overall patient health. PAs can also encourage communities to consider fluoridation programs and other activities that promote public health, educate other health care providers and childhood educators about the oral systemic connection, and offer education programs for parents, teachers, or other health professionals to build the community's oral health literacy.

Below are important actions to improving overall oral health when seeing patients:

- Conduct an oral health risk assessment as part of the routine exam by taking an oral health history, including questions about toothache or pain, swollen or bleeding in gums, or problems with eating, vomiting, etc. Ask patients if they have a regular dental provider and when they had their last dental visit.
- Check the patient's mouth for problems including bleeding gums, swollen or untreated decay, signs of infections, lesions, or trauma.
- Where appropriate, and in consideration of state practice laws, apply fluoride varnish as part of a routine office visit.
- Explain the importance of oral health care to the patient as part of an overall strategy for prevention of illness; include a discussion of potential medication side effects or physical states (i.e., pregnancy) that could affect their oral health. Emphasize the importance of early care—the American Academy of Pediatric Dentistry (AAPD) recommends that children see a dentist by age one or within six months of the emergence of their first tooth.
- Advise patients about appropriate oral health care in culturally and linguistically appropriate ways, making oral health an integral part of the comprehensive health plan for all patients.
- Document findings in the medical record and make any necessary referrals to a dentist for follow-up care.
- If the patient does not have a dental home, facilitate referrals to dentists who will accept new patients from various socioeconomic backgrounds.

It is clear from recent IOM reports and historical research that one strategy for improving access to preventive services for oral health is to expand the use of non-dental professionals. Primary care providers who integrate oral health into their practice and work with other professionals to increase oral exams, risk assessments, and anticipatory guidance can help prevent oral disease, especially in children. Physician assistants can work as part of a team with other providers and families to promote good oral health and increase the quality of overall patient health and well-being.

REFERENCES

Ahovuo-Saloranta, A., Hiiri, A., Norblad, A., Worthington, H., & Makela, M. (2008). Pit and fissure sealants for preventing dental decay in the permanent teeth of children and adolescents. *Cochrane Database of Systematic Reviews,* (4):CD001830.

Bureau of Labor Statistics. (2013). Employment projections: Fastest growing occupations. http://www.bls.gov/emp/ep_table_103.htm

Centers for Disease Control and Prevention, National Center for Chronic Disease Prevention and Health Promotion, Division of Oral Health. (2011). *Oral health: Preventing cavities, gum disease, tooth loss, and oral cancers: At a glance.* Retrieved from http://www.cdc.gov/chronicdisease/resources/publica-tions/aag/pdf/2011/oral-health-aag-pdf-508.pdf

Centers for Medicare & Medicaid Services. (2013). *National health expenditures 2012 highlights.* http://www.cms.gov/Research-Statistics-Data-and-Systems/Statistics-Trends-and-Reports/NationalHealthExpendData/Downloads/highlights.pdf

Deery, C., Heanue, M., Deacon, S., Robinson, P., Walmsley, A., Worthington, H., Shaw, W., & Glenny, A. (2004). The effectiveness of manual versus powered toothbrushes for dental health: A systematic review. *Journal of Dentistry, 32*(3), 197–211.

Dietrich, T., Culler, C., Garcia, R. I., & Henshaw, M. M. (2008). Rachial and ethinic disparities in children's oral health: The National Survey of Children's Health. *Journal of the American Dental Association, 139*(11), 1507-1517.

Dye, B. A., Tan, S., Smith, V., Lewis, B. G., Barker, L. K., Thornton-Evans, G., et al. (2007, April). Trends in oral health status: United States, 1988–1994 and 1999–2004. National Center for Health Statistics. *Vital and Health Statistics, 11*(248).

Everett, C. M., Schumacher, J. R., Wright, A., & Smith, M. A. (2009). Physician assistants and nurse practitioners as a usual source of care. *Journal of Rural Health, 25*(4), 407–414.

Fox, M., Moore, J., Davis, R., & Heintzelman, R. (2003). Changes in reported health status and unmet need for children enrolling in the Kansas Children's Health Insurance Program. *American Journal of Public Health, 93*(4), 579–582.

Gelskey, S. C. (1999). Cigarette smoking and periodontitis: Methodology to assess the strength of evidence in support of a causal association. *Community Dentistry and Oral Epidemiology, 27*(1), 16–24.

Gies, W. J. (1926). *Dental education in the United States and Canada: A report to the Carnegie Foundation for the Advancement of Teaching* (Bulletin No. 19). New York: Carnegie Foundation for the Advancement of Teaching.

Gift, H. C., Reisine, S. T., & Larach, D. C. (1992). The social impact of dental problems and visits. *American Journal of Public Health, 82*(12), 1663–1668.

Institute of Medicine and National Research Council. (2011). *Improving Access to Oral Health Care for Vulnerable and Underserved Populations.* Washington, DC: The National Academies Press.

Jacques, P. F., Snow, C., Dowdle, M., Riley, N., Mao, K., & Gonsalves, W. C. (2010). Oral health curricula in physician assistant programs: A survey of physician assistant program directors. *Journal of Physician Assistant Education, 21*(2).

Kaiser Family Foundation, Kaiser Commission on Medicaid and the Uninsured. (2012, June). *Children and oral health: Assessing needs, coverage, and access.* (Publication No. 7681-04). Retrieved from http://kaiserfamilyfoundation.files.wordpress.com/2013/01/7681-04.pdf

Kenney, G. (2007). The impacts of the State Children's Health Insurance Program on children who enroll: Findings from then states. *Health Services Research, 42*(4), 1520–1543.

Klein, J. D., Shone, L. P., Szilagyi, P. G., Bajorska, A., Wilson, K., & Dick, A. W. (2007). Impact of the state children's health insurance program on adolescents in New York. *Pediatrics, 119*(4), e885-e892.

Liu, J., Probst, J. C., Martin, A. B., Wang, J. Y., & Salinas, C. F. (2007). Disparities in dental insurance coverage and dental care among U.S. children: The National Survey of Children's Health. *Pediatrics 119*(1), S12–S21.

McBroome, K., Damiano, P. C., & Willard, J. C. (2005). Impact of the Iowa S-SCHIP program on access to dental care for adolescents. *Pediatric Dentistry, 27*(1), 47–53.

Mofidi, M., Slifkin, R., Freeman, V., & Silberman, P. (2002). The impact of a state children's insurance program on access to dental care. *Journal of the American Dental Association, 133*(6), 707–714.

National Association of Dental Plans, Health Care Reform. (2009, March). *Dental benefits improve access to dental care.* Retrieved from http://www.nadp.org/Libraries/HCR_Documents/nadphcr-dentalbenefitsimproveaccesstocare-3-28-09.sflb.ashx

National Institute of Dental and Craniofacial Research. (2000). Oral Health in America: A Report of the Surgeon General—Executive Summary. Retrieved from http://www.nidcr.nih.gov/datastatistics/surgeongeneral/report/executivesummary.htm

National Institute of Dental and Craniofacial Research. (2003). A National Call to Action to Promote Oral Health (NIH Publication No. 03-5303). Retrieved from https://www.nidcr.nih.gov/NR/rdonlyres/C133CA2D-4A12-474-A856-3F778DEA49F7/0/NtionalCallToAction.pdf

National Institute of Dental and Craniofacial Research. (2014). Dental caries (tooth decay) in children (age 2 to 11). Retrieved from http://www.nidcr.nih.gov/DataStatistics/FindDataByTopic/DentalCaries/DentalCariesChildren2to11

Neuhauser, L. (2010, June 28). *Communicating with patients: A survey of dental team members—preliminary results*. Paper presented at a meeting for the Committee on an Oral Health Initiative, Washington, DC.

Otto, M. (2007, February 28). For want of a dentist. *The Washington Post*. Retrieved from http://www.washingtonpost.com/wp-dyn/content/article/2007/02/27/AR2007022702116.html

Palacio, H., Hilton, J. F., Canchola, A. J., & Greenspan, D. (1997). Effect of cigarette smoking on HIV-related oral lesions. *Journal of Acquired Immune Deficiency Syndromes and Human Retrovirology, 14*(4), 338–342.

Rozier, R. G., Horowitz, A. M., & Podschun, G. (2011). Dentist-patient communications techniques used in the United States. *Journal of the American Dental Association, 142*(5), 518–530.

The Office of Minority Health. (2010). Racial and ethnic specific oral health data. Retrieved from http://minorityhealth.hhs.gov/templates/browse.aspx?lvl=3&lvlid=209

Truman, B. I., Gooch, B. F., Sulemana, I., Gift, H. C., Horowitz, A. M., Evans Jr., C. A., & Carande-Kulis, V. G. (2002). Reviews of evidence on interventions to prevent dental caries, oral and pharyngeal cancers, and sports-related craniofacial injuries. *American Journal of Preventive Medicine, 23*(1), 21–54.

Walsh, T., Worthington, H. V., Glenny, A. M., Appelbe, P., Marinho, V. C., & Shi, X. (2010). Fluoride toothpastes of different concentrations for preventing dental caries in children and adolescents. *Cochrane Database of Systematic Reviews*, (1):CD007868.

Wang, H., Norton, E. C., & Rozier, R. G. (2007). Effects of the State Children's Health Insurance Program on access to dental care and use of dental services. *Health Services Research, 42*(4), 1544–1563.

World Health Organization. (2014). Oral health: Risks to oral health and intervention. Retrieved from http://www.who.int/oral_health/action/risks/en/

World Health Organization, Commission on Social Determinants of Health. (2008). *Closing the gap in a generation: Health equity through action on the social determinants of health* (Final Report). Retrieved from http://whqlibdoc.who.int/publications/2008/9789241563703_eng.pdf

EYELID SURGERY AMONG THE NACIREMA

Toward Asian American Understanding

By Nicholas Daniel Hartlep

"Societies in part create the disease they experience and, further, they materially shape the way in which diseases are to be experienced."

Susser et al., 1985, p. 17

INTRODUCTION: ASIANS IN THE NACIREMA

I n his classic 1956 allegorical anthropological article, "Body Ritual Among the Nacirema," Horace Miner described the cultural practices of the Nacirema, a seemingly strange and scary people. The Nacirema initially appear to readers to behave in grotesquely savage and inhumanely cruel ways, implying low levels of cultural sophistication. At some point though—perhaps not until after the article has been read and ruminated over—the reader, invariably, has an epiphany and recognizes the irony in Miner's ploy: the Nacirema are Americans! In fact, Nacirema is simply A-m-e-r-i-c-a-n spelled backward. Although written from an anthropological perspective, Miner's (1956) article has much relevance to an issue of medical importance for the Asian American population as well as to its providers in primary care and health care (e.g., nurse practitioners [NP], physician assistants [PA], medical doctors [MD, DO]). The images and ideas of white beauty affect Asian identity to some extent and, hence, affect health, both mentally and physically. This important issue, and consequently the focus of this chapter, can be considered among the social determinants of health related to white racial images and the model minority stereotype.

This chapter aims to educate readers about specific medical and moral issues affecting the health (physical, social, psychological) of Asian Americans, the fastest-growing segment in the United States (Lai and Arguelles, 2003). Introducing Western medical practices to Asian Americans in ways they will understand within their own cultural practices and paradigms is important, but to do this, health care providers must first confront the social conditions that more or less determine health status and outcomes for diverse and stigmatized populations, Asian Americans in particular, in critical and significant ways (Ma, 2009).

Education, socioeconomic status, growing inequality, and sociopolitical factors are inextricably linked and at play when discussing the health and well-being of Asians in the United States. This chapter does not attempt to provide a comprehensive analysis on the social factors that determine one's health. Rather, the focus will be on one unique aspect of white racial images and perspectives (such as the model minority stereotype) that influence or dictate a type of maladaptive health outcome (Marsh, 2011).

STARTLING STATISTICS: HEALTH STATUS AND ASIAN AMERICANS

It is important to understand that statistics often homogenize Asian Americans as a group, treating them monolithically, despite their incredible amounts of intergroup and intragroup diversity. Homogenization reinforces the model minority stereotype (e.g., see Chang, 1998; Chen and Hawks, 1995; Conchas and Perez, 2003; Endo and Della-Piana, 1981; Jang and Surapruik, 2009; Lee and Rotheram-Borus, 2009; Lester, 1992; Lai and Arguelles, 2003; Zhang, 2010; Zhao and Wiu, 2009). Asian Americans are heralded as "model minorities." What this means is that society views them positively and as American success stories. As it pertains to health, this myth inaccurately posits that Asian Americans, compared with their minority counterparts (African Americans, Latinos, and Native Americans), have few, if any, needs when it comes to health care or social services. This perception, however, has been found to be faulty by empirical and social scientific research. In other words, Asian Americans struggle as much as other people of color. While Asian American homogenization is not the focus of this chapter, it certainly affects the ways in which health care providers perceive the medical needs of Asian American patients that they interact with and serve—needs that largely remain invisible (Zhan, 1999). Moreover, many texts do not adequately examine their health status and outcomes as a population (Patel and Rushefsky, 2008). These realities necessitate a discussion on the social determinants of health.

Social determinants

Social determinants of health are the economic and social conditions (*viz.* determinants) under which people live that determine their health (Marmot and Wilkinson, 1999). Consider them to be societal "risk conditions" in contrast to individual "risk factors" since *condition* implies a conditional state, whereas a *factor* implies a relatively

Photo taken in subway system of Seoul, South Korea illustrating the pervasiveness of Asian Eyelid Surgery. Copyright © Nicholas D. Hartlep.

fixed or permanent state. Social determinants of health either increase or decrease the risk of acquiring disease/infection. Interestingly, many books have been written about the social determinants of health, but none have specifically focused on Asian Americans' needs (e.g., see Marmot and Wilkinson, 1999, 2005). A chief way that the social, psychological, and health care needs of Asian Americans are homogenized is through aggregated statistical data.

But according to Chang (1998), "Statistics are like a bikini. What they reveal is suggestive, but what they conceal is vital" (p. 367). Keeping Chang's (1998) comments in mind, health care providers will profit professionally by reading some of the following revelatory, albeit startling, health statistics regarding Asian Americans. The following section details selected determinants of health that affect Asians in the United States.

Household

In the past several years, the field of public health has moved away from a disparity-specific model to assess "root causes" of disproportionate burdens of illness. Public health experts now embrace a more comprehensive approach that takes into account not only individual factors, but contextual factors as well, including socioeconomic status, home and work environment, access to transportation, and educational attainment.

In response, government agencies and health professionals emphasize addressing the social determinants of health and improving social and physical conditions, such as the "built environment," to enable healthy minds and healthy bodies.

Income and Poverty

- Nearly one in three working families in the United States is struggling to meet basic needs (Roberts, Povich, and Mather, 2011).
- People in the highest income group can expect to live, on average, at least six and a half years longer than those in the lowest (*Unnatural Causes*, 2001).
- *Allostatic load* increases for Asian Americans who live in constant states of stress caused by economic poverty (Jensen, 2009). Allostatic load refers to the psychological consequences of chronic exposure to stress (in various forms), which can lead to negative health outcomes (McEwen, 2000).
- In 2010, Asian Americans (12 percent) had a higher poverty rate than non-Hispanic Whites (9.9 percent) (Brown and Boteach, 2011, p. 21).
- Asian Americans' absolute and relative rates of poverty are higher than non-Hispanic whites (Takei and Sakamoto, 2011; Toji and Johnson, 1992). Moreover, the following Asian nationalities have a higher-than-average rate of poverty: Cambodian (29.3 percent), Laotian (18.5 percent), and Vietnamese (16.6 percent) (Brown and Boteach, 2011, p. 21).
- The poverty rate for Asian American seniors aged sixty-five and over (12.3 percent) is higher than the national average for seniors (9.9 percent) (Brown and Boteach, 2011, p. 21).
- The locations where Asian Americans live matters significantly: New York (15.5 percent), Massachusetts (14.7 percent), and Pennsylvania (14.8 percent) have some of the highest poverty rates among Asian Americans in the country (Brown and Boteach, 2011, p. 21).

Education

- Education is thought to be able to remedy society's sundry inequalities, but it cannot (Marsh, 2011) since it was created to divide and sort students (Duncan-Andrade and Morrell, 2008).
- Asian Americans are perceived to be educational "model minorities," a status that adversely affects their overall health (e.g., see Jang and Surapruik, 2009; Lee and Rotheram-Borus, 2009; Lin-Fu, 1988).
- Asians receive inequitable education in the United States (Redondo, Aung, Fung, and Yu, 2008).

Access to Health Care

- Hepatitis B infection among Asian American youths occurs at a rate approximately thirty times greater than that for white children (Trinh-Shevrin, Islam, and Rey, 2009).
- Overweight and obesity rates have climbed faster for Asian American and Pacific Islander children than for any other US population (Trinh-Shevrin, Islam, and Rey, 2009).
- In 2008, 17.6 percent of Asian Americans lacked health insurance, compared with 15.4 percent in the United States overall (Bread for the World, 2010).
- The rate and number of uninsured increased significantly for Asians, according to information collected in the 2011 and earlier Current Population Survey Annual Social and Economic Supplements (CPSASEC) conducted by the US Bureau of the Census (DeNavas-Walt, Proctor, and Smith, 2011).
- Uninsured rates vary among Asian subpopulations—Koreans and Southeast Asians are more likely to be uninsured than Chinese, Japanese, Filipinos, and South Asians (Ku and Waidmann, 2003, pp. 4–5).

Language and Culture Linked to Health Outcomes

- Statistical disaggregation is an important practice for health care providers since Asian Americans are a "bimodal-distributed" population (Chang and Kim, 2010; Woo, 2000) that encompasses more than twenty nations, sixty ethnic groups, and speaks more than one hundred languages and dialects (Africa and Carrasco, 2011; CARE, 2008, 2010, 2011; Hsia, 1988; Lee and Kumashiro, 2005). The population is *bimodal* because there are both *highly healthy* and *highly unhealthy* Asian Americans.
- Southeast Asian American high school students have been found to be ideologically blackened, affecting their sense of belonging. This blackening was found to be correlated with their socioeconomic status. In other words, the poorer a Southeast Asian American student was the higher the likelihood he or she would be viewed negatively (akin to African American peers). This weight of worrying to fit in socially can cause educational and health problems due to "stereotype threat," which results in increased cortisol levels for Asian Americans (Bucholtz, 2004; Jensen, 2009; Steele, 2010; *Unnatural Causes*, 2001).

Racism and Health Outcomes

- Racial battle fatigue, racial weathering, micro-insults, and racial micro-aggressions—all of which are forms of racism—impact Asian Americans' overall health (Lin, 2010; Sue et al., 2007; Sue, 2010a, 2010b).

- Anti-Asian American racism results in increased risk for suicidal ideation and committing suicide (Leong, Leach, Yeh, and Chou, 2007).
- Asian Americans are more at risk than white Americans to have diabetes. Moreover, the diabetes rates among Asians in the United States are much higher than Asians living in Asia (ICHS, 2010).
- Heart disease risk and death rates are high among Native Hawaiians and Asian Indians, partly because of their higher rates of obesity, diabetes, and high blood pressure (ICHS, 2010).

ASIAN NACIREMA CULTURE AND DOUBLE-EYELID SURGERY

Asian Americans and Westernized ideals of beauty have a very long history. Lee, Wong, and Alvarez (2009) write that "[i]n efforts to escape the perpetual foreigner label, some Asian Americans may even alter their bodies to appear more like European Americans. These efforts to look less Asian may include wearing colored contact lens, coloring hair, and even plastic surgery" (p. 79). Rondilla and Spickard (2007) echo these same sentiments by writing that "Asian American women inhabit a marginal position as members of a *model minority* who are socially acceptable but *not quite White*. For some of them, cosmetic surgery presents itself as a way to try to jump the racial gap" (p. 117, italics added).

From a health provider's standpoint, what are the social and psychological consequences for Asian Americans who have been labeled by Tuan (1998) as "honorary" whites, and who at times are thought to "out-white" whites (e.g., see Chen, 2004b; *Newsweek*, 1971)? This topic will be traversed through the examination of the most quintessential (and physically aggressive) form of assimilation, the supposed cosmetic body enhancement of plastic surgery.

According to Park (2007), the first eyelid operation was performed in Japan in 1896 by Mikamo, who read Hotz's 1880 German publication on entropion—a procedure to correct the turning in of the eyelid after an infection. Consequently, Asian eyelid surgery, or blepharoplasty, became incredibly popular after World War II, when Asians desired to look more "Western" (Harahap, 1981). Blepharoplasty is a medical procedure, whereby a plastic surgeon cuts and creates two newly shaped eyelids, turning what is an otherwise healthy eyelid into one that is more cosmetically desirable. This medical procedure makes the individual appear less Asian and more Caucasian (Chen, 2006; McCurdy and Lam, 2005)[1].

---

1   This chapter intentionally uses the term *Caucasian* not only because others have, but also because the word contains the word *Asian*.

Asian eyelid surgery is not a contemporary phenomenon (Chen, 2006). Indeed, the double-eyelid surgery was developed in Japan in the late 1800s during an epoch where geisha women were the procedure's largest clienteles. The development of the surgery continued well into the Vietnam War era, when many Vietnamese women were exposed to American GIs and consequently assimilated formal Western beauty by having the cosmetic procedure performed (Adetuyi, 2000; Wong, Rainwater-McClure, Reed, and Kramer, 2003).

Insidiously, many textbooks on Asian American health preclude discussions on Asian eyelid surgery and its consequences (e.g., see Trinh-Shevrin, Islam, and Rey, 2009). Worse yet, these very same textbooks also fail to discuss the stigmatized stereotypes of Asian eyes that are codified in the anthropological annals of the eighteenth century (e.g., slit and slanted eyes being perceived to indicate Asians as sneaky, sinister, and snaky). Without a discussion of such historical importance, many are left to believe that the "West is best" and that Asian American patients' decision to have their eyelids surgically enhanced is a wholly benign and a culturally neutral choice.

Does mainstream society, through white supremacy and its ideals of Western beauty, contribute to Asian Americans' desire to disfigure their own bodies?[2] Who benefits from the imprimatur of whiteness? The word "Caucasian" may contain the word "Asian," but most important is that those who were in power defined Caucasian historically to mean "beautiful." They did this to maintain and consolidate their hegemonic power (Painter, 2010). Thus, it is imperative to realize that "power" and "beauty" became mutually inclusive, especially with the Oriental approximating the Occidental (Park, 2007). In some respects the body ritual of the Asian Nacirema is just as much a societal and sociological issue as a medical one.

What compels Asian Americans to undergo expensive and painful surgical procedures? According to Park (2007), in 2006 there were eleven million cosmetic surgery procedures performed in the United States, constituting an $11.4 billion industry. Moreover, among ethnic nonwhite patients from 2004 to 2006, the number of Asian Americans who sought plastic and cosmetic surgery rose sharply by 55 percent. More recently, in 2010, Asians who had double-eyelid surgery contributed to the $10.1 billion spent on cosmetic procedures in the United States, which was up 1.2 percent from 2009 (American Society of Plastic Surgeons, 2010). Blepharoplasty can cost upward of $3,500 and it "is estimated that 40 percent of young Korean women undergo this eye surgery" (p. 227). Adetuyi (2000) points out that Asians tend to develop larger scars (raised and wider) after the blepharoplasty surgery, while Oullette (2009) writes that blepharoplasty "surgery poses the risk of hematoma, asymmetry, and drooping," adding that "[r]ecovery may be uncomfortable" (p. 16). The costs are great; are the benefits of blepharoplasty greater?

One only has to visit the World Wide Web and type the words *Asian eyelid surgery* into the search engine to see how widespread the surgery is globally. Many medical centers in the

2 Television commercials reinforce ideals of whiteness as beautiful. Korean Air commercials highlight female Korean Air flight attendants who have Westernized facial features and light-skinned complexions.

United States specialize in blepharoplasty. The maxim, "beauty is in the *eye* of the beholder" is scary and metaphorical in both senses of the word (e.g., see Mok, 1998). What are the risks and rewards for Asian Americans who get blepharoplasty work done? Before they are able to provide culturally relevant patient care, health professionals have a responsibility to recognize that although Asian Americans are thought to be "model minorities," they do experience racism (Chou and Feagin, 2008; Teranishi, 2010), issues of identity struggle (Pang and Cheng, 1998), depression (Lai and Arguelles, 2003), and suicide ideation (Noh, 2007; Wong, Chiu, Mok, Koo, and Tran, 2011).

Health care officials should be cognizant of the mind-set of some young Asian American girls who believe they will gain more attention from males if they have more Western-looking eyes. Keep in mind that Asian American youth are also subjected to a commercialized culture (*viz*. media, entertainment, fashion, advertisements, etc.) saturated with images of Asians with white-appearing eyes, which unavoidably influences cultural aesthetics that value larger eyes (Rondilla and Spickard, 2007). If Asian Americans believe their eyes and eyelids are slit and slanted (both of which are racialized), they will be more likely to have lower self-esteem and to internalize a feeling of inferiority. There is a Chinese expression that the eyes are the windows to your spirit, so health professionals have an obligation to understand what exactly motivates Asian Americans to undergo this invasive surgical procedure while counseling and consulting prospective patients.

One social consequence of Asian Americans getting this cosmetic and elective procedure done is that women who have their eyelids surgically altered are appropriating Westernized and idealized beauty. Thus, they are reaffirming the hierarchy of racial distinction, naturalizing the idea that white features are indeed the most beautiful features. All of this assimilation comes with a huge psychological price tag. Furthermore, internalized ethnoraical self-hatred caused by internalized racism may be a contributing factor to why a patient is choosing to have his or her eyelids "enhanced" (e.g., see Heyes, 2009; Kaw, 1993). Why do Asian American patients feel the need to enhance their eyes? Hegemony is likely a reason. In her Steven Polgar Prize-winning essay, "Medicalization of Racial Features: Asian American Women and Cosmetic Surgery," Kaw (1993) writes:

> These associations that Asian American women make between their features and personality characteristics stem directly from stereotypes created by the dominant culture in the United States and by Western culture in general, which historically has wielded the most power and hegemonic influence over the world. Asians are rarely portrayed in the U.S. popular media and then only in such roles as Charlie Chan, Suzie Wong, and "Lotus Blossom Babies" (a.k.a. China Doll, Geisha Girl, and shy Polynesian beauty) (p. 80).

It is androcentric and white hegemonic societal/sociological inclinations that motivate Asian Americans, the majority women, to have their eyelids "enhanced" (Heyes, 2009). Different than breast augmentation (implants can be removed), eyelid surgery is permanent (nearly impossible to be reversed). The following section outlines important health and cultural implications of blepharoplasty for Asian Americans.

The Future of Asian Eyelid Surgery

Asian American identity viewed through the dominant culture, including standards and ideals of beauty, serves to imprison and self-silence Asian Americans and their health needs. Hollywood, by its outright omission or distorted portrayals of Asian Americans, reinforces servile stereotypical depictions of the Asian body, fetishizing elements it likes and tossing out those it despises. Health care providers need to realize that the health needs (social, physical, psychological) of Asian Americans largely go unrecognized.

The practice of double-eyelid surgery affects the ethnic identity of Asian Americans whether health care providers wish to acknowledge it or not (Wong, 2009). The eyelid surgery industry is a big and lucrative business (Rainwater-McClure, Reed, and Kramer, 2003, p. 226). In fact, it is the most sought-after surgical procedure among Asians (Dolnick, 2011). Health care providers must comprehend the health needs of Asian Americans and their social determinants or social causes.

CONCLUDING THOUGHTS

"Eyelid Surgery Among the Nacirema: Toward Asian American Understanding" has presented a healthcare situation related to Asian Americans with the intent to begin furthering health care providers' limited understanding of Asian American health care needs and problems, as well as the social determinants of health affecting this heterogeneous and bourgeoning population. Sadly, unless it is through reinforcement of the model minority stereotype, Asian Americans remain an invisible population (e.g., see Hartlep, forthcoming). With so much attention devoted to their supposed exceptional achievements in the areas of education, citizenship, and workforce, their health needs remain obfuscated and ordinarily overlooked (Karkhanis and Tsai, 1989). In addition to the issues surrounding blepharoplasty surgery— foremost that it is a dangerous elective procedure usually undertaken by individuals solely for the purpose of looking more like Caucasians—it is essential that health care practitioners be conscientious of the multifaceted and variegated needs related to their Asian American patients. Asian Americans, who were 5 percent of the US population in 2005, will be 9 percent in 2050 (Passel and Cohn, 2008). For the reasons outlined above, if not due to a demographic imperative, Asian Americans should not continue to be misunderstood.

Growing social inequality (Marsh, 2011; Wilkinson, 2005; Wilkinson and Pickett, 2010) must also be addressed because it has been shown that inequality makes people sick (e.g., see Marsh, 2011; *Unnatural Causes,* 2001). As noted in this chapter's epigraph, Susser et al. (1985) observed that "[s]ocieties in part create the disease they experience and, further, they materially shape the way in which diseases are to be experienced" (p. 17). Thus, it is my belief that Nacirema society has the power to meet the health needs of all of its citizens; this requires increasing equity and equality of the social determinants of health (equalizing household incomes, reducing and eventually eliminating poverty, improving education for all, increasing access to health care, and valuing diversity in terms of languages and cultures).

Recommendations and Suggestions

In order for medical providers and medical trainees—i.e., PAs, NPs, MDs, DOs—to provide culturally sensitive and socially just medicine, it is vital that they reflect on how the social determinants of health, discrimination, and racism impact the lives of their Asian American patients. The social determinants of health are racialized; why else would nonwhite minorities live shorter lives than their white counterparts (e.g., see *Unnatural Causes,* 2001)? The model minority myth influences Asian Americans' health, and may be one of many reasons so many Asian Americans are getting blepharoplasty surgery. The three suggestions that follow are important for health care providers to consider when working with Asian patients:

1. **Recognize** that the health needs for Asian Americans are not uniform because Asian Americans constitute a heterogeneous and bimodal population;
2. **Understand** the ways that social position affect Asian Americans' health and well-being; and
3. **Become** better adept at understanding how the "model minority" stereotype and the inequality embedded within it, along with the social determinants of health, affect Asian American patient care and the livelihoods of Asian American patients.

All forms of inequality are color-conscious; if inequality were colorblind, then people's health and life expectancy would be uniform (*Unnatural Causes,* 2001). This means that the body ritual (eyelid surgery), and ultimately the overall health of the Asian Nacirema, can be radically improved through increased awareness, equity/equality efforts, and the reduction of prejudice, biases, and stereotypes by medical providers and practitioners.

REFERENCES

Adetuyi, A. (2000). *Skin Deep: Asian to Caucasian*. Kelowna, B.C: Filmwest Associates.

Africa, J. & Carrasco, M. (2011, February). *Asian-American and Pacific Islander Mental health: Report from a NAMI listening session*. Arlington, VA: National Alliance on Mental Illness.

American Society of Plastic Surgeons. (2010). *Report of the 2010 Plastic Surgery Statistics*. Retrieved on January 29, 2012, from http://www.plasticsurgery.org/Documents/news-resources/statistics/2010-statisticss/Top-Level/2010-Fullquickfacts-cosmetic-surgery-minimally-invasive-statistic-demographics.pdf.

Bread for the World. (2010). *Fact Sheet: Poverty and Social Indicators among Asian-Americans*.

Retrieved on February 9, 2012, from http://www.bread.org/what-we-do/resources/fact-sheets/asian-american-facts.pdf.

Brown, D. & Boteach, M. (2011). "Poverty in the United States Today: Knowing Where We Stand So We Know Where to Begin." In Half-In-Ten (ed.), *Restoring Shared Prosperity: Strategies to Cut Poverty and Expand Economic Growth* (pp. 14–33). Washington, DC: Half-In-Ten. Retrieved on January 31, 2012, from http://halfinten.org/uploads/support_files/2_Indicators_chapter_1.pdf.

Bucholtz, M. (2004). "Styles and Stereotypes: The Linguistic Negotiation of Identity Among Laotian American Youth." *Pragmatics*, 14(2/3), 127–147.

Chang, C. (1998). "Streets of Gold: The Myth of the Model Minority." In G. Colombo, R. Cullen, and B. Lisle (eds.), *Rereading America: Cultural Contexts for Critical Thinking and Writing* (4th ed.) (pp. 366–375). Boston, MA: Bedford Books.

Chang, E. T. & Kim, B. W. (2010). "Korean Americans." In E. W. Chen, and G. J. Yoo (eds.), *Encyclopedia of Asian American Issues today* (Vol. 1) (pp. 41–50). Santa Barbara, CA: Greenwood Press.

Chen, C. H. (2004a). *Mormon and Asian American Model Minority Discourses in News and Popular Magazines*. Lewiston, NY: Edwin Mellen Press.

Chen, C. H. (2004b). "'Outwhiting the Whites': An Examination of the Persistence of Asian American Model Minority Discourse." In R. A. Lind (ed.), *Race, Gender, Media: Considering Diversity Across Audiences, Content, and Producers* (pp. 146–153). Boston, MA: Allyn and Bacon.

Chen, W. (2006). *Asian Blepharoplasty and the Eyelid Crease* (2nd ed.). Philadelphia, PA: Elsevier.

Chen, M. S. & Hawks, B. L. (1995). "A Debunking of the Myth of Healthy Asian Americans and Pacific Islanders. *American Journal of Health Promotion*, 9(4), 261–268.

Chen, C. H. & Yorgason, E. (1999). "'Those Amazing Mormons': The Media's Construction of Latter-Day Saints as a Model Minority." *Dialogue: A Journal of Mormon Thought*, 32(2), 107–128.

Chou, R. & Feagin, J. R. (2008). *The Myth of the Model Minority: Asian Americans Facing Racism*. Boulder, CO: Paradigm Publishers.

Conchas, G. & Perez, C. (2003). "Surfing the 'Model Minority' Wave of Success: How the School Context Shapes Distinct Experiences Among Vietnamese Youth." *New Directions for Youth Development, 2003*(100), 41–57.

DeNavas-Walt, C., Proctor, B. D., & Smith, J. C. (2011). *Income, Poverty, and Health Insurance Coverage in the United States: 2012 (Current Population Reports, P60–239)*. Washington, DC: US Government Printing Office. Retrieved on January 11, 2012, from http://www.census.gov/prod/2011pubs/p60-239.pdf.

Dolnick, S. (2011, February 18). "Ethnic Differences Emerge in Plastic Surgery." *New York Times*. Retrieved on January 27, 2012, from http://www.nytimes.com/2011/02/19/nyregion/19plastic.html?pagewanted=all.

Du Bois, W. (2003). *The Souls of Black Folk*. New York, NY: Barnes & Noble Books.

Duncan-Andrade, J. & Morrell, E. (2008). *The Art of Critical Pedagogy: Possibilities for Moving from Theory to Practice in Urban Schools*. New York, NY: Peter Lang.

Endo, G. T. & Della-Piana, C. K. (1981). "Japanese Americans, Pluralism, and the Model Minority Myth." *Theory Into Practice, 20*(1), 45–51.

Goto, S. G. & Abe-Kim, J. (1998). "Asian Americans and the Model Minority Myth." In T. M. Singelis (ed.), *Teaching About Culture, Ethnicity, & Diversity: Exercises and Planned Activities* (pp. 151–157). Thousand Oaks, CA: Sage Publications.

Hall, C. (1995). "Asian Eyes: Body Image and Eating Disorders of Asian and Asian American Women." *Eating Disorders: The Journal of Treatment and Prevention, 3*(1), 8–19.

Harahap, M. (1981). "Blepharoplasty for Orientals." *Journal of Dermatologic Surgery and Oncology, 7*(4), 334–339.

Hartlep, N. D. (In-Press). *The Model Minority Stereotype: Demystifying Asian American Success*. Charlotte, NC: Information Age Publishing.

Heyes, C. J. (2009). "All Cosmetic Surgery is 'Ethnic': Asian Eyelids, Feminist Indignation, and the Politics of Whiteness." In C. J. Heyes and M. Jones (eds.), *Cosmetic Surgery: A Feminist Primer* (pp. 191–205). England, UK: Ashgate.

Hsia, J. (1988). "Limits of affirmative action: Asian American access to higher education." *Educational Policy, 2*(2), 117–136.

ICHS. (2010, July). *2010 Asian & Pacific Islander Health: Community Needs Assessment Overview*. Retrieved on November 6, 2012, from http://www.ichs.com/File/Publications/2010%20CNA%20Overview.pdf.

Jang, D. & Surapruik, A. (2009). "Not the Model Minority: How to Address Disparities in Asian American Health Care." *Asian American Policy Review,* 18, 91–106.

Jensen, E. (2009). *Teaching With Poverty In Mind: What Being Poor Does to Kids' Brains and What Schools Can Do About It.* Alexandria, VA: ASCD.

Lai, E. Y. P. & Arguelles, D. (2003). *The New Face of Asian Pacific America: Numbers, Diversity & Change in the 21st Century.* San Francisco, CA: Asian Week.

Lee, S. & Rotheram-Borus, M. J. (2009). "Beyond the 'Model Minority'; Stereotype: Trends in Health Risk Behaviors Among Asian/Pacific Islander High School Students." *Journal of School Health,* 79(8), 347–354.

Lee, S. J. & Kumashiro, K. K. (2005). *A Report on the Status of Asian Americans and Pacific Islanders in Education: Beyond the 'Model Minority' Stereotype.* Washington, DC: National Education Association.

Lee, S. J., Wong, N. A., & Alvarez, A. N. (2009). "The Model Minority and the Perpetual Foreigner: Stereotypes of Asian Americans." In N. Tewari and A. N. Alvarez (eds.), *Asian American Psychology: Current Perspectives* (pp. 69–85). New York, NY: Psychology Press.

Leong, F., Leach, M., Yeh, C., & Chou, E. (2007). "Suicide Among Asian Americans: What Do We Know? What Do We Need To Know?" *Death Studies,* 31(5), 417–434.

Lester, D. (1992). "Suicide Among Asian Americans and Social Deviancy." *Perceptual and Motor Skills,* 75(3) 1134.

Lin, A. I. (2010). "Racial Microaggressions Directed at Asian Americans: Modern Forms of Prejudice and Discrimination." In D. W. Sue (ed.), *Microaggressions and Marginality: Manifestation, Dynamics, and Impact* (pp. 85–103). Hoboken, NJ: John Wiley & Sons.

Lin-Fu, J. S. (1988). "Population Characteristics and Health Care Needs of Asian Pacific Americans." *Public Health Reports,* 103(1), 18–27.

Karkhanis, S. & Tsai, B. L. (eds.). (1989). *Educational Excellence of Asian Americans: Myth or Reality.* New York, NY: The Asian/Pacific American Librarians Association.

Kaw, E. (1993). "Medicalization of Racial Features: Asian American Women and Cosmetic Surgery." *Medical Anthropology Quarterly,* 7(1), 74–89.

Ku, L. & Waidmann, T. (2003). *How Race/Ethnicity, Immigration Status and Language Affect Health Insurance Coverage, Access to Care and Quality of Care Among the Low-Income Population.* Washington, DC: Kaiser Family Foundation. Retrieved on January 11, 2012, from http://www.kff.org/uninsured/up-load/How-Race-Ethnicity-Immigration-Status-and-Language-Affect-Health-Insurance-Coverage-Access-to-and-Quality-of-Care-Among-the-Low-Income-Population.pdf.

Ma, G. X. (2009). *The Culture of Health: Asian Communities in the United States.* Westport, CT: Bergin & Garvey.

Marmot, M. G. & Wilkinson, R. G. (1999). *Social Determinants of Health.* Oxford: Oxford University Press.

Marmot, M. & Wilkinson, R. (2005). *Social Determinants of Health* (2nd ed.). Oxford: OUP Oxford University Press.

Marsh, J. (2011). *Class Dismissed: Why We Cannot Teach or Learn Our Way Out of Inequality.* New York, NY: Monthly Review Press.

McCurdy, J. A. & Lam, S. M. (2005). *Cosmetic Surgery of the Asian Face* (2nd ed.). New York, NY: Thieme.

McEwan, B. S. (2000). "Allostasis and allostatic load: Implications for neuropsychopharmochlogy." *Neuropsychopharmochlogy,* 22(2), 108–124.

Miner, H. (1956). "Body Ritual Among the Nacirema." *American Anthropologist,* 58(3), 503–507.

Mok, T. A. (1998). "Asian Americans and Standards of Attractiveness: What's in the Eye of the Beholder?" *Cultural Diversity and Ethnic Minority Scholarship,* 4(1), 1–18.

Newsweek. (1971, June 21). Success Story: Outwhiting the Whites. 24–25.

Noh, E. (2007). "Asian American Women and Suicide: Problems of Responsibility and Healing." *Women and Therapy,* 30(3–4), 87–107.

Oullette, A. (2009). "Eyes Wide Open: Surgery to Westernize the Eyes of an Asian Child." *Hastings Center Report,* 39(1), 15–18.

Painter, N. I. (2010). *The History of White People.* New York, NY: W. W. Norton & Company.

Pang, V. O. & Cheng, L.-R. L. (1998). *Struggling to be Heard: The Unmet Needs of Asian Pacific American Children.* Albany, NY: State University of New York Press.

Park, R. M. (2007). *Neverperfect* [DVD]. New York, NY: Cinema Guild.

Passel, J. S. & Cohn, D. (2008). *U.S. Population Projections: 2005–2050.* Pew Research Center. Retrieved on January 31, 2012, from http://www.pewhispanic.org/files/reports/85.pdf.

Patel, K. & Rushefsky, M. E. (2008). *Health Care in America: Separate and Unequal.* Armonk, NY: M. E. Sharpe.

Rainwater-McClure, R., Reed, W. & Kramer, E. M. (2003). "A World of Cookie-Cutter Faces." In E. M. Kramer (ed.), *The Emerging Monoculture: Assimilation and the "Model Minority"* (pp. 221–233). Westport, CT: Praeger.

Redondo, B., Aung, K. M., Fung, M., & Yu, N. W. (2008). *Left in the Margins: Asian American Students and the No Child Left Behind Act.* New York, NY: Asian American Legal Defense and Education Fund. Retrieved on March 21, 2012, from http://www.aaldef.org/docs/AALDEF_Leftinthe Margins_NCLB.pdf.

Roberts, B., Povich, D., & Mather, M. (2011). *Overlooked and Underpaid: Number of Low-Income Working Families Increases to 10.2 Million.* Washington, DC: Working Poor Families Project.

Rondilla, J. L. & Spickard, P. (2007). *Is Lighter Better?: Skin-Tone Discrimination Among Asian Americans.* Lanham, MD: Rowman & Littlefield.

Steele, C. (2010). *Whistling Vivaldi: And Other Clues to How Stereotypes Affect Us.* New York: W. W. Norton & Company.

Sue, D. W., Capodilupo, C. M., Torino, G. C., Bucceri, J. M., Holder, A. M., Nadal, K. L., & Esquilin, M. (2007). "Racial Microaggressions in Everyday Life: Implications for Clinical Practice." *American Psychologist, 62*(4), 271–286.

Sue, D. (ed.). (2010a). *Microaggressions and Marginality: Manifestation, Dynamics, and Impact.* Hoboken, NJ: John Wiley & Sons.

Sue, D. (ed.). (2010b). *Microaggressions in Everyday Life: Race, Gender, and Sexual Orientation.* Hoboken, NJ: John Wiley & Sons.

Susser, M., Watson, W., & Hopper, K. (1985). *Sociology in Medicine.* New York, NY: Oxford University Press.

Takei, I. & Sakamoto, A. (2011). "Poverty Among Asian Americans in the 21st Century." *Sociological Perspectives, 54*(2), 251–276.

Teranishi, R. T. (2010). *Asians in the Ivory Tower: Dilemmas of Racial Inequality in American Higher Education.* New York, NY: Teachers College Press.

The National Commission on Asian American and Pacific Islander Research in Education (CARE). (2010). *Federal higher education policy priorities and the Asian American and Pacific Islander community.* Retrieved February 8, 2012, from http://apiasf.org/CAREreport/2010_CARE_report.pdf.

The National Commission on Asian American and Pacific Islander Research in Education (CARE). (2008). *Asian Americans and Pacific Islanders. Facts, not Fiction: Setting the record straight.* Retrieved February 8, 2012, from http://www.nyu.edu/projects/care/ CARE_Report-Revised.pdf.

Toji, D. S. & Johnson, J. H. (1992). "Asian and Pacific Islander American Poverty: The Working Poor and the Jobless Poor." *Amerasia Journal, 18*(1), 83–91.

Trinh-Shevrin, C., Islam, N. S. & Rey, M. J. (eds.). (2009). *Asian American Communities and Health: Context, Research, Policy, and Action.* San Francisco, CA: Jossey-Bass.

Tuan, M. (1998). *Forever Foreigners or Honorary Whites? The Asian Ethnic Experience Today.* New Brunswick, NJ: Rutgers University Press.

Unnatural Causes ... Is Inequality Making Us Sick? [DVD]. (2001). San Francisco, CA: California Newsreel.

Wilkinson, R. G. (2005). *The Impact of Inequality: How to Make Sick Societies Healthier.* New York, NY: New Press.

Wilkinson, R. G. & Pickett, K. (2010). *The Spirit Level: Why Greater Equality Makes Societies Stronger.* New York, NY: Bloomsbury Press.

Wong, J. (2009). *Viewing the World Through Small Eyes: Asian Double-Eyelid Surgery and the Implications of this Practice for Asian American Ethnic Identity.* [Master's thesis].

Wong, Y. J., Chiu, Y.-C., Mok, Y., Koo, K., & Tran, K. K. (2011). "Asian American College Students' Suicide Ideation: A Mixed-Methods Study." *Journal of Counseling Psychology,* 58(2), 197–209.

Woo, D. (2000). *Glass ceilings and Asian Americans: The New Face of Workplace Barriers.* Walnut Creek, CA: AltaMira Press.

Zhan, L. (ed.). (1999). *Asian Voices: Asian and Asian-American Health Educators Speak Out.* Sudbury, MA: Jones and Bartlett Publishers.

Zhang, Q. (2010). "Asian Americans Beyond the Model Minority Stereotype: The Nerdy and the Left Out." *Journal of International and Intercultural Communication,* 3(1), 20–37.

Zhao, Y. & Qiu, W. (2009). "How Good Are the Asians? Refuting Four Myths About Asian-American Academic Achievement?" *Phi Delta Kappan,* 90(5), 338–344.

THE EFFECTS OF LIVING WITH RACE-BASED DISCRIMINATION AND STRESS

The Impact on the Body and Mental Health

By Darron T. Smith, Ph.D., PA-C

The Negro death rate and sickness are largely matters of [social and economic] conditions and not due to racial traits and tendencies . . .

–W. E. B. Du Bois

INTRODUCTION

Health status follows a social gradient that mirrors larger societal patterns of inequalities. Think of a social gradient as a ladder on which individuals and groups move up or down according to income and wealth variables (Marmot, 1978). Social factors, more so than individual behavioral factors alone, adversely affect population health, and these determinants are linked by social position along a graduated continuum of lower, middle, and upper classes—a social gradient of health—that correlate class status with better health (Marmot, 2004). In other words, socioeconomic status (i.e., level of income, occupational position, and household income) and the relative distribution of society's resources are inversely associated with all major indicators of health status including the distribution of disease-specific mortality and morbidity, which occurs at every step within and along the social hierarchy (Center for Health Statistics study, 2008). These associations are often explicitly materialized in the stark differences in income between populations. Those at the top of the income ladder enjoy wide advantages in life expectancy and quality of life while those near the bottom experience startling differences in life expectancy, with as many as seven years between income groups (Sorlie et al., 1995).

It is no accident that African Americans, the poor, and other Americans of color disproportionately occupy the lower rungs in society, given what has transpired over the past four hundred years. People of color in US society persistently experience discrimination-related issues in all areas of life, including housing, employment, and the school-to-prison pipeline that affects communities and the people residing in them. The resulting macro-societal determinants such as residential segregation also affect both health and health outcomes. The poor, uneducated, unemployed or underemployed are hit particularly hard, and they are more vulnerable to disease as a result of their life circumstances than more advantaged populations.

The reality of race in America is ever-present, and the historical implications of income inequality and race-based stratification are corrosive to all Americans. Social scientists have maintained that the structure of social life is deeply rooted in systems of oppression and the opportunities (or lack thereof) available to racial and ethnic groups in the United States, which can "result in predictable patterns of risks and stressors" (Aneshensel, Rutter, and Lachenruch, 1991). The space in which minority populations live and exist in the social hierarchy influences their health and well-being.

Ironically, the United States is a democratic society that tolerates its disadvantaged remaining trapped in unequal circumstances of resource scarcity, and often, these very people are blamed for developing negative health-related coping behaviors such as smoking, excessive alcohol consumption, high-risk sexual behavior, and drug use (Lynch, 1997). Given the degree of modern-day forms of stress that Americans endure, it is easy to understand why so many turn to maladaptive ways of coping, including violence. Conditions of deprivation can encourage the practice of unhealthy behavior as people find alternative ways to cope with the vagaries of life (Williams and Collins, 2001). It is important, nevertheless, to look beyond individual health behaviors as the sole cause of ill health. Although these actions contribute to poor health outcomes, poor health is also (in part) a result of living in a modern world where daily stressors no longer include potential physical threats from a charging predator, but more emotional and mental stress—from the workplace to home and everywhere in between.

Contemporary medicine can no longer rely solely on an outdated "biomedical" mode of disease causation, which generally posits that infectious organisms are the primary source of debilitating illness and poor health (Flint, 1989). Due to considerable public health advances in the nineteenth century, such as improvements in housing, food preparation, decent work hours, clean water and sewage, vaccinations against infectious agents, and other biomedical innovations, particularly in Western market-based democracies, the human lifespan has been considerably lengthened. In the developed world, modern medical killers are no longer a result of infectious disease, but instead function around the physiology of stress and how it plays out on the body.

In the United States, differences in health status between Whites and stigmatized minority groups are worsened by the persistence of contemporary forms of racial prejudice and discrimination, typically facilitated by public policy and societal structure (and often unconsciously by white America). Even if these forms of micro-aggressions are simply *perceived*, the body responds the same, engaging its "fight or flight" response, and thus, hastening the physiological processes that speed up the progression of disease.

Social factors are important in determining various aspects of population health. And the less examined social factor of *perceived* discrimination brought on by centuries of American racism (Sondik et. al., 2010) is a constant reminder that race still matters (Bonilla-Silva, 2003; Feagin, 2001). Therefore, increasing the knowledge, awareness, and understanding among clinically practicing health care providers (i.e., MDs, DOs, PAs, and NPs) and medical trainees on how human health is connected to the social structure will improve patient outcomes and clinical decision making through the refining of provider-patient interaction.

It is essential that medical training facilities (i.e., medical schools, physician assistant schools, and nurse practitioner schools) include in the curriculum well-known research that emphasizes the significance of social and environmental circumstances that produce stressful events, along with how they contribute to the causation of bodily disease and mental health decline (McEwen, 1998; Sapolsky, 1993; Marmot, Shipley, and Rose, 1984). The increasing awareness by the medical profession concerning the relationship between the social environment, negative health behaviors, and disease formation—the social determinants of health—is an important epidemiologic shift and signals greater acceptance among the medical establishment of the relationship between the mind, the body, and chronic illness (IOM, 2004).

DISCRIMINATION: ONE MAJOR SOCIAL FACTOR AFFECTING DISEASE

African Americans live with an inordinate amount of stress compared with white Americans as they continue to endure daily forms of race-based insults and micro-aggressions—e.g., being ignored, misunderstood, stereotyped, labeled incompetent, excluded, avoided, socially isolated, and treated with less deference—in a variety of social locales and daily happenings (Ong et al., 2009). Those with low socioeconomic status (SES) as measured in income, occupation, and educational standing experience these stressors to a greater degree (James,

1994; Xanthos, Treadwell, and Holden, 2013). For example, chronic exposure to modern-day forms of stress and stressors such as joblessness, not being able to pay bills, or living in a community where the threat of crime, drugs, and other social dynamics keeps the body in a constant state of tension over the course of months to years. And still, colorblind policies of white stakeholders in a host of institutions and workplace settings deepen this divide between Blacks and Whites across class lines. Even high-SES African Americans succumb to stress-related disease and early death more commonly than Whites in the same social class (Kitagawa and Hauser, 1973; Eberly et. al., 2010; Epstein et. al., 2010). The reasons are multifactorial, but what is certain is the grinding and enduring exposure to race-based discrimination in both subtle and not so subtle ways.

Deeply embedded within the American politico-economic system of emerging capitalism, white Americans have conjured up mythmaking and race-based assumptions about black bodies. And these subjective notions about black Americans and other Americans of color have created certain ingrained ideas and institutional practices, thus, restricting group uplift. Much of the discord in American society has to do with human relationships. In health care, this manifests often as patient-provider interaction. In other words, provider perceptions of difference and the ways in which white health care providers have been racially socialized to see difference often results in poor communication and distrust, leaving many providers with the belief that black patients are less sophisticated, less attentive to their health, and less compliant than white patients, regardless of social economic class and position (Van Ryn et. al., 2011).

Structural racism is morally divisive and economically corrosive to civil society, especially to those industrialized nations struggling with profound challenges of addressing centuries-long, race-based discrimination. Despite the government's Healthy People 2020 initiative to eliminate disparities between subgroups, structural racism continues to blight the life chances inside communities of color. This legacy can now be felt among racial and ethnic minority groups and in the various health inequities they experience (Williams and Sternthal, 2010; William and Jackson, 2005).

Perceived Discrimination

Researchers consistently find that individuals who self-report acts of racism are at increased risk for mental and physical illness, regardless of whether the events were real or perceived (Brondolo et al., 2009; Fuller-Rowell et. al, 2012). Forces outside our control largely shape how we see ourselves as human beings. The social self is a reflection of historical processes of unequal power relations based on arbitrary markers of differences across race, class, and gender; determinants deemed important enough for society to single out and scrutinize. Subjective perceptions of unfair and unjust treatment have an effect on higher order cognition, which can deepen human misery in self-deprecating ways. Being made to feel as though one does not matter much in the world creates pressure within the lived reality of a world at odds with itself over the principles of equality enshrined in and guaranteed in the Constitution. This imagined community remains illusive and unrealized for throngs of African Americans and other Americans of color living on the fault lines of race.

The tension is historical in nature and looms large, threatening self-esteem and self-worth through the constant judgments and negative appraisals of others. Thus, the context of this lived reality gives way to self-doubt with the goal of creating a protective environment where feelings of caution prevail amid hostility, but which ultimately undermines productivity. Some researchers have defined this phenomenon of perceived discrimination a result, in part, of "social-evaluative threat" (Dickerson and Gruenewald, 2004). Unfortunately, the *threat* of racism, whether *actual or perceived*, is enough to cause slow physiological damage in the bodies of its victims through the chronic over-activation of the body's physiological systems responsible for the maintenance of normal equilibrium in the face of physical and other social mediated demands (Smedley, Stith and Nelson, 2003; McEwen, 1998).

There are different explanatory models used to operationalize perceived discrimination. Two predominate models are social-evaluative threat and stereotype threat. Both frameworks are effective measures of shame-related cognitive processes on vulnerable populations such as African American males and other Americans of color. Threats to the "social self" are situations that provide the potential for loss of self-esteem, social status, or social acceptance characterized by the rejection of some primary aspect of one's identity (i.e., racial group affiliation, skin tone, intelligible capacity) that could be judged by others as deficient, defective, or inferior (Gilbert, 1997). Shaming is a central emotional component undergirding both models, and there is strong evidence that different emotions arouse areas of the brain and central nervous system responsible for the preservation of the social self (Canli et. al, 2001). Race-related events and other micro-aggressions require preserving the self. Perceived negative-evaluative threats are, likewise, accompanied by increases in mental health disorders as well as increases in biological inflammatory markers (e.g., C-reactive protein and cortisol).

African Americans—particularly black males—have been historically marginalized and restricted from opportunities afforded to white Americans, a reality that can leave many African Americans susceptible to stressful feelings of inadequacy and insecurity. Living with everyday racism and bearing the brunt of white supremacist inclinations exacerbates individual and group deprivation felt by the oppressed, thus, accelerating the development of certain types of mental illness and preventable diseases (Sapolsky and Mott, 1987). With centuries of marginalization of African Americans, many are left with the legacy of attempting to filter out what situations and interactions are formed out of racial historical context, intentional or not. Yet, even if the interactions are purely innocent and devoid of any racial context, the process of filtering and deciphering in one's mind and the mere threat of this possibility leaves damaging marks inside the mind and body of those on the disadvantaged side of the interaction.

Mental Health

Research has uncovered much about the health consequences of perceived discrimination. And what most Americans do not realize is that constant race-based battles over one's right to exist in the world can lead not only to physical and/or mental exhaustion, but also physiological fatigue with the chronic over-activation of the body's "fight or flight" response caused by stress. Smith (2002) coined "racial battle fatigue" (RBF) as mental exhaustion that develops as a result of institutional racism. In other words, mistreatment and the perception of difference attributable to stigma are types of stressors on the body that are mentally draining, leaving its victims weary.

Like military personnel who experience symptoms of mental health collapse after long years of deployments in dangerous combat areas, such as in the Middle East, RBF develops in response to daily and cumulative distressing mental/emotional conditions and environments that result from facing daily forms of race-related harassment and aggression. According to Smith, these stressors include racial slights, workplace conflict, shaming, blaming, recurrent indignities and irritations, unfair treatment (including a contentious classroom), and potential threats or dangers under tough to violent, and even life-threatening, conditions (Smith, 2004). Such constant duress increases the likelihood of developing PTSD, depression, and/or anxiety.

Many African Americans persistently endure these dehumanizations in one form or another, whether rich or poor. Some African Americans have developed coping skills either through the received wisdoms and collective experiences of family members or through the school of "hard knocks" where they develop a tough exterior shell that becomes difficult to penetrate emotionally. But regardless of the coping, the mental and emotional self takes a pounding. What most Americans and even health care providers don't realize is the toll that these situations take on the physical body.

Preponderance of Stress and Other Psychosocial Factors in African American Health

Persistent discrimination directed at African Americans and other Americans of color continues to blight their life chances. The enduring wealth gap that has widened in recent years as well as the protraction of poverty, social isolation, residential segregation, and other social factors have been shown to be causative for the development of systemic disease secondary to stress and environment.

But disease does not exist in a vacuum. Social factors such as discrimination and perceived discrimination affect the progression of disease via the stress response of the body. Stress hormones have a profound and lingering effect on the body. This influence on health is greatest in early childhood (including prenatal, antenatal, and postpartum) where stress can have an impact on complex brain circuitry involved in cognition and mental health as well as other tissues and organs formed during and after birth (Koehl et. al, 1999; Seckl, 2008).

The process of not being heard combined with enduring daily stressors creates conditions that give rise to a perfect storm for disease deep within the physiology of the patient. The psychoneuroendocrine system in the human body is generally well equipped to adjust to situational fluctuations of daily stress. When the brain perceives a stressor, whether real or imagined, a coordinated physiological response is activated that involves the autonomic, neuroendocrine, metabolic, and immune systems. The initial stress response begins in the brain through a pathway known as the "fight or flight" response that occurs in seconds to minutes, thus preparing the body to cope with a specific threat, whether real or imagined.

Envision being robbed at gunpoint. Indeed, just thinking about a stressful event is enough to stimulate the body's stress response. The energy demands on the body are much greater during times of stress. What typically occurs are increases in heart rate, blood pressure, and respiration as well as the production, release, and utilization of blood sugar and free fatty acids circulating through the vasculature when the adrenal gland is triggered in a reflex response to produce adrenaline and noradrenaline (otherwise known as epinephrine and norepinephrine). The stress response is our biological alarm system that was designed for human survival, especially when our ancestors wandered the plains in search of food. Stress for our ancestors was typically acute and situational. Upon seeing a predator, the pupils constricted to make the vision sharper, respiration increased to take in more oxygen, the heart rate accelerated to pump more blood (and, hence, oxygen) to the extremities, and the body prepared to utilize the quick energy source of glucose in a mad dash. The animal charged and your ancestor would run to survive or would die trying. Today, threats from charging predators are less likely, but our hard-wired stress response remains intact and responds to acute physical threats just the same. What's more, our body's stress response cannot differentiate between types of stress (eustress or distress); thus, it also responds the same way to the more common daily stressors of modern times: socially mediated stressors or psychological stress.

Although the initial stress response can still be helpful in today's settings under such acute situations as being held at gunpoint, a secondary, extended stress response is maintained more consistently in the body in the course of persistent stressors. And these persistently elevated stress levels can be physiologically damaging. Under sympathetic control, the stress response is acutely activated, and once the acute situation resolves, the parasympathetic nervous system should return the body back to normal function. This process is known as homeostasis. But this does not always happen efficiently, especially in the bodies of African Americans where stressors tend to linger, keeping the body's stress response in a continued state of heightened awareness.

The body thus responds by activating the HPA axis, which is a longer-acting stress response. This takes several minutes to activate yet remains high for much longer. In the HPA axis, that same adrenal gland is stimulated by a hormone, which culminates in the production of cortisol. Though cortisol is necessary for the body in short bouts to decrease inflammation, among other functions, it is well documented in the research literature on stress as having a pernicious effect on the body the longer it remains elevated (Marmot and Shipley, 1996). With long-term exposure, cortisol has a blunting effect on systemic immunity, leaving the body more vulnerable to disease. Metabolically, for example, the dysregulation of gluconeogenesis or energy production via the liver leaves excess circulating glucose in the blood stream, which is unable to penetrate the muscle for energy. Stress can lead to a metabolic imbalance on the body with a greater propensity toward weight gain, especially in the abdomen where more fat around the visceral organs is dangerous. Increases in abdominal girth can potentially lead to diabetes, high cholesterol, cancer, hypertension, depression, anxiety, and other forms of lifestyle-related disease (Melfi et. al, 2000).

Despite the evidence that social factors contribute to disease formation and earlier death for African Americans, the medical community continues to rely on an outdated "biomedical model" of disease causation that is largely reductionist and individualistic regarding the approach to patient care and disease. That the patient is nothing more than a constellation of symptoms caused by an infectious host is an archaic concept taken from the Middle Ages when the majority of deaths were due to disease, secondary to lack of cleanliness and immunizations. Today, the majority of deaths in the developed world are due to preventable disease, and our current medical approach is obsolete and without any regard to the social conditions of racism in which African Americans have been made to endure.

In other words, white physicians and other health care providers often politely ignore or even deny social factors (knowingly or not) such as poverty, the black-white income and wealth gap, unemployment, and lower educational expectation and performance that contribute to the advancement of disease, often blaming individuals for engaging in inappropriate negative health behaviors. In actuality, biomedical science has revealed the importance of social factors such as race, class, gender, and geographic location as significant social determinants of health (Satcher, 2003; Williams, 1999).

According to the 2011 report of the Association of American Medical Colleges (AAMC), "A complete medical education must include, alongside physical and biological science, the perspectives and findings that flow from the behavioral and social science" (p. 5). Psychosocial factors are those determining aspects of psychological well-being such as social status, social networks, and stress in early childhood. Such are the seeds of discontent. Medical providers receive very little training in recognizing those groups that experience relative deprivation within a society and also in understanding that these groups are more at-risk for developing chronic disease disproportionate to the primarily white and upper-middle-class population. The distribution of society's valued resources has more to do with social causation factors in disease and illness than any other factor today.

To successfully improve the health of the nation and reduce the inequities between desperate populations, training facilities need to better educate their students to the reality of how the social world informs health. Additionally, training programs should use this knowledge to teach and integrate various aspects of why social factors matter in respect to patient care, teaching students that they are culpable in the perpetuation of health care disparities. PA schools can use the new medical school teaching model to incorporate social medicine into the curriculum. The bar should be equal to if not higher than medical schools. And of more importance, schools must strive to robustly admit more qualified students of color, and hire and retain more faculty of color to successfully mentor these students, in efforts to maintain a high degree of integrity and rigor common in professional school curricula. This is especially important since evidence-based research reveals that providers typically return to communities similar from where they came. As health care professionals and educators entrusted to train the next generation of preprofessional students, it is negligent to allow students to matriculate from their programs without equipping them with an understanding of the impact that social factors such as institutional racism and discrimination have on health.

As providers and educators, it is necessary to recognize that black adults and children are less likely to receive appropriate guideline-concordant attention and cutting-edge medical care than their white American counterparts (Van Ryn et. al., 2011). Subsequently, frequent exposure to race-based discrimination and its cumulative effects place black Americans as a group at greater risk for the development of mental and physical disease (Mays et. al, 2006).

CONCLUSION

Each psychosocial component plays a vital role in the overall health and well-being of a population, and it begins with the premise that human beings are exceedingly sensitive to what others think, whether real or imagined. No longer are biological explanations for disease solely adequate, since they fail to capture the disparate situations in which human populations are made to eke out an existence under grossly unequal circumstances.

With so many advances in public health and epidemiology, one of the greatest enemies of human health in contemporary life can be found in our primary social organ, the human brain. Our relationships with one another and whether or not we are made to feel that we matter in the world weigh heavily in our psyche. Our sensitivities to self-doubt and the evaluations by others, brought about by gross societal inequities in material resources and life chances, greatly affect our morbidity and mortality. In recognizing that patients' situations and life circumstances can have a deleterious effect on the body, physician assistants can begin the process of healing and preventing some of America's most pressing medical concerns and leading causes of death.

Racism remains a stable force in US society. Individual racism is generally believed by the American public to be acts of meanness committed by one person against another of a differing race. By this standard, any one person, regardless of skin tone, can commit indiscriminate racial acts of meanness. While black people can also be prejudiced, often their interpersonal feelings generally do not disadvantage others in the same way. This time-honored popular understanding of racism as nothing more than interpersonal conflict reduced to name calling and cross burning is severely misguided, since it does not explain the persistence of structural inequalities that stubbornly exist in health care, public and higher education, crime and punishment, housing, and many other institutions.

Social analysts have long maintained that racism operates at different levels in US society, from the individual to the institutional level (Feagin, 2001; Jones, 2000). Given, for example, the institutional racist practices, procedures, law making, and educational reasoning that established popular knowledge concerning race, it should be no surprise by now that African Americans are among the highest group to self-report acts of discrimination. Because systemic racism is still a reality, African Americans live with and have more stress to manage than any other stigmatized minority group (with the exception of Native Americans), which essentially translates into increased mortality and morbidity. These additional stresses that they carry are unfathomable to most white Americans.

Cultural and institutional racism have proven much harder to uncover in a society fixated on colorblindness as an acceptable form of intervention. Policies and interventions aimed at changing the interpersonal aspects of racism do very little to alter the footprint of our nation's past. A thoughtful health care provider must be given additional intellectual tools during their training years to consider not only the social and environmental complexities of patient care, but also to understand the deeply engrained structures that additionally shape the lives and life chances of communities of color.

REFERENCES

Aneshenel, C. S., Rutter, C. M., & Lachenbruch, P. A. (1991). "Social Structure, Stress and Mental Health: Competing Conceptual and Analytic Models." *American Sociological Review,* 56: 166–78.

Institute of Medicine. (2004). "Improving Medical Education: Enhancing the Social and Behavioral Science Content of Medical School Curricula." *National Academy Press.*

Association of American Medical Colleges. *Behavioral and Social Science Foundations for Future Physicians.* Association of American Medical Colleges, 2012. 4p. https://www.aamc.org/download/271020/data/behavioralandsocialsciencefoundationsforfuturephysicians.pdf (accessed April 16, 2012).

Center for Health Statistics Study. *Behaviors: The Actual Leading Causes of Death.* http://www.dchd.net/files/Behavioral%20Risk%20Factors.pdf (accessed April 17, 2012).

Salpolsky, R. M. (1993). "Endocrinology alfresco: psychoendocrine studies of wild baboons." *Recent Prog. Horm. Res.,* 48, 437–68.

Marmot, M. G., Shipley, M. J., & Rose, G. (1984). "Inequalities in death—specific explanations of a general pattern." *Lancet* i, 1003–6.

Marmot, M. G. (2004). *Status syndrome.* Bloomsbury, London.

Du Bois, W. E. B. (2003). "The Health and Physique of the Negro American." *American Journal of Public Health,* 93: 272–276.

Flint, V. J. (1989). "The Early Medieval 'Medicus', the Saint—and the Enchanter." *Social History of Medicine,* 2(2): 127–46.

Sondik, E. J., Huang, D. T., Klein, R. J., & Satcher, D. (2010). "Progress toward the Healthy People: 2010 Goals and Objectives." *Annual Review of Public Health,* 31(1): 271–281.

Carmichael, S. & Hamilton, C. V. (1967). *Black Power: The Politics of Liberation in America*: New York: Vintage Books.

Jones, C. P. (2000). "Levels of Racism: A Theoretic Framework and a Gardner's Tale." *American Journal of Public Health,* 98(Supplement 1):S16.

Feagin, J. (2010). *The White racial frame: Centuries of racial framing and counterframing.* New York: Routledge.

Smith, D. T. (2011). "Dirty Hands and Unclean Practices: How Medical Neglect and the Preponderance of Stress Illustrates How Medicine Harms Rather Than Helps." *Journal of Black Masculinity,* 2(1), special edition 11–33.

Brondolo, E., Brady ver Halen, N., Pencille, M., Beatty, D., & Contrada, R. J. (2009). "Coping with Racism: A Selective Review of the Literature and a Theoretical and Methodological Critique." *Journal of Behavioral Medicine, 32*(1): 64–88.

Mays, V. M., Cochran, S. D., & Barnes, N. W. (2006). "Race, Race-based Discrimination, and Health Outcomes among African Americans." *Annual Review of Psychology,* 58: 201–225.

Smith, W. A., Yosso, T., & Solorzano, D. (2007). "Racial primes and Black misandry on historically White campuses: Toward a critical race accountability." *Educational Administration Quarterly, 43*(5), 559–585.

Bartley, M. (2003). "Health inequality and societal institutions." *Soc. Theory. Hlth.* 1, 108–29.

Ard, J. D. (2007). "Unique Perspective on the Obesogenic Environment." *J Gen Intern Med.* 2007 July; 22(7): 1058–1060. Published online May 23, 2007. doi: 10.1007/s11606-007-0243-z.

Diez-Roux, A. V., Link, B. G., & Northridge, M. E. (2000). "A multilevel analysis of income inequality and cardiovascular disease risk factors." *Social Science and Medicine,* 50 (5): 673–87.

Lynch, J. W., Kaplan, G. A., & Shema, S. J. (1997). "Cumulative impact of sustained economic hardship on physical, cognitive, psychological, and social functioning." *N Eng.J. Med.,* 337, 1889–95.

Salpolsky, R. M. & Mott, G. E. (1987). "Social subordinance in wild baboons is associated with suppressed high density lipoprotein–cholesterol concentrations: the possible role of chronic social stress." *Endocrinology,* 121, 1605–10.

Melfi, C. A., Croghan, T. W., Hanna, M. P., & Robinson, R. L. (2000). "Racial variation in anti-depression treatment in a Medicaid population." *Journal of Clinical Psychiatry,* 61, 16–21.

Koehl, M. et al. (1999). "Prenatal stress alters circadian activity of hypothalamo-pituitary-adrenal axis and hippocampal corticosteroid receptors in adult rats of both gender." *J. Neurobiol,* 40, 302–315.

Seckl, J. R. (2008). "Glucocorticoids, developmental 'programming' and the risk of affective dysfunction." *Prog. Brain Res.,* 167, 17–34.

Healthy People (2010). *Executive Summary: Goal 2: Eliminate Health Disparities.* http://www.healthy-people.gov/Data/midcourse/html/execsummary/Goal2.htm (assessed April 1, 2012.)

Feagin, J. (2001). *Racist America: Roots, current realities, and future reparations.* New York: Routledge.

Williams, D. R. & Sternthal, M. (2010). "Understanding Racial-ethnic Disparities in Health: Sociological Contributions." *Journal of Health and Social Behavior,* 51(S): S15–S27.

Williams, D. R. & Jackson, P. B. (2005). "Social Sources of Racial Disparities in Health." *Health Affairs,* 24(2): 325–334.

Dalton, S. (2007). "Our Vulnerable Children: Poor and Overweight." *Southern Medical Journal:* January 2007, vol. 100, issue 1 pp. 1–2 doi: 10.1097/01.smj.0000252993.86981.0c.

Jones, C. P. (2000). "Levels of Racism: A Theoretical Framework and a Gardner's Tale." *American Journal of Public Health*, 90(8): 1212–1215.

James, S. A. (2008). "Confronting the Moral Economy of US Racial/Ethnic Health Disparities." *American Journal of Public Health*, 98 (supplemental 1): S16.

Ong, A. D., Fuller-Rowell, T. E., & Bonanno, G. A. (2010). "Prospective predictors of positive emotions following spousal loss." *Psychol. Aging,* 25, 653–660.

Gee, G. C. (2002). "A Multilevel analysis of the relationship between institutional and individual racial discrimination and health status." *Am. J. Public Health,* 92, 615–623.

McEwen, B. S. (1998). "Protective and damaging effects of stress mediators." *N. Engl. J. Med.,* 338, 171–179.

Williams, D. R. & Collins, C. (2001). "Racial residential segregation: A fundamental cause of racial disparities in health." *Public Health Reports,* 116(5), 404–416.

Marmot, M. G. & Shipley, M. J. (1996). "Do socioeconomic differences in mortality persist after retirement? 25-years follow up of civil servants from the first Whitehall study." *British Medical Journal,* 313, 1177–1180.

Williams, D. R. (1999). "Race, socioeconomic status, and health: the added effects of racism and discrimination." *Annals of the New York Academy of Sciences,* 896, 173–188.

Satcher, D. (2003). "Overlooked and underserved: Improving the health of men of color." *American Journal of Public Health*, 93(5), 707–709.

Sorlie, P. D., Backlund, E., & Keller, J. B. (1995). "U.S. mortality by economic, demographic, and social characteristics: the national longitudinal mortality study." *Am. J. Public Health,* 85:949–56.

Kitagawa, E. M. & Hauser, P. M. (1973). *Differential Mortality in the United States: A Study of Socioeconomic Epidemiology.* Cambridge, MA: Harvard Univ. Press.

Eberly, T., Davidoff, A., & Miller, C. (2010). "Managing the Gap: Evaluating the Impact of Medicaid Managed Care on Preventative Care Receipt by Child and Adolescent Minority Populations." *Journal of Health Care for the Poor and Undeserved,* 21(1): 92–111.

Epstein, A. J., Gray, B. H., & Schlesinger, M. (2010). "Racial and Ethnic Differences in the Use of High-Volume Hospitals and Surgeons." *Archives of Surgery,* 145(2): 179–186.

Noguera, P. A. (2003) "Schools, Prisons and the Social Implications of Punishment." *Theory to Practice,* 42(4).

Alexander, M. (2010). *The New Jim Crow: Mass Incarceration in the Age of Colorblindness.* The New Press. New York

Pager, D. (2007). *Marked: Race, Crime, and Finding Work in an Era of Mass Incarceration.* The University of Chicago Press.

Kelly, E., Moy, E., Stryer, D., Burstin, H., & Clancy, C. (2005). "The National Healthcare Quality and Disparities Reports: An Overview." *Medical Care*, 43(3 Supplemental): 13–8.

Van Ryn, M., Burgess, D. J., Dovidio, J. F., Phelan, S. M., Saha, S., Malat, J., Griffin, J. M., Fu, S. S., & Sylvia, P. (2011). "The Impact of Racism on Clinician Cognition, Behavior, and Clinical Decision Making." *Du Bois Review*, 8:1 (2011) 199–218.

McEwen, B. S. (1998). "Protective and damaging effects of stress mediators." *New England Journal of Medicine*, 338, 171-179.

Fuller-Rowell, T. E., Doan, S. N., & Eccles, J. S. (2012). "Differential effects of discrimination on the diurnal cortisol rhythm of African American and Whites." *Psychoneuroendocrinology*, 37, 107–118.

Gilbert, P. (1997). "The evolution of social attractiveness and its role in shame, humiliation, guilt, and therapy." *British Journal of Medical Psychology*, 70, 113–147.

Canli, T., Zhao, Z., Desmond, J. E., Kang, E., Gross, J., & Gabrieli, J. D. (2001). "A fMRI study of personality influences on brain reactivity to emotional stimuli." *Behavioral Neuroscience*, 115 (1), 33–42.

Xanthos, C., Treadwell, H. M., & Holden, K. B. (2013). *Social Determinants of Health Among African American Men*. Jossey-Bass: San Francisco.

AUTHOR CREDITS

Darron T. Smith, Ph.D., PA-C
Assistant Professor
Department of Physician Assistant Studies
University of Tennessee Health Science Center

Tasha E. Sabino, MPAS, PA-C, ATC
Adjunct Faculty/Instructor
Physician Assistant Program
Christian Brothers University

Cardell Jacobson, Ph.D.
Professor of Sociology
Brigham Young University

Vasco Deon Kidd, DHSc, MPH, PA-C, MS
Visiting Assistant Professor
Physician Assistant Program
Riverside Community College

Michelle DiBaise, MPAS, PA-C, DFAAPA
Associate Clinical Professor
Physician Assistant Program
Northern Arizona University

Lisa Hines, Ph.D., MSW
Assistant Professor
School of Social Work
Wichita State University

Jim Anderson, MPAS, PA-C, ATC, DFAAPA
Physician Assistant and Teaching Associate
Department of Anesthesiology and Pain Medicine
University of Washington School of Medicine
Physician Assistant
Evergreen Treatment Services Opiate Treatment Program, Seattle, WA

Patricia J. Devine, MLS
Medical Librarian
National Network of Libraries of Medicine
Pacific NW Region

Cherise B. Harrington, Ph.D., MPH
Assistant Professor
Department of Prevention and Community Health
School of Public Health and Health Services
The George Washington University

James F. Cawley, MPH, PA-C, DHL (hc)
Professor
Department of Prevention and Community Health
Director, PA/MPH Program
School of Public Health and Health Services
Professor of Physician Assistant Studies
School of Medicine and Health Sciences
The George Washington University

J. Leocadia Conlon, PA-C, MPH
Assistant Professor
Physician Assistant Studies
Shenandoah University
Education Advisor
American Academy of Physician Assistants

Daniel S. Goldberg, J.D., Ph.D.
Assistant Professor
Department of Bioethics & Interdisciplinary Studies
Brody School of Medicine
East Carolina University

Susan LeLacheur, DrPH, PA-C
Associate Professor of Physician Assistant Studies
School of Medicine and Health Sciences
The George Washington University

Anita Duhl Glicken, MSW
President and CEO
The nccPA Health Foundation
Associate Dean and Professor Emerita
University of Colorado School of Medicine

Nicholas D. Hartlep, Ph.D.
Assistant Professor of Educational Foundations
Department of Educational Administration and Foundations
Illinois State University

CPSIA information can be obtained at www.ICGtesting.com
Printed in the USA
BVOW06s1022120614

356171BV00003B/14/P